The Great Psychological Crime: The Destructive Principle of Nature in Individual Life

John Emmett Richardson, Florence Huntley

The Great
Psychological Crime

The Destructive Principle of Nature
In Individual Life

Edited by

FLORENCE HUNTLEY

Author of

"Harmonics of Evolution"

and

"The Dream Child"

COPY OF A MINIATURE SCULPTURE BY J. OTTO SCHWEIZER

A Psychological Study----The Artist's Imagination crystal-
lizes the modern spirit of greed and selfishness, and
presents a somber Reality

HARMONIC SERIES

VOL. II

FIFTEENTH EDITION

CHICAGO, ILLS.
INDO-AMERICAN BOOK CO.
5707 So. Blvd.
1915

The Great
Psychological Crime

The Destructive Principle of Nature
In Individual Life

Edited by
FLORENCE HUNTLEY
Author of
"Harmonics of Evolution"
and
"The Dream Child"

HARMONIC SERIES
VOL. II

FIFTEENTH EDITION

CHICAGO, ILLS.
INDO-AMERICAN BOOK CO.
5707 So. Blvd.
1915

Copyright, 1902,
By Florence Huntley.

Published 1915

ADDRESSED

TO

THE PROGRESSIVE INTELLIGENCE OF THE AGE.

The Great Psychological Crime
In Three Parts

Modern Hypnotism

Spiritual Mediumship

Retributive Justice

Part I—Modern Hypnotism

CHAPTERS

Part II—Spiritual Mediumship

CHAPTERS

CONTENTS

Part III—Retributive Justice

CHAPTERS

Supplement—Theories of "The Wise Men"

The Genesis of Dogma

Topics

Facts and Theories.
Differences and Distinctions.
Transmigration.
Metempsychosis.
Transubstantiation.
Reincarnation.
The Missing Link.
Evolution.
Conditional Immortality.
Inherent Immortality.
Psychical Reinvestiture.
The "Wages of Sin."
The "Second Death."
Individual Extinction.

UNIV. OF
CALIFORN.

Modern Hypnotism

CHAPTER I.

PSYCHOLOGICAL CRIME.

1. A Psychological Crime is a crime against the intelligent Soul or essential Entity of Man.

2. A *Great* Psychological Crime is such a crime against the intelligent Soul of Man as deprives it of any of the inalienable rights, privileges, benefits, powers or possibilities with which God or Nature has invested it.

3. THE GREAT PSYCHOLOGICAL CRIME is that crime against the intelligent Soul or essential Entity of Man which constitutes the central theme of this volume, wherein it is defined, analyzed, illustrated and elucidated.

CHAPTER II.

New Definitions.

A work of science or philosophy, to be of value, must be free from ambiguity, and of the utmost exactness in its terminology.

No more difficult task is laid upon a writer than that he shall reach a satisfactory standard in either of these respects.

The most that will here be attempted is to approach such a standard as closely as may be possible under all the circumstances, and then rely upon the intelligence and good conscience of the reader to catch the real intent wherever the expression or the terminology may prove to be at fault.

To accomplish the purpose of this work in the fullest measure possible it is necessary that the exact meaning of certain terms be specifically defined at the outset, as they are hereinafter to be employed and understood. This is especially important, for the reason that through the indiscriminate manner in which writers have hitherto employed them they have become involved in such ambiguity as to entirely destroy their scientific value.

For the purpose of this work, therefore, special attention is called to the following definitions:

Hypnotist.—A person in the physical body who voluntarily controls the will, voluntary powers and sensory organism of another physically embodied person.

It will be observed that this definition has reference to a certain relation existing between physically embodied persons only; that is, between human beings. Attention is called to this particular limitation, for the reason that upon it depends an important distinction between a "hypnotist" and a "control," as the latter is defined in Part II of this volume.

Subject.—A physically embodied person whose will, voluntary powers and sensory organism are under the domination and subject to the control of a hypnotist.

Hypnotism.—The process by and through which a hypnotist obtains, holds and exercises control of the will, voluntary powers and sensory organism of his subject. Also the psychic relation which exists between the two parties during the continuance of the hypnotic process.

HYPNOTIC "SUGGESTION."—A "suggestion"—so-called—made by a hypnotist to his subject while the latter is under the hypnotic control of the former.

INDEPENDENT SUGGESTION.—A suggestion made by one person to another while both are in full and complete control of their own voluntary powers and rational faculties; that is, while neither is under hypnotic control. In this case each person acts independently and of his own free will.

TELEPATHIC SUGGESTION.—Independent suggestion made by one person to another by mental processes alone, without the aid of the usual physical means of communication.

As this term may be employed in contradistinction to the term hypnotic "suggestion," it is important to note that telepathic suggestion is independent, while hypnotic "suggestion" is not.

MAGIC.—The individual exercise and use of the natural powers of the body, spirit and soul in controlling and applying the forces, activities and processes of Nature.

WHITE MAGIC.—The right individual exercise and use of the natural powers of the body, spirit and soul in controlling and applying the forces, activities and processes of Nature in such manner as to supplement and conform to Nature's Constructive Principle.

BLACK MAGIC.—The wrong individual exercise and use of the natural powers of the body, spirit and soul in controlling and applying the forces, activities and processes of Nature in such manner as to supplement and conform to Nature's Destructive Principle.

In the framing of these definitions no attempt has been made to conform to the specific limitations of any lexicographer or author. There is a good and valid reason for this seeming repudiation of established authorities. It will be found in the following brief explanation:

In the discussion and consideration of the particular subjects in which these terms are of specific importance, writers, more especially of the modern schools, seem to have become confused. By reference to their writings it will be found that the same term is often employed to express either a diametrically opposite or a wholly different meaning. The remarkable extent to which this ambiguous use of terms has been carried in recent writings has done much to envelop the whole subject of psychological and metaphysical study and research in a dense cloud of mysticism.

The present intent, therefore, is to take these particular words out from their environment of uncertainty and give to them specific and definite meanings for the purposes of this particular work. We are, therefore, not concerned with the objections or criticisms which may, and very likely will, be volunteered by other writers, nor does it appear either necessary or desirable to enter the field of controversy for the purpose of justifying the lexicology upon which these definitions are based. It is sufficient if the reader alone shall understand them. It is assumed that, whatever may be his individual views upon the various phases of the subject to be considered, he is nevertheless honest in his desire to understand the exact meaning and intent of the writer.

In order that he may be successful in this undertaking, he is therefore asked, for the purposes of this particular work, to accept these definitions without qualification.

CHAPTER III.

Pertinent Admissions.

A judge before whom a cause is to be tried at court is always pleased if opposing counsel will come together and submit to him what is known in law as an agreed statement of facts. This saves the time, labor and energy of the court and counsel which would otherwise be consumed in impaneling a jury, examining witnesses, taking testimony, eliminating from the record that which is irrelevant, immaterial and incompetent, and sifting out the facts which have a legitimate and proper bearing upon the subject matter of the case under consideration. This leaves nothing to be done but determine what is the law that covers the particular facts agreed upon.

In the matter here to be adjudicated it is desirable, as far as may be possible, that the reader occupy the position of the court. Even though he may, perchance, be prejudiced in favor of or against one side or the other, this fact will not disqualify him, as it might in a trial at court. Indeed, the ethics to be observed in the present instance are so free from restrictions that he may, without offense or impropriety, act as judge and opposing counsel at the same time.

In any event, it is here agreed in advance that whatever may be his present convictions or prejudices, no motion will be made for a change of venue nor appeal taken from his decision. It is fair to assume that his honesty and love of justice will prompt him to render his decision in strict conformity with the law and the facts, and this is all that could be asked of the most open-minded and unbiased judge.

In accordance with the foregoing suggestions the following admissions are offered as a part of the record upon which the questions hereinafter raised are to be tried and determined. They are alleged by all hypnotists to be facts, and for the purpose of avoiding all unnecessary controversy concerning them it is preferred to here admit them as such. It then but remains to determine the law applicable to these particular facts:

1. It is admitted that hypnotism is a fact.

2. It is admitted that there are numerous methods or processes by means of which it is possible for a hypnotist to obtain control of the will, voluntary powers and sensory organism of his subject.

3. It is admitted that a hypnotist who thus has control of his subject can, under certain conditions, produce a very wide range of phenomena which are usually classified as hypnotic.

4. It is admitted that through the effects of hypnotism a subject may, for the time being, be made unconscious of physical pain. This fact is known and quite generally acknowledged. It has been often demonstrated in medical schools, colleges, clinics and hospitals throughout the country.

5. It is admitted that very painful surgical operations may be performed upon hypnotized subjects without conscious physical suffering. This has been demonstrated so often that it has come to be quite generally known and acknowledged.

6. It is admitted that by hypnotic "suggestion," so-called, a subject may be temporarily relieved from some physical disabilities, and that some habits of long standing may be thus temporarily overcome.

7. It is admitted that a very large percentage of men, women and children everywhere might, under favorable conditions therefor, be made subjects of hypnotic control.

8. It is admitted that a very large percentage of men, women and children would be able, with instruction and practice, to develop some degree of hypnotic power.

9. It is admitted that hypnotic power may be so used as to command wealth, luxury, notoriety and the subserviency of many people. This has been demonstrated all too often, and the demonstrations still continue.

10. It is admitted that the practice of hypnotism is a most fascinating diversion, and can be made to afford much interest and amusement to those who are without conscience, and those who are ignorant of the laws, principles, forces, activities and processes involved.

11. It is admitted that the mischievous and destructive effects of hypnotic control do not generally manifest themselves at once to the observer nor to the subject himself.

12. It is admitted that there are some hypnotists who are honest, and who would not knowingly and intentionally engage in any practice which does violence to a primary and fundamental law of individual life, growth and development.

13. It is admitted that much has been written by students, investigators, hypnotists and men of professional standing, on the general subject of hypnotism, which is at variance with the position taken in this work.

The impression made by these admissions will very largely depend upon the character of the intelligence to which they are submitted, the nature and scope of his personal experiences, and the measure, liberality and value of his educational training.

If he should chance to be a professional hypnotist, or a sympathetic student of hypnotism, or a mere believer in the merit of the hypnotic process, he might, perhaps, obtain the impression that his position is not only admitted, but also justified and approved. If so, he is asked to follow the subject matter through to the end before he renders his final decision and judgment.

If a lawyer, or any other person acquainted with the logical determination of difficult problems, he cannot fail to see that these admissions furnish the only substantial basis upon which the errors, mistakes, fallacies and misconceptions of hypnotism may be successfully disclosed and corrected.

Whoever the reader may be, by whatever scientific or philosophic convictions he may be influenced, he cannot fail to understand and appreciate the following facts, viz.:

1. There is no intention, desire nor disposition on the part of the writer to deny, ignore, evade or minimize any of the relevant and material facts which are in any manner pertinent to the subject under consideration.

2. That an honest and earnest effort will be made to deal with the subject in a fair and impartial manner, and

with courteous consideration for the sensibilities of all those who may hold opinions, beliefs, convictions or prejudices at variance with the results hereinafter obtained.

It is hoped that Part I of this volume will command the especial attention and thoughtful consideration of physicians and surgeons, hypnotists and hypnotic students and subjects, investigators and students of psychic phenomena, and all liberal minded and intelligent students and thinkers who are not bound by the subtle power of scientific bigotry, dogmatism, prejudice or personal interest.

CHAPTER IV.

WHAT IS HYPNOTISM?

Hypnotism is the process by and through which one person—called a hypnotist—obtains, holds and exercises control of the will, voluntary powers and sensory organism of another person—called a subject. It also includes the psychic relation which exists between the two persons during the continuance of the hypnotic process.

It is well understood in advance that this definition will hardly meet the approval of every hypnotist or writer upon the subject, for reasons which will become more apparent as we proceed. In anticipation of the objections which are likely to be offered against it a clear analysis of its exact meaning will here be given. This is deemed advisable for the reason that it is of first importance to fix in mind the exact scope, as well as the expressed limitations of the definition, before proceeding to a consideration of the subject in chief.

The definition involves the following propositions, viz.:

1. A hypnotist controls the Will (as well as the voluntary powers and sensory organism) of his subject during the continuance of the hypnotic process.

2. Within the meaning of the definition hypnotism involves a relationship between at least two persons.

3. One of these persons is in a state of subjection to the Will of the other. Therefore one dominates or controls and the other is dominated or controlled.

4. The limitations of the definition entirely exclude what is commonly known as "Auto-Hypnotism," or "Self-Hypnotism." This particular subject will be considered in another chapter.

It will be observed from the foregoing analysis of the definition that no attempt is here made to conform to any of the generally accepted theories of hypnotism heretofore promulgated by our western writers and acknowledged authorities. The reader is entitled to know the reason for this seeming disregard of "authority" in a matter of such vital importance. It is equally due the writer that he shall not be subject to the charge of discourtesy in the treatment of his theme.

In view of all the interests involved, the following brief explanation would seem to be both pertinent and necessary:

1. "Hypnotism" is a word of comparatively modern origin. It was first employed by Dr. Braid, an eminent English author and student of psychic phenomena. It seems to have been adopted by him for the express purpose of marking a distinction between his own theory and that of Mesmer, with whom he disagreed.

Those who are familiar with the subject are already aware that Mesmer advocated what is commonly known as the "Magnetic" theory. He endeavored to establish as a scientific fact that magnetism is at the basis of all phenomena produced under the process which he invoked, and which afterwards came to be known as "Mesmerism." All his methods of operation, both in the matter of inducing the Mesmeric sleep and in the production of psychic phenomena, were made to conform to his theory of magnetism.

Dr. Braid, however, discovered that the condition of artificial sleep may be induced by simply causing the subject to gaze steadily at a bright object, without employing any of the magnetic methods of Mesmer. He therefore concluded that Mesmer was mistaken in assuming that magnetism is at the basis of the process, or, in fact, had anything to do with it. In order to give to his own theory a name which should properly distinguish it from the magnetic theory of Mesmer, he adopted the term "Hypnotism." From that time to the present the word has been in common use, and is now the word most generally employed by all the leading authorities.

2. Since the time of Dr. Braid, however, a flood of light has been thrown upon the subject by the investigations which have been carried on by eminent men of science in both this country and Europe. Many of the facts have been carefully classified in the hope of discovering a fundamental principle underlying all phenomena of a psychic nature.

Quite independently, however, it has been known by the

School of Natural Science for many centuries that all such phenomena, under whatever name designated, naturally divide themselves into two classes, upon what may be appropriately termed the principle of causation.

The first of these two classes includes all such phenomena which are produced while the will of the subject is under control of an operator whom we will name, in accordance with the definition, a hypnotist.

The second class is confined to those which occur independently of hypnotic control.

The first class falls strictly within the meaning of the definition at the head of this chapter, while the second is entirely excluded. And this is the exact purpose of the definition.

The distinction is of the most vital importance. It goes to the very essence of the subject, and involves a principle which lies at the foundation of all ethics, as well as of life itself.

The vital necessity for this distinction will be better understood and more fully appreciated when it is recalled that our modern writers and authorities generally seem to have overlooked it entirely, or noted it in such manner as to suggest its lack of importance.

3. The term "Hypnotism," by the indiscriminate manner in which it has been employed, has been made to include both classes of phenomena, as well as the various processes by and through which they are produced. This entire lack of scientific discrimination is more conspicuously noticeable in the writings of our modern western authorities.

It must be apparent to every intelligent student whose attention is called to it that such a lack of discrimination is both unscientific and unfortunate. Indeed, the first prerequisite of all progressive work in the field of exact science is a terminology free from ambiguity. Without this confusion and chaos are inevitable.

A single illustration will be sufficient. Suppose, for instance, that instead of the words "positive" and "negative," with meanings exactly opposite, our scientists had employed but the one word "positive," to express either meaning or both, what would have been the effect upon the science of our age?

Or, suppose we employed to-day but a single term to signify "fact," "fiction," "truth," "falsehood"; is there anyone who could possibly hold that such a substitution would be admissible?

Most assuredly not. Such a course would introduce into our language confusion, ambiguity and contradiction to such an extent as to make scientific expression an impossibility, and destroy the foundation upon which rests all our progress in both ethics and religion.

The logic of the situation is beyond all question. The word "Hypnotism" cannot, with propriety, be employed to define two separate, distinct and radically unlike processes. Neither can it be made properly to cover two different classes of phenomena which are the results of wholly different causes. Any attempt to do so must necessarily result in still further intensifying the mysticism in which this subject has already become involved.

The question then arises as to the propriety of using the word at all. That is to say, has it become so irrevocably involved in uncertainty and confusion as to destroy its availability or usefulness as a scientific term in the future? This is indeed an important question. Any view we may take of it discovers difficulties in our way. We can scarcely hope to avoid them entirely. Our only alternative, therefore, is to overcome them as far as may be possible.

In the accomplishment of this result two different methods of procedure suggest themselves, viz.:

1. With perfect consistency we might eliminate the word entirely, upon the theory that its past promiscuous and unfortunate associations wholly unfit it for service in the future. In this event, however, it would then become necessary to invent or adopt other terms and give to them definite scientific meanings. This is never desirable so long as it is possible to avoid such a course.

2. On the other hand, we might continue to employ the

term, but in so doing limit its meaning in such manner and to such extent as to divest it of all its present elements of ambiguity and give to it an exact and scientific significance.

This latter method would appear to be the least objectionable, all things duly considered, and has therefore been adopted. The term will therefore be employed in this work and its meaning will be limited to the process and the relation involved in the definition at the beginning of this chapter. It is therefore important that special note be taken of the limitations referred to. The value and importance of this suggestion will soon become apparent.

It is a fact, with which every student who is at all familiar with the literature of the subject is acquainted, that the leading exponents of hypnotism are widely at variance upon almost every essential phase of the subject. They disagree in their methods of "inducing" the hypnotic state or condition. They differ widely in their theories as to the nature of the process in operation during the continuance of the hypnotic state. They are at variance as to the forces employed in hypnotic processes. They cannot agree as to the nature of the relation which exists between the hypnotist and his subject during the continuance of the hypnotic state or condition. They contradict each other in their efforts to define the hypnotic process. And finally, they disagree as to the natural results of hypnotism upon the subject.

Indeed, it would appear that they unanimously agree in but a single phase of the subject, namely, in ignoring the fundamental principle of individual life which underlies the entire problem.

This statement of their inharmonious views and theories upon the basic principles of the subject is not made in the spirit of criticism. On the contrary, this general confusion and conflict of opinion is interpreted as a most healthful indication of future possibilities. It very strongly indicates the spirit of independence in which each investigator has approached his subject, and the strength of purpose with which he has made his investigations. It indicates that each one has entered upon his task fearlessly, unfettered by professional ethics and free from the prejudices of conventional thought. It is to be accepted as a guaranty that each has studied such facts as he has been able to discover, and has drawn his independent conclusions from them. If his deductions have been at variance with those of his fellows, he has declared them nevertheless and has done his best to maintain them.

In the midst of this general disagreement and the spirit of controversy and criticism which it has developed, whoever shall venture to enter the arena must be prepared to receive or parry the blows and thrusts of many assailants. For, whatever attitude he may assume, it is safe to predict that he will be compelled either to defend himself or retreat.

And so it is anticipated that the hosts who have broken spears and javelins and lances over each other's heads in the battle royal which they have waged among themselves will declare an armistice for the express purpose of punishing anyone who may venture to invade the field or enter the lists from a new quarter.

In other words, it is here anticipated that the definition of hypnotism at the beginning of this chapter will be resented by almost every professional hypnotist and writer upon the subject of hypnotism throughout the country who shall give this work the courtesy of a thoughtful reading. The limitations which have been set about the word, as it is there defined, raise a vital issue with many of the leading western authorities upon the subject. This issue is raised with full knowledge of its importance, and with the deliberate purpose of pressing it to trial and final judgment before the bar of the reader's best intelligence.

It is maintained by some of the leading authorities in our own country, as well as in Europe, that the relation between hypnotist and subject does not involve a question of either domination on the part of the hypnotist or subjection on the part of the subject. By these writers it is held that the will and voluntary powers of the subject are never, at any time, under control of the hypnotist.

The direct question to be considered, therefore, is whether

a hypnotist, under any circumstances, controls the will or voluntary powers of his subject.

By reference back to the definition and to the analysis which follows thereafter, it will be observed that there is no uncertainty as to the position here taken. The purpose of the definition is, in truth, to raise this issue as directly as may be possible. For this reason it is here again declared without qualification that a hypnotist does control the will and voluntary powers of his subject during the continuance of the hypnotic relation established between them. It is at the same time admitted that this declaration raises a vital issue which goes to the very essence of the subject under consideration.

The importance of the issue here defined is such that its presentation is reserved for another chapter.

CHAPTER V.

The Deadly Parallel.

Does a hypnotist control the will or voluntary powers of his subject during the continuance of the hypnotic relation?

Upon the results of absolute, scientific demonstration it is again declared that he does.

Moreover, in so far only as this is true does hypnotism exist at any time. In just so far as the will or voluntary power of the subject is dominated or controlled by the hypnotist, in just that degree is the process invoked and the relation established hypnotic in character. And conversely, in just so far as the will or voluntary power of an individual is under his own independent control, to that degree is he free from hypnotic control.

As previously stated, the School of Natural Science has demonstrated the truth of the foregoing declarations in such manner as to leave not the least possible room for doubt or uncertainty. It would therefore be entirely admissible to rest the case upon their demonstration and throw the burden of proof upon whomsoever may desire to controvert it.

This position is not only admissible, but would be equally desirable if it were not for the possibility, as well as the probability, that there may be interested parties who are not prepared to accept the authority of this School as sufficient or its demonstrations as scientifically conclusive. To such as these other evidence would be necessary. For the benefit of any who may, perchance, make such a demand, other evidence will be furnished of such a character as to meet the requirements of the most hostile opponent or incredulous skeptic.

Under the law of evidence it is held that the "admissions of a party against his own interests" are to be regarded as evidence of the highest character. In practice such evidence is generally considered to be as nearly conclusive as any that can be adduced.

For illustration: Suppose a party is on trial charged with

the commission of some public offense. At the trial of the case he is placed on the witness stand and of his own volition admits that the charge against him is true. In such case his free and voluntary admission is held to be evidence of the strongest possible character.

This is precisely the character of evidence to be introduced upon the question here at issue. Various eminent hypnotists all over the world have gone upon the witness stand in the trial of this question, and have there voluntarily offered their testimony to the world for what it is worth. They have testified from the standpoint of "parties in interest."

They have been publicly accused of the serious offense of practicing a profession and invoking processes which involve the control of the will or voluntary powers of their subjects. If this accusation is sustained it means slavery of the most unhappy character. The human soul and human reason protest against slavery. Public conscience condemns it. Every moral sentiment or lofty emotion resents it. Therefore these men stand before the world charged with the offense of practicing an art which has for its purpose the enslavement of the souls of their fellow-men. But the crime of which they stand accused before the bar of public conscience is not that of mere physical slavery. It is the slavery of the human soul.

It has been necessary for them to defend themselves. The only defense possible in a case of this nature is a general denial of the charge. This defense has been entered by them, and the issue is therefore squarely joined. They deny the charge. In other words, they plead "Not guilty." They allege by way of defense that the processes of hypnotism do not involve the control of the will or voluntary powers of the subject in the least degree. This is the only possible defense they could make without seriously jeopardizing their cause at the very outset.

Unfortunately, however, for the position they have thus assumed, and with equally good fortune for the cause of truth, they have been compelled to make certain admissions in their testimony which are fatal to their entire cause. It is the purpose of this chapter to call attention to these fatal admissions. It is hoped and believed that this may be done in such manner as to avoid all offense to the sensibilities of those who in good faith have advocated the cause of hypnotism. To do this the several witnesses will be allowed to tell their stories in their own way, and the reader will be asked to simply note the admissions as the case proceeds.

The first witness called is John Duncan Quackenbos, M. D., Professor Emeritus of Columbia University, who is also one of the principal defendants on trial. Prof. Quackenbos has for many years been considered one of the ablest exponents of hypnotism in all its varied phases in this country. His reputation for both intelligence and honesty seems to be above suspicion. His writings are among the acknowledged authorities of our western world, and may be found in our leading public and private libraries. His prominent position as a public educator is one which entitles him to a respectful hearing. His experience covers many years of active practice and demonstration and has been of such a character as to enable him to speak with as much assurance as any defendant in the case. Indeed, his testimony may be regarded as that of an expert, from his point of view.

It is due him, as well as his many students and friends all over the country, to state that the moral tone of his writings is above reproach. No one can read his works without a feeling of respect for the man himself, as well as for the order of his intelligence. It is for this very reason, however, that his public utterances upon this question are all the more dangerous.

His testimony, here to be presented, is embodied in a work entitled *"Hypnotism in Mental and Moral Culture."* This is his most recent work, and therefore represents his best knowledge and most mature judgment upon the question at issue.

At page 268 he says:

"Will-power has nothing to do with hypnotic suggestion, neither the will-power of the operator nor that of the subject. Paralysis of the will, which is the *bête noire* of the popular mind, is inconceivable. The mesmerizee (subject) is inspired or empowered, as the case may be, and works out his own salvation in his own objective life without conscious effort of any kind. . . . Above all, he is in no degree subject to another Will."

This brief quotation from the concluding chapter of his book is sufficient to clearly define his position upon the particular question here under consideration. It will be observed that he unqualifiedly holds that a hypnotist does not control the will or voluntary powers of his subject. It is for this reason that he is made a party defendant. For the same reason he is called as a witness in this case.

But while he is on the witness stand we have the right, and it is not only our right but our duty as well, to carefully weigh and consider all the testimony he has offered. In this manner only shall we be able to do him full justice as "a party in interest."

The opening sentence of his testimony is at page 3 of the same work and reads as follows:

"Hypnotism, or hypnotic sleep, implies a mind condition in which the mental action and the will-power of a sensitive subject are under the control of an operator who has induced the state."

Compare this, his definition of hypnotism, with his subsequent declaration above quoted, that "will-power has nothing to do with hypnotic suggestion, neither the will-power of the operator nor that of the subject." Then lay it down by the side of his further declaration that "above all, he (the subject) is in no degree subject to another will." We are then led to ask what could possibly induce any man of intelligence to voluntarily place himself in so compromising and so equivocal a position before an enlightened and truth-loving public.

The importance of these conflicting declarations entitles us to set them in parallel columns for the purpose of more careful analysis and more critical study. Here they are. Examine them carefully:

Page 3.	Page 268.
"Hypnotism, or hypnotic sleep, implies a mind condition in which the mental action and the will-power of a sensitive subject are under the control of an operator who has induced the state."	"Will-power has nothing to do with hypnotic suggestion, neither the will-power of the operator nor that of the subject. * * * Above all, he (the subject) is in no degree subject to another will."

Again, we are constrained to ask what motive, or double

motive, could prompt any man of intelligence and moral perception to thus freely and voluntarily impeach, discredit and utterly destroy the value of his own testimony in a matter of such importance to himself as well as to the world in general?

To one whose life and work have made the study of the human mind in all its activities, moods and motives a necessity, there is but one answer, namely—a conflict between acknowledged truth and personal interest. This, however, does not necessarily imply deliberate dishonesty nor intentional deception, for the influence of personal interest is often so powerful in its effect upon the intelligence as entirely to obscure the application of the most exact and definite knowledge.

When the author above quoted took his pen and proceeded to deliver his message to the world he was full of his subject. His long experience and study entitled him to feel that he had acquired something of value to his fellow-men. The spirit of truth and the honest desire to serve mankind prompted him to write. With no particular thought of himself, nor of the necessity for his subsequent vindication, justification or defense, but with a clear consciousness of the truth alone, based upon his own personal and repeated demonstrations, and an untroubled conscience, the first words he penned were these:

"Hypnotism, or hypnotic sleep, implies a mind condition in which the mental action and the will-power of a sensitive subject are under the control of an operator who has induced the state."

Upon the basis of this (his own definition of hypnotism), which is exact, explicit and true as far as it goes, he then proceeds for more than 250 pages to reiterate, elaborate, elucidate and expound the subject of hypnotism in a clear and forceful manner. But when he is almost ready to lay down his pen and say, "It is finished," his attention is called to the fact that the "popular mind" condemns the practice of hypnotism on the ground that it involves a "paralysis of the will."

His intelligence at once recognizes the fact that "paralysis of the will" is a most undesirable achievement. He is therefore compelled, as an honest and intelligent gentleman, to observe that the will and voluntary powers of every intelligent individual constitute the very foundation of his individual responsibility. He knows that individual responsibility is the very corner stone of the entire social and moral structure. It therefore occurs to him that any process, practice or profession which involves a paralysis of the will must be deemed a menace to the individual, and therefore inimical to the highest interests of society and morals.

He therefore feels that his profession and practice, as well as the processes and forces he employs, are under the ban of suspicion. For the time being he forgets the meaning of his definition and realizes only that it is incumbent upon him to defend himself and his profession from the accusing attitude of the "popular mind."

He sees that there is but one method by which he can do this. That is by an unqualified denial of the justice of popular sentiment and popular judgment. There is nothing left for him to do but reverse them. It is then that he declares with all the earnestness of an injured party that "Paralysis of the will, which is the *bête noire* of the popular mind, is inconceivable."

It is then that personal interest overrides the power of acknowledged truth. For the time being his opening definition and all his work based thereon pass from his memory and their meaning from his consciousness. With all his faculties and powers awake and actively engaged in an effort to combat the "popular mind," he is, for the time being, utterly oblivious to the fact that by his own admissions he stands condemned. Then it is that he pens "The Deadly Parallel."

Had he been content to rest his case upon its merit, he would have stood before the world a notable exception, and must then have challenged the admiration of all honest and intelligent men.

To fully appreciate the overwhelming manner in which the testimony of this defendant must stand as his own most powerful accuser, it is necessary to read his book through from beginning to end. A few brief quotations, however, will be sufficient to illustrate the complete manner in which he has "turned state's evidence" in the case at issue.

At pages 5 and 6 he says:

"It has long been known that a human being can be thrown into an artificial sleep, during which he sustains such a relation to an operator who has induced it that he is sensitive only to what the operator tells him he is sensitive to, and is wholly subject, so far as his mental operations and physical actions are concerned, to the volition of his hypnotist. A hypnotized person sees, hears, tastes, smells and feels what the operator says that he sees, hears, tastes, smells and feels—and nothing else. For the time being his individuality is surrendered to the person who has hypnotized him."

Special attention is called to the admission herein contained to the effect that the subject "is wholly subject, so far as his mental operations and physical actions are concerned, to the volition of his hypnotist." In this connection also let it be remembered that "volition" is nothing more nor less than the "active Will." Then note the parallel:

Page 5.	Page 268.
"He is wholly subject, so far as his mental operations and physical actions are concerned, to the volition of his hypnotist."	"Above all, he is in no degree subject to another will."

Comment is unnecessary.

Again, at page 11, after a most vivid portrayal of the process by which he proceeds to obtain control of his subject, he says:

"And in a few moments a profound breath is taken, the lids close, . . . and I know that I have been given possession of that soul for such time as I may prescribe, *to do with it what I will.*"

Once more we are compelled to note the parallel:

Page 11.	Page 268.
"I know that I have been given possession of that soul for such a time as I may prescribe to do with it what I will."	"Above all, he is in no degree subject to another will."

And so we might proceed throughout his entire work, and upon almost every page produce cumulative evidence of the same general character. It is only when he finds it necessary to meet the accusing attitude of the "popular mind" that he turns from the logic of his own experiments and demonstrations. But the "Deadly Parallel" has done its work.

Much more space and consideration have been given to the testimony of this witness than would otherwise have been done but for the following reasons:

1. He is a conspicuous educator of acknowledged ability and a professor in one of the leading universities of the country.

2. He is a modern writer of the Occidental school, whose interest in the subject under consideration has kept him before the public mind in a most conspicuous manner.

3. So far as known to the writer he is a man of clean moral life and excellent professional standing.

4. He stands as an acknowledged authority upon the subject of hypnotism among his western contemporaries.

5. His long experience as a professional man, together with his many years of active investigation and practice as a hypnotist entitle him to speak with as much assurance as any writer of his time who has written upon this subject.

6. His treatment of the subject under consideration is identical in all its essential features with that of other leading western authorities.

7. The fatal contradictions in which he has involved himself in his efforts to justify the practice of hypnotism are of the same general nature as are those of every other authority who has denied that the will or voluntary power of the subject is under control of his hypnotist.

8. He therefore stands as a typical defendant in this case, possessing the highest character and attainments, and for these reasons is in position to set up as strong a defense as can be made.

With as much brevity as the importance of the subject will admit, the testimony of other authorities will now be presented.

From a work entitled "Eastern Manners," by Jameson, the following quotation concerning the effects of the "Evil Eye"—as he has chosen to designate the hypnotic gaze—is reproduced. He says:

"The first effect of the malignant glance is to deprive the individuals subject to it of the capability to exercise their will. They are brought under the absolute control of the possessor of the 'Evil Eye.'"

There can be no mistaking the meaning of this quotation. It stands as another unqualified admission of the fact that the hypnotist does control the will or voluntary powers of his subject.

One of the most useful works of reference, perhaps, to be found, covering this subject, is entitled *"Private Instructions in the Science and Art of Organic Magnetism,"* by Miss Chandos Leigh Hunt, of London, England. This is also a comparatively recent publication. Its special value, in this connection, is in the fact that the author has supplied us with a literal reproduction of the separate and distinct methods or processes employed by some fifty or more of the leading hypnotists, from whose writings she quotes extensively.

As plainly as words can be employed in the expression of intelligent ideas, these various authors have only described their differing methods of reaching the same result. But what is the result reached? It is nothing less than the subjection of the will or voluntary powers of the subject to the domination and control of the operator, whom we name the "hypnotist."

In describing her own method of obtaining such control, she leads to the point at which the subject becomes unable to open his eyes, and then she says:

"Being unable to open them by his volition" (which is only another way of saying that he no longer possesses the will or voluntary power to do so), "open his eyes, . . . making him fix his eyes upon yours, and draw him toward you by drawing-passes. He is now controlled, and you may proceed at once to the production of experimental phenomena."

Note the expression, *"He is now controlled,"* etc. There can be no possible mistake as to the meaning of these words. They state the fact in all its simplicity and truth. He is indeed "controlled."

A little further on, at page 31, she says:

"When you are operating upon a subject, you must *Will* that he cannot open his eyes," etc.

At page 32 she further says:

"The *Magnetic-Will* must be employed. . . . You will then

be able to draw him towards you, provided you fully **express your Will**," etc.

More than one hundred similar expressions may be found in her "Instructions," each of which clearly and unqualifiedly indicates but one fixed and definite purpose on the part of the hypnotist, and that is to obtain control of the will or voluntary powers of her subject. The process which she so cleverly describes merely discloses the several objective steps by which this one purpose is accomplished.

Dr. Gregory says:

"It is necessary to act with a cool, collected mind, and a firm *Will*, while the patient (subject) is perfectly passive," etc.

It is also said of Dr. Darling:

"A very large proportion is found, on examination, to be more or less subject to his *Will*. . . . In like manner *he controls the Will*, so that the subject is *compelled* to perform a certain act," etc.

Professor Gregory says of Mr. Lewis:

"He adds certain gestures and passes, all of which are most deeply imbued with that energetic concentration of the *Will* which I have never seen so strongly developed," etc.

Captain James says:

"It is recommended that the operator should concentrate his energies, and earnestly *Will*," etc.

Kluge says:

"The Magnetist should make that pass with all the force and continuance of *Will*, as if pressing strongly upon the patient," etc.

Baron Dupotet says:

"To establish the art of magnetizing, all then consists in recognizing at first the properties (fixed and unalterable) of the Magnetic agent, then all these wherewith we can ourselves invest it by the imprint of our *Will*.

"Directing a continuously fixed look upon a subject with premeditated intention, and after some minutes upon another person, it is possible to cause, by strong *Will*, the subject to become furious against that person.

"It is by the immaterial power of the soul that all these faculties are brought into play; it is by this exorbitant *Will* that man possesses, that he can violently enter, by the energy of his *Will*, into the soul of another man, and install himself there. . . . The simple *Will* can profoundly overthrow the physical, intellectual and moral organization of another man."

The following definition of hypnotism may be found in Foster's Encyclopædic Medical Dictionary:

"An abnormal state into which some persons may be thrown . . . by the exercise of another person's *Will*; characterized by *suspension of the Will* and consequent obedience to the prompting of 'suggestions' from without."

Dr. James R. Cocke, of our own country, in his recent work on the subject of hypnotism, at page 9, says:

"Briefly, then, hypnotism may be induced by impressing profoundly the mentality through all the senses. The intellect, the reason, the *Will,* the emotions, are all children of the senses."

Page 12:

"I had one man tell me that he did it all for amusement, and that he was not in any way *under my control,* but I soon convinced him of his mistake by hypnotizing him one day and telling him that he had drunk a number of flies with his cup of coffee, for he immediately vomited his whole breakfast."

Page 13:

"I have recently made a very curious experiment in order to determine whether a person *paralyzed by hypnotic suggestion* would act in the same way as he would if he were paralyzed from organic disease of the brain."

Italics supplied by the author.

Page 21:

"The hypnotized subject will become physically blind at the operator's *Will.*"

Page 35:

"The moralists who are careful of human dignity, and who are preoccupied with the thought of such great possibilities of danger, are in the right. They are right to condemn a practice which may rob a man of his free will without the possibility of resistance on his part; they would be a thousand times right if the remedy were not side by side with the evil."

Particular attention is called to the admission that the practice of hypnotism is one *"which may rob a man of his free will without the possibility of resistance on his part."* This confesses all that has been claimed thus far. The concluding clause of the quotation which suggests that a remedy is "side by side with the evil," involves an assumption, pure and simple, which the following pages will fully demonstrate.

Dr. Luys, of the Charity Hospital of Paris, in his Clinical Lectures, says:

"You can not only oblige this defenseless being (hypnotized subject), who is incapable of opposing the slightest resistance, to give from hand to hand anything you choose, but you can also make him sign a promise, draw up a bill of exchange, or any kind of agreement. You can make him write an holographic will (which according to the French law, would be valid), which he will hand over to you, and of which he will never know the existence. He is ready to fulfill the minutest legal formalities, and will do so with a calm, serene and natural manner, which would deceive the most expert law officers. The somnambulist will not hesitate either, you may be sure, to make a denunciation, or bear false witness. *They are, I repeat, the passive instruments of your Will.*"

Prof. De Lawrence, in his recent work on "Hypnotism," says:

Page 77:

"There is a way in which a shrewd hypnotist can succeed in putting people under the influence who really do not care to be hypnotized."

Page 78:

"The author has, during his years of experience, discovered and successfully used a method by which he has succeeded in hypnotizing a great many people against their will, who had never been operated on before."

Page 79:

"You can then proceed by a few well chosen suggestions to put him dead asleep and induce somnambulism or trance in the regular way. *He will ever afterwards be your subject* if you understand your business in giving post-hypnotic suggestions."

To the same general effect the testimony of other witnesses of equal professional standing might be continued indefinitely. The writer here asserts, without the least fear of contradiction, that there is not a single acknowledged authority on the subject of hypnotism but will furnish evidence of the same general tenor and effect as that here submitted.

The reader is asked to specially note this statement. It is of the most vital importance for the reason that it makes every hypnotist a witness against hypnotism. An exhaustive research through the literature of the subject will establish the truth of the declaration here made and fully justify the position here taken.

It now remains to close the case with the testimony of witnesses who are able to speak from a definite knowledge based upon absolute personal experiences which are above and beyond the power of controversy. These witnesses are hypnotic subjects in whose behalf this work is presented to the world. These are the most important of all the "parties in interest" and are therefore entitled to be heard.

The first witness of this character is a colored boy of twenty years who was the unhappy and unwilling victim of one of the leading professional hypnotists of this country whose name is familiar to almost every student of the subject.

It is a fact with which every professional hypnotist is familiar, that the colored race is peculiarly susceptible to hypnotic influence. Colored people, both men and women, make excellent subjects for experimental purposes.

The young man whose experience is offered in evidence, lived in one of our southern cities. His first hypnotic experience was at a public entertainment given by the hypnotist with whom he afterwards traveled. He was called to the platform from the audience for the purpose of experimentation. He was assured that he would not be injured in any way and that the process was entirely harmless. After much persuasion, in which some of his friends joined, he finally consented to go upon the platform and submit to the test. He proved to be a most susceptible subject, and upon the second or third trial was completely hypnotized. Under the hypnotic spell he was made to furnish entertainment for his friends and proved a valuable acquisition to his hypnotist.

A proposition was made to him the next day to travel and submit to hypnotic tests whenever required. He refused to go on any terms whatever. But he attended another entertainment, and was again hypnotized. After that day he was the helpless instrument of the man who had thus dethroned his will. When the hypnotist left the city the colored boy went with him. For the first few weeks he was kept under hypnotic control much of the time in order to overcome his lingering desire to return to his home and parents. For a period of two years he was the helpless instrument under the control of the relentless will of his hypnotist.

At last his mind gave way under the strain and he became a raving maniac. In this condition he was carried to an asylum, and, so far as the writer knows, is still an inmate of that institution.

The next witness is a young man of Swedish parentage, who was induced under similar circumstances to first submit himself to a public test. He fell an easy victim to hypnotic influences. In a similar manner he was compelled to follow the fortunes of an unscrupulous hypnotist and submit himself to public tests whenever required.

The writer chanced to attend one of the public entertainments at which this young man was subjected to the most cruel and inhuman treatment it has ever been his misfortune to witness. The next day, through an unexpected incident, the writer and the young man were brought together under conditions which made it possible to obtain the facts here narrated.

The young man pleaded for help to break the spell which bound him as the helpless slave of an unscrupulous master. His story pictured each day as a living hell. Many times he tried to run away and conceal himself. He had even tried to commit suicide to escape the mental clutches of his tormentor. Every effort for liberty only bound the chains of hypnotic influence more securely upon him.

As he told the story his face blanched with fear and his body shook with suppressed agony. In his eyes was the look of the hunted deer. He seemed to realize that his very soul was slowly but surely being consumed by the strange power which had overwhelmed all his voluntary faculties and powers. He too became a mental wreck inside of eighteen months from the time of his first hypnotic subjection, and was abandoned by the man who had wrecked his life, but by mere chance was found by relatives and cared for by them.

The third witness is a young and beautiful girl whose life was full of brightness and promise until the fateful day when she first submitted to the seductive charm of the hypnotic trance. She was exhibited for three days upon the stage in her country town and then left home, friends and loved ones to follow the man who had overthrown her powers of resistance. Insanity and suicide ended the earthly career of this beautiful girl, and her murderer is still permitted to practice his black art upon others equally ignorant and equally innocent.

These are but three of the many witnesses of this class whose testimony is unanswerable. Comment is unnecessary. These three speak for the multitudes. They do not theorize nor speculate nor argue. They speak with absolute authority. There is none who dares dispute them. They testify from a personal experience. Their testimony is conclusive.

What hypnotic control has done for these three it will do for as many more as submit to its influence under similar conditions. The fact that it has overthrown the will and voluntary powers of but a single individual is sufficient to discredit the testimony of all the so-called "authorities" whose observations and speculations have led them to declare that such results are impossible or "inconceivable."

The reader is asked to note the fact that among all the authorities who have arrayed themselves upon the defense, not one is able to speak from the standpoint of exact and definite knowledge. Their testimony invariably takes the form of argumentation or disputation. Not one is able to say, "I know."

As a typical illustration, attention is called to the work of Thomson Jay Hudson, LL. D., entitled "The Law of Psychic Phenomena." This author devotes an entire chapter of twenty closely written pages to the subject of "Hypnotism and Crime." His purpose is to show, among other things, the "utter impossibility of victimizing virtue and innocence by means of hypnotism."

He takes the position that it is impossible for a hypnotist to so far control the will of his subject as to compel him to do that which he knows, or conscientiously believes to be wrong. He then lays down a number of suppositions and with these suppositions as a premise proceeds to an elaborate argument in which he endeavors to sustain his position.

His argument is ingenious and interesting, from the standpoint of mere speculation, but, after all, it is nothing but an argument. Moreover, it is an argument which is entirely answerable even from the basis of his own premises. Aside from this, however, it cannot stand in the face of facts demonstrated. Under the relentless logic of personal experience and personal demonstration it must yield to the immutable law of gravity and fall to the ground.

Let it be remembered that the definite purpose of this

chapter is to establish in the mind of the reader one fundamental fact, and one only, namely—that a hypnotist does control the will or voluntary powers of his subject during the continuance of the hypnotic relation.

The establishment of this fact is here based upon three distinct and separate lines of direct evidence either of which, under all the rules for determining the value of testimony, would be deemed sufficient in law, even though it stood alone and unsupported. These three lines of evidence are as follows:

1. The absolutely positive, definite and uncontroverted testimony of the School of Natural Science, based upon the most exact, personal and scientific demonstration.

2. The voluntary, public admissions of hypnotists themselves, whose profession, practice and personal interest have together impelled them to take the witness stand in their own defense. These admissions, upon examination, are found to be of the most positive and unqualified character, and coming as they do from the defendants on trial, must be regarded as evidence of the most conclusive character.

3. The evidence of hypnotic subjects whose ruined lives and shattered reason tell the story of the despotic master and his helpless victim, with a force and pathos which puncture every sophistry and silence all ridicule.

By the authority and sanction of Natural Science, by the voluntary, public admissions of hypnotists themselves, by the wrecked lives and dethroned reason of hypnotic subjects, and finally, by the personal demonstrations and definite knowledge of the writer, it is declared as an indisputable and a demonstrable fact that a hypnotist does control the will and voluntary powers, as well as the sensory organism of his subject during the continuance of the hypnotic relation.

In like manner it is again declared that hypnotism is the process by and through which a hypnotist obtains, holds and exercises control of the will, voluntary powers and sensory organism of his subject, and only in so far as such control exists is the process hypnotic.

CHAPTER VI.

MAN AND HIS TWO ORGANISMS.

No adequate conception of the true nature of hypnosis is possible until the threefold nature of man is understood and appreciated as a scientific proposition. This subject has been fully and carefully presented in "Harmonics of Evolution" (Volume I, of this series), chapter III, to which the reader is referred for full and complete data. The following extracts from that work are here reproduced as the basis of our present analysis.

Vol. I, p. 39, *et seq.*:

"Man is composed of body, spirit and soul. This means that man has a physical body and a spiritual body which are controlled and operated by the highest entity, the intelligent ego, the soul. The physical body is composed of physical matter. The particles which are coarse in texture move at a correspondingly low rate of vibratory action. The physical body is provided with physical sensory organs. Nature has conditioned these organs to receive and register the vibrations of physical matter only. These vibrations are registered upon the physical brain, through which instrument they become cognizant to the intelligent soul. By aid of these organs the intelligent ego or soul becomes cognizant of different external, physical objects, elements and conditions. The recognition by the ego of these external, physical objects, elements and conditions constitutes what we term physical sensation. Each of the physical organs of sensation receives and registers a different range of vibration.

"Through the operation of these several physical organs, each one registering a different range of vibration, the intelligent ego is brought into conscious relations with a very wide range of vibratory activity of physical matter. . . .

"It must now be clear that the physical sensory organs are adapted to receive and register only the vibrations of physical matter. It must also be clear that they are adapted to receive only a limited range of physical vibrations.

"The spiritual body of a man is composed of 'spiritual material.' That is, of matter much finer than the finest physical matter, and moving at a higher rate of vibration than the finest particles of physical matter moving at their highest possible rate. The spiritual body permeates the physical and constitutes the model upon which physical matter integrates. The spiritual body, like the physical, is provided with five sensory organs. They are adapted to receive and register vibrations of spiritual matter only; that is, of matter lying upon the same plane of vibratory action as the spiritual body itself. By the aid of these organs the intelligent ego becomes cognizant of different external, spiritual objects, elements and conditions. The recognition by the ego of these objects, elements and conditions constitutes what we term spiritual sensation. Each one of the spiritual sensory organs receives and registers a different range of vibration.

"By use of these spiritual organs, each registering a different range of vibratory activity upon the spiritual plane, the intelligence or soul is brought into conscious relation with a very wide range of vibrations of spiritual material.

"These spiritual organs register the vibrations of spiritual material only. They are also limited in their capacity on the spiritual plane in a manner analogous to the limitations of the physical senses.

"That which is important in this connection is the fact that the spiritual sensory organs do not register the vibrations of physical matter.

"It now becomes possible to conceive of two planes of matter, life and intelligence, correlated yet separated by apparently impassable barriers. This knowledge explains how matter upon one plane is invisible and intangible to intelligence upon another. It explains how sound on one plane is silence on the other; how the light of one plane is darkness upon the other.

"The earth man is, therefore, the inhabitant and operator of two distinct instruments for the uses of his intelligence. Each performs functions peculiar to its own plane of matter. Neither body is more than a mere vehicle for the uses of the operating ego. Both are important. Both are indispensable to the soul seeking knowledge of itself and its environment."

In the light of this analysis it would appear that Paul knew what he was talking about when he declared to the Corinthians in such exact and unqualified terms that: "There is a natural body, and there is a spiritual body." (I Cor., 15, 44.) It is also evident that Christ fully understood the relation of these two bodies to the third and highest element in the triune nature of man when he asked the searching and vital question: "For what shall it profit a man, if he shall gain the whole world, and lose his own soul?" (Mark, 8, 36.)

From the foregoing analysis it will be understood that the physical body is but a coarser duplicate of the spiritual, and that each and every physical organ has its spiritual duplicate. There is a spiritual brain as well as a physical brain. There is a spiritual organ of sight as well as a physical one. There are spiritual organs of touch, taste, smell and hearing, just as there are physical organs of these several senses. In other words, for each separate physical organ of the brain there is a corresponding spiritual one. This being a scientific fact, it will not be difficult to understand its natural corollary, which is, that under given conditions the intelligent soul which owns and operates these separate organisms may receive impressions through either set of its sensory organs.

But man in the physical body is generally so conditioned that his intelligence operates far more consciously through the physical organism than it does through the spiritual. Just why this is true is not so much a matter of importance at this time as the fact that it is one of the provisions of nature with which science must deal in its solution of the question here under consideration.

It is also a fact that wherever this condition obtains the individual is concerned with and absorbed in the impressions which reach his consciousness from the physical world only. The action of the spiritual organism, however, is not entirely suspended, as might be inferred. It is merely obscured or covered up, as it were, by that condition of nature which fixes the attention upon the physical plane.

But even in this condition the spiritual organism sometimes conveys its impressions in a dim way to the consciousness of the individual, and when it does so we call them "intuitions."

The following illustration may serve to present the facts and the principle more clearly to mind:

Go into one of the large, steel manufacturing establishments of the country while the machinery is in full operation and there attempt to carry on a conversation with a person twenty feet distant from you. However much you may both exert yourselves you will be unable to hear a word he says. The noise of the machinery and the general confusion of the factory will make it impossible. His voice is drowned in the general uproar and fails to make a sufficiently strong impression upon your consciousness to be recognized with distinctness. You are too busily engaged with the various and conflicting impressions made upon your consciousness by the thunder, clang and turmoil of the factory.

But the sound of the voice is there, just the same. More than this, it even makes an impression upon your sensory organism. Why, then, do you not recognize the fact? It is only because your consciousness is so preoccupied with the more intense impressions of the louder noises of the factory, for the time being, that you fail to distinguish the sound of the voice.

In a somewhat analogous manner the average man seems to be shut out and away from all conscious touch with the spiritual world. But this is only a seeming condition, for it is not true in fact. He is merely so absorbed, for the time being, in the more intense impressions which reach his consciousness through the physical senses that the spiritual do not impress themselves upon him with sufficient relative force to be so identified or distinguished by him.

Carrying the illustration still further, it is an interesting fact that a worker in the steel factory, in course of time, trains his sense of hearing to distinguish the sound of the human voice even in the midst of the din and blast of the factory which at first made such a thing impossible. The question naturally arises as to how he acquires this remarkable power. The answer is simple.

It is necessary for him to communicate with his fellow workmen in some manner. The only adequate means of communication with which he is familiar is the sound of the human voice. In the midst of the noise of the factory, therefore, he must still depend upon his sense of hearing and upon its ability to distinguish the sound of the human voice. He unconsciously begins a course of systematic training to accomplish the desired result. He may be, and generally is, wholly ignorant of the law involved. But, "Necessity is the mother of invention," and without knowing it he begins to train his ear to the new condition of things.

His attention is constantly fixed upon the thing to be accomplished. His consciousness gradually responds. By the continued exercise of his conscious faculties and powers he slowly but surely learns to differentiate between the impressions which the various noises make upon his consciousness. In course of time and constant training his power of perception is intensified until the human voice once more distinctly registers its impressions, and to his trained consciousness stands out fully distinguishable from the general turmoil of his environment. He has simply developed his power of attention to the thing desired until his consciousness responds to the new demands thus made upon it.

By a method which is somewhat analogous to this it is possible for anyone who possesses the necessary Intelligence, Courage and Perseverance and the right desire, together with the time, opportunity and proper instruction, to accustom his consciousness to take note of the impressions which are being constantly registered upon it through the spiritual sensory organs.

(It may not be out of place to here suggest that the development of this subject, together with an exposition of the laws, principles and processes involved, is reserved for another volume of this series.)

But while man is in touch with his fellow man upon the physical plane and with the plane of physical nature generally, his attention is absorbed upon that plane. He does not feel the necessity for employing other means or using other channels of communication. In most instances he does not even know that they exist. And so long as there is no absolute necessity for the development of the finer senses he continues to be absorbed with those more familiar to him. Just so long as his attention is thus confined to a plane of existence entirely below that of the spiritual his consciousness distinguishes nothing higher than *the plane of his attention*.

Other illustrations concerning the physically blind and deaf might be given which would carry the principle still further, but this is a digression which would distract attention from the distinct subject now under consideration.

CHAPTER VII.

HYPNOTISM AND THE THREE BRAINS.

The threefold nature of man, body, spirit and soul, constitutes the fundamental fact from which it is possible to obtain a rational understanding of hypnotism in its physiological, pathological and psychological aspects.

The physical brain is the primary physical organ of the Soul or essential Intelligence. It is the central organic instrument by and through which the individual intelligence receives impressions from the outside world of physical nature. It is also the physical instrument first employed by the intelligent soul in communicating its impressions, ideas and thoughts to other intelligences.

Whatever affects the intelligent faculties, capacities and powers of the soul from the purely physical plane is necessarily related to the central physical organ of the soul—the physical brain.

Any adequate understanding of the physiological action of hypnosis, therefore, calls for definite knowledge of the relation of the hypnotic process to the physical brain itself. This opens a broad subject of the most profound and absorbing interest. Its complete exposition would require a volume in itself. The purpose and limitations of this work, however, forbid more than a very brief outline of the subject, leaving the interested student to complete his purely physiological studies by an examination of the standard works upon that particular branch of the subject here under consideration.

The outline here given will nevertheless be sufficient, it is hoped, to disclose some of the popular fallacies in which the subject of hypnotism has become involved.

By the term brain, as here employed, is meant that part of the central nervous organism which is inclosed within the cavity of the human skull. This organ of the intelligence is divided into three distinct parts. For the purpose of this work these three distinct parts or general divisions constitute three distinct and separate brains which, according to scientific nomenclature, are designated as follows:

1. *Medulla Oblongata.* This, to the uninstructed observer, would appear to be little more than the enlarged upper end of the spinal cord. It lies just inside the opening through which the spinal cord enters the skull at its base. It is somewhat in the form of a pyramid, and is about one and one-fourth inches long by one inch broad at its broadest part. It is continuous with the spinal cord below, and seems to be nothing more than an extension of it. It is connected above with both the other brains by a bridge of nervous tissues, technically known as the *Pons Varolii.*

2. *Cerebellum,* or little brain. This brain occupies the lower back portion of the skull cavity, somewhat back of the Medulla. It is connected with the Medulla and also the upper brain by the bridge above named.

3. *Cerebrum,* or great brain. This brain entirely fills all the front and upper parts of the skull cavity and is known as the intellectual brain. It is connected below with both the other brains by the same bridge of nervous tissues above referred to.

Each of these three brains is divided into two parts, right and left. In the Cerebrum and Cerebellum these two halves are called hemispheres or lobes. For a full and complete description and illustration of these organs, together with special information as to their anatomy and physiology, the reader is referred to any standard, modern work on these subjects.

For the sake of easy reference the three brains will be hereinafter designated in the order above mentioned, as the primary, secondary and third brains, the Medulla being designated as the primary, the Cerebellum as the secondary and the Cerebrum as the third brain.

This sequence is adopted for the reason that it represents the exact order in which Nature has evolved the animal brain. That is to say, the lowest forms of animal life, such for instance as the mollusk, have only the primary brain. This is found to be but an enlarged terminal section of a central nerve cord. To this extent it is analogous to the central nerve organism of man—minus the second and third brains.

As might be anticipated, the intelligence manifested through such a brain is of the lowest type and the most limited in its scope and operation. It seems to be confined almost entirely to the one line of activity which has to do with the struggle for nutrition. Even here in this narrowly limited field of operation, it seems to be little more than a reflex of the purely physical demand for food. It seeks its nourishment with little more evidence of an individualized intelligence than is manifest in the sunflower when it turns its face to the sunlight. It seems to operate almost as an automatic instrument under the control of natural law, as if it were so impelled by the great Universal Intelligence which lies back of all life.

Ascending the scale of animal life in the order of evolutionary development, the second brain is slowly evolved. In proportion as this fact is accomplished the individualizing of intelligence is evidenced. The range of its activity is enlarged. The number and nature of the animal demands increase and become more and more complex. But still the character of intelligence is such as to suggest that its operations are much more nearly a mere reflex of the operation of natural law than the result of individual intelligence operating independently.

Nature continues this process of brain evolution until the third, or intellectual brain, makes its appearance in higher forms of animal life. This third brain reaches its climax of development in the highest type of human life. While there are many species below the level of human life in which the third brain is present in varying degrees of development, yet in man it finds its highest proportional development. The nascent or slumbering intelligence of the lower animal becomes the wakeful, self-conscious, rational and voluntary power in man.

These facts of physical science are of fundamental importance to a clear understanding of what occurs when a human being is subjected to the blighting power of hypnotic control. They will be more fully considered in that connection. A further study of the anatomy and physiology of the three human brains would develop many other facts of interest and value, but the limitations of this work exclude a more extended inquiry in this direction.

The science of phrenology is based on the hypothesis that each faculty or capacity of the human mind manifests itself through a special organ of the brain. This is evidenced in so many different ways that it has come to be generally accepted as a scientific fact. It is upon this basis that the different sections of the human brain have been assigned to different mental characteristics and activities. While it is conceded that phrenology is, as yet, very far from being an exact science, it is nevertheless an undoubted fact that, in a general sense, its groupings of the organs of the brain are correct.

Surgery has in recent years demonstrated the correctness of the phrenological hypothesis. It has definitely traced the action of various organs of the body to certain specific areas in the cortex of the brain. It has even platted the surface of the brain in such manner as to show what portions are directly related in their action to the various organs of the body.

Following this line of suggestion it is a fact which science has come to recognize, that those particular convolutions of the third brain through which we exercise our perceptive faculties and rational powers are located in the front portion of the upper brain cavity just above and back of the eyes. That is to say, the organs through which we perceive physical form, size, weight, color, locality, number, order, events, time, tune, language, causality and exercise the power of reason, all lie within a comparatively small space mainly above and just back of the eyes. These are the organs which give prominence and elevation to the forehead of man as compared with that of the animal.

It is important to note the fact that through the action of these perceptive organs we come into intelligent and rational touch with the outside or objective world. Because of this these are also frequently, and very aptly, designated as the "objective faculties" of the mind. It is through these that Mr. Hudson's "Objective Mind" operates. Through these the purely intellectual processes of the mind find expression. When we observe a physical object, note its form, size, weight and color, and then compare it with other objects with which we are familiar, and reason upon its probable composition, purpose and value, we are making use of our objective, perceptive, and rational faculties and powers through these organs.

That portion of the skull cavity just above and back of these perceptive or objective organs of the mind is supposed to contain the particular convolutions of the brain through which the emotional nature of man mainly finds expression.

Those convolutions of the brain which occupy the posterior portion of the third brain cavity are in some way related to the physical appetites, passions and desires.

The chief function of the second or middle brain thus far specifically identified by physical science is that of co-ordinating the motions of the physical body. By this is meant that process by and through which the entire body, as a single instrument, is brought under control of the individual will.

For instance: In the process of walking many individual muscles are brought into action. The power of the will to so co-ordinate the action of all the different muscles as to direct the body, as a whole, in the desired manner, is referable to the second brain.

Among the most important functions of the primary brain (the Medulla), thus far fully identified by physical science, attention is called to the following:

1. It acts as a conductor of both motor and sensory impressions from all parts of the body.

2. It constitutes a reflex center for numerous special nerves governing respiration, circulation, deglutition, the voice, etc.

In view of that which follows, it is of special interest to recall the historic fact that among the ancients the primary brain, now known to science as the Medulla Oblongata, was believed to be the seat of the soul. A study of the physiology of hypnotism will disclose the interesting fact that this ancient belief was not wholly without foundation.

Although the foregoing is but a mere suggestion of the anatomy and physiology of the human brain, all too brief and incomplete, yet it may serve to furnish the foundation for a more definite understanding of the physiological action of the forces, activities and processes involved in the exercise of hypnotic control.

CHAPTER VIII.

The Physiology and Pathology of Hypnotism.

It is important to bear in mind that there are all shades and degrees of hypnosis, ranging from the lightest form of hypnotic influence through all the deepening stages to the most profound state of complete functional suspension of the physical organism.

In the incipient stages the subject appears to be almost entirely conscious of all that is transpiring about him on the physical plane. But as the state is intensified he gradually loses control of his independent faculties and capacities as well as his voluntary powers, and his impressions from the outside, physical world about him. In the deeper state of complete lethargy or catalepsy his consciousness is wholly out of touch with his physical sensory organism. In this condition he becomes an automatic instrument under the control of the operator's will.

What physiological transformation or psychic inversion has occurred to produce this abnormal condition?

Science has been able to demonstrate that the primary physiological action of the hypnotic process is registered upon the physical brain of the subject. Moreover, it operates upon the physical brain in the reverse order of its evolutionary development. That is to say, its first apparent effects are registered upon the third or intellectual brain, its deeper effects upon the secondary brain and its final effects upon the primary brain, or Medulla Oblongata.

More than this, it is also found that the process has its inception in the extreme front portion of the third brain in the region of the physical organs of perception. Thence, as the hypnotic state deepens, it sweeps backward through the third brain, downward through the second brain, and in its final stages is communicated to the primary brain.

Every student of hypnotism is more or less familiar with the data bearing upon this phase of the subject, and will recognize their meaning and value as they are presented in this connection, as follows:

1. One of the most invariable manifestations which follow the inception of the hypnotic process is the inability of the subject to control the objective and perceptive faculties of the mind. His physical sensory organism becomes confused in its reports from the objective world of physical nature. The subject begins to receive mixed and imperfect impressions.

But when these impressions are analyzed they are found to be a composite of those received through the physical sensory organs from his physical environment, and those which are produced by the mental impulses of the operator's will. To these are also often added the results of imagination. This clearly indicates that the hypnotic process interferes with the natural action of those organs of the physical brain through which the objective and perceptive faculties of the mind operate.

2. As the hypnotic condition is intensified those convolutions of the third brain which lie immediately above and back of the eyes pass into a state of complete anaesthesia, or temporary paralysis. As a natural result the voluntary perception of the objective, physical world is destroyed. Consciousness is driven backward from the objective and rational plane. The will of the operator comes into partial control of the channels through which the consciousness of the subject is reached upon the spiritual plane.

However remarkable this statement may appear to the uninitiated, it is nevertheless susceptible of scientific demonstration. There are many collateral evidences of its truth with which every student of the subject is already familiar

For illustration: When this stage of hypnosis has been attained the operator is able to produce many and various effects upon the consciousness of his subject by simple impulses of his will. In the language of no less an authority than Prof. John Duncan Quackenbos, of Columbia University, "He (the hypnotized subject) is sensitive only to what the operator tells him he is sensitive to, and is wholly subject, so far as his mental operations and physical actions are concerned, to the volition of his hypnotist. He sees, hears, tastes, smells and feels what the operator says that he sees, hears, tastes, smells and feels—and nothing else. For the time being, his individuality is surrendered to the person who has hypnotized him."

The operator, for instance, wishes the subject to obtain the impression that he is giving him an apple to eat. Although the physical eyes of the subject are wide open and apparently looking straight at the object, instead of an apple the operator hands him a piece of wood, or a book, or substitutes any other object which happens to be handy. The subject invariably accepts whatever is given him under the impression that it is an apple, and unless restrained will proceed to eat it, or endeavor to do so, and will manifest every evidence of perfect satisfaction in the process. The physical sensory organs being in a state of anaesthesia, or temporary paralysis, convey no impression whatever to his consciousness. How, then, does he receive the impression of the apple, if not through the physical sensory organs?

The answer is that it is projected upon his consciousness by the mental impulse of the hypnotist, through the spiritual sensory organs of the subject. In this condition the spiritual sensory organism of the subject is within the power and under the domination and control of the operator's will, and as an automatic instrument responds to its impulses.

One phase of this experiment might appear, at first view, to contradict this statement. For instance, it will be observed that the operator speaks to the subject just as he would do if the subject were wide awake and in full possession of all his physical senses. He tells him in spoken words which anyone in the room might hear, that the object he presents to him is an apple. The subject also acts just as he might be expected to do if he had heard the spoken words through the medium of his physical sensory organs of hearing. The natural presumption, therefore, would be that he did so hear them. Such, however, is not the case wherever hypnosis has reached the stage here referred to.

A simple illustration will be sufficient to prove the accuracy of this statement. Let the subject's physical ears be completely muffled in such manner as to entirely shut out all physical sound of the operator's voice. Repeat the experiment under these conditions and it will be found that the subject will hear just the same and will obtain exactly the same impression as before.

Or, reverse the process. Instead of muffling the subject's physical ears to shut off the physical sound of the operator's voice, let a dozen or more of the spectators present (or a hundred for that matter) create all the noise and confusion possible. Let them carry this to a point where it is impossible for anyone in the room to hear a word the operator says. Under these conditions repeat the experiment. It will be found that exactly the same results will obtain. The physical noise which would otherwise drown the operator's voice will have not the least effect upon the subject. He will seemingly hear every word the operator says and will implicitly obey his every command.

Or, again: When the hypnotist has acquired complete control of all the channels through which the consciousness of the subject is approached, he may convey the same impression without an audible word. In this case it is not even necessary for him to present to the subject a physical object of any kind. A simple impulse of the will is sufficient.

Every one who is at all familiar with the processes of telepathy will understand how it is possible to convey an exact impression, or thought, or impulse of the will, to the consciousness of another quite independently of the physical senses. Independent telepathy, however, must not be confused with the hypnotic process, for it is no more related to hypnotism than it is to the ordinary process of telegraphy.

It should be remembered that an impulse of the mind formulated in a thought is a wholly different thing from the words in which that thought is clothed. It requires the spoken words to convey an exact thought from one mind to another through the instrumentality of the physical auditory nerve. In like manner, it requires the printed letters and words to convey the thought of a writer to the mind of his reader through the agency of the physical optic nerve. Although words are necessary in both instances, nevertheless, the words themselves do not constitute the thought in either case. They do not even constitute any part of the thought.

In the first instance they are merely a combination of physical sounds so arranged and modulated as to convey to the listener's consciousness through his physical sense of hearing the thought in the mind of the speaker. In the other they are only a set of physical signs so arranged as to convey the same thought from one mind to another through the physical sense of sight. In both cases they are simply used as instruments or vehicles for carrying thoughts from one intelligence to another.

Moreover, it is a scientific fact which anyone may demonstrate in course of time, under proper instruction, that the impulse of the human soul formulated into a definite thought is a force. This force, under proper conditions, may be impressed upon the consciousness of another intelligent soul without the aid of words either spoken, written or printed. This may be done without the use of the physical sensory organs at all. It may be accomplished through spiritual agencies exclusively. And the channels through which this may be accomplished are the spiritual sensory organs which are analogous to the physical sensory organs in both number and character, except that they operate upon a higher plane of refinement and vibratory activity.

This is precisely what occurs in that stage of hypnosis above referred to. The physical sensory organism is, for the time being, completely paralyzed. It conveys no impressions whatever to the imprisoned consciousness of the subject. In this condition his spiritual sensory organism becomes a mere instrument under the control of the hypnotist's will. All the channels of ingress to the subject's consciousness, therefore, are under control of the operator, who is, for the time being, an absolute censor, possessing unlimited authority and power. Complete fascination or enchantment of the subject's consciousness is the result. He sees nothing, hears nothing, feels nothing; is, in fact, conscious of nothing whatsoever save the dominating presence and power of his hypnotist's will.

A careful study and analysis of this condition of the subject and of the relation which his consciousness sustains to the will of the operator will reveal many of the seeming mysteries of hypnotic control.

For instance, the hypnotic subject in the deep lethargic condition is insensible to physical pain. In this condition the most painful surgical operations may be performed upon him without the least indication of physical suffering.

What physiological action or condition is responsible for this startling result? The answer is, paralysis of the physical sensory organism, by means of which the channels of consciousness upon the physical plane are entirely cut off.

The question has also been often asked by hypnotists themselves, why it is that in this condition the subject invariably accepts without question every suggestion or impression coming to his consciousness from the mind of the hypnotist. Often the operator has been surprised to find that his unexpressed thoughts and impulses have been indelibly impressed upon the consciousness of his subject. For instance, the author above quoted, at page 269 of his recent work on hypnotism says:

"I have often been startled by having patients tell me days after hypnotization of feelings and incentives to action of which I had said nothing, but which I knew to be in the background of my consciousness at the time of treatment."

It is worth while to pause and contemplate for a moment what must have been the results had the impulses and incentives to action "in the background" of the operator's consciousness at the time of treatment been of a vicious and immoral character.

This phase of the subject will explain one of the most common fallacies of hypnotists who claim to have made many experiments which tend to show that a subject cannot be impelled by hypnotic processes to commit a crime. The experiments, when fully understood, prove the exact reverse of the claim they make.

For instance, the average experiment is something as follows: The subject is first hypnotized. He is then strongly impressed with the "suggestion" that a certain person in the audience has deeply wronged him and deserves to be killed. He is then given a knife and commanded to kill the person so designated. He proceeds to carry out the command. He even carries it to the point of stealthily approaching the victim and raising the knife over him. But he will not strike the fatal blow. Why is this? Why does he stop at this critical point in the experiment?

In the light of the facts above stated, the answer is simple. The subject is impelled by the *real* motive and intention in the mind of his hypnotist, and not by the spoken word of command. In this condition and relation words mean nothing to the subject, unless they convey the real intent of the soul that projects them. In fact, the subject does not hear the words of command at all. He receives only the conscious intent of his hypnotist.

In other words, a hypnotist cannot possibly project a murderous intent or impulse unless he actually feels it. He cannot inspire his subject to commit a murder unless he has murder in his own soul. As the author above quoted very aptly expresses it, he cannot project the impulse of murder upon his subject unless there is "in the background" of his own consciousness the criminal impulse which inspires murder.

In all the public so-called tests, such as the one above suggested, the hypnotist does not intend that his subject shall carry the experiment to the final act of murder. There is "in the background" of his consciousness all the time the protecting reservation. The real intent in his soul is that the subject shall carry the experiment to the very point where he stops. He does not intend that he shall actually strike the fatal blow. He could not inspire such an act unless he were a murderer at heart and fully intended that his subject should execute the murderous design in his own soul. The subject is impelled by the *real* impulse in the soul of his hypnotist and not by the spoken words of command.

Let the operator once project the real murderous impulse upon the consciousness of his subject under the conditions named and murder will be the result in every instance.

The *rationale* of these wonderful results is not difficult to understand in the light of the foregoing analysis. In his normal state man depends upon his physical senses to furnish him information as to his immediate physical environment. In most instances he has not yet come to know that he has a spiritual organism. It has never been called into action by him in such manner as to identify it to his consciousness as something apart from his physical. But as the physical sensory organism yields to the paralyzing effects of the hypnotic process, the spiritual continues its activity to a certain extent independently of the physical. This is true even in the final stages of hypnosis. In this partial independence of the spiritual organism it takes the place of the physical, for the time being, in its relation to the consciousness of the subject. For the time, therefore, it is the only channel through which he receives impressions from without. Whatever he receives through this channel, therefore, is as much a verity to his consciousness as are the impressions which come to him through the physical sensory organs in his normal condition, and are accepted by him just as if they were of physical origin and reached him through the physical sensory organism.

The impulses of the operator's will are as much a fact to him in this condition of complete subjectivity as are the objects of Nature which impress the physical sensory organism in his natural, waking condition. Every thought of the operator, every impulse of his will, is a thing, something which makes its impress upon the subject's consciousness as definitely as do the tangible objects of Nature under other conditions. Its integrity is no more a matter of doubt to him in this state than is the sight of any physical object with the physical eyes in his normal, waking condition.

In the state and condition here referred to the mind and will of the hypnotist take the place of the physical world in their relation to the consciousness of the subject. They, in truth, constitute the only world with which the subject is, for the time being, in conscious touch. It is, therefore, not strange but perfectly natural that "he sees, hears, tastes, smells and feels what the operator says that he sees, hears, tastes, smells and feels—and nothing else."

The author just quoted unwittingly explains the reason for this when he further says that "for the time being his individuality is surrendered to the person who has hypnotized him."

This is but another method of saying that the operator has obtained absolute control of all the active channels through which the conscious intelligence of the subject may be reached and impressed. These channels are, for the time being, the spiritual, sensory organs. The operator who controls these channels is in position to impress upon the consciousness of the subject whatever mental impulses he may desire. He is likewise in position to enforce the execution of his will through the same channels.

During the continuance of this relation his mind and will are the sole governing factors in the conscious life of the subject. The only impulses the subject has, for good or ill, while in this state are those which come to him from the will of his hypnotist. He can no more disobey the will of the operator, during this relation, than he can disobey his own will in his normal condition. This follows from the fact that the only will he has during the continuance of the hypnotic relation, at this particular stage, is the will of the hypnotist to whom "his individuality is surrendered."

3. The final stage of hypnosis to which reference need here be made is one seldom successfully produced by our western practitioners. It involves the complete suspension of physical animation. In this state every function of the physical organism is wholly arrested. Even respiration ceases. Circulation stops. The body, in some instances, becomes cold and rigid. To every outward appearance physical death has actually occurred.

In its physiological aspect complete functional suspension of the physical organism has occurred. In its downward sweep through the central nervous organism the hypnotic process has at last overwhelmed the primary brain and the involuntary or reflex centers of nervous energy. In this condition the physical body is no longer an active part of the individual.

Remarkable as this may all appear, those who have been reckless enough to carry their experiments to this point have been astonished to find that, notwithstanding this complete suspension of all functional activity of the physical organism, the subject is even more intently conscious of every thought, intention and mental impulse of the hypnotist than he is during any of the less profound states of hypnosis which precede this condition.

This has never been satisfactorily explained by the School of Physical Science. Indeed, it does not seem to be consistent with their purely materialistic view of the relation of mind to matter. To those, however, who understand the three-fold nature of man, consisting of physical body, spiritual body and intelligent soul, there is a scientific explanation.

In proportion as the consciousness of the subject is acted upon through the physical organism, his attention is absorbed in the impressions made through those dominant channels, and correspondingly diverted from all other impressions. But as these physical organs are silenced and gradually paralyzed by the power of hypnosis the impulses which reach his consciousness through the spiritual sensory organism become more and more distinct to him. The relatively stronger of the two sets of impulses is the one which absorbs the attention so long as its dominance continues.

When the final state of profound hypnosis above referred to has been attained the physical world is entirely cut off from the consciousness of the subject. All impressions from that source cease. In this condition, therefore, there is nothing to divert his attention from the impressions which now reach him through the spiritual sensory organism alone.

But these channels of ingress to the imprisoned consciousness of the subject are under control of the hypnotist. He therefore commands the absolute and undivided attention of his subject. Hence it is that in exact proportion as this state of hypnosis is attained the consciousness of the subject responds to the will of the operator, and his attention becomes more and more completely riveted upon all that the hypnotist conveys to him.

This will also explain why it is that the hypnotist can, by a simple command or impulse of the will, waken his subject from even this profound condition of seeming physical death. His ability to thus waken his subject is at all times commensurate with the degree of control he is able to exercise over him. If, perchance, in the condition above referred to, some accident should occur to break the control of the hypnotist, the physical death of the subject would instantly follow. For, at this stage of hypnosis, the operator's will is the only power in existence that holds the two organisms together.

In this state of complete functional suspension of the physical organism it is even possible for the operator to force a complete temporary separation of the two organisms, and by the power of his will alone unite them again. In such case he is able to send the temporarily liberated spiritual body and soul of his subject to distant points and there enforce implicit obedience to his commands within certain well defined limitations. He may thus obtain definite information concerning matters at a distance of which he is at the time entirely ignorant.

Before passing to the consideration of another phase of the subject attention is here called to the interesting and significant fact that the three human brains correspond to the triune nature of man, body, spirit and soul. The action of hypnosis upon the three physical brains has a corresponding correlative effect upon the three sides of his triune nature. This phase of the subject will be more fully considered in subsequent chapters.

From the foregoing exposition of the subject, the physiological action of hypnosis, in so far as it has been here considered, may be very briefly summarized as follows:

1. Hypnosis acts both directly and indirectly upon the central nervous organism, the three physical brains.

2.   Its action upon this central nervous organism produces anæsthesia and paralysis.

3.   Its effects upon the central nervous organism are first registered upon that part of the third or intellectual brain through which the objective and perceptive faculties of the mind operate.

4.   In its progressive action hypnosis proceeds from this point backward through the third brain, downward through the second brain, and finally through the primary brain, until all parts of the physical nervous organism are brought under its complete control.

5.   Its impelling force is the will of the hypnotist.

It will be observed that consideration of the subject has been strictly confined thus far to such physiological action of the hypnotic process as may become apparent to everyone who has either experienced its results or been in position to observe them.

The more deeply scientific subject of the cellular action of hypnosis has been purposely omitted for the following reasons:

1.   Its consideration leads directly into the field of technical scientific treatment.

2.   Such treatment of the subject at this time could appeal to none but those few scientists who happen to be directly interested in the technical study of psychic phenomena. It would, in all human probability, require a century, through this channel, to bring the matter to the attention of the great world of humanity that needs to know the simpler facts and principles for self-protection.

3.   The purpose of this work is to reduce the subject to its simplest possible form. By so doing it is hoped to bring it within the easy comprehension as well as the personal interest of every man, woman and child who shall be able to read and understand the simplest expression of the English language.

Professional hypnotism has progressed to the point where it has become a most serious menace to individuals and to society. In one form or another it now threatens almost every home within the limits of our country. The dangers which lurk beneath the murky folds of its black mantle are many and threatening. They are fascinating and seductive. They present themselves in every charming disguise to mislead the innocent and deceive the thoughtful.

It is hoped that this work, in its simplicity, directness and freedom from all technicality, may carry into many homes the needed warning, together with a practical understanding of the principles and processes involved.

CHAPTER IX.

"Auto-Hypnotism" a Misnomer.

There is no such thing as "Auto-Hypnotism."

The term is a misnomer. "Auto" means "Self," and "Auto-Hypnotism," therefore, means, in its literal signification, "Self-Hypnotism."

This would convey the impression that it is possible for an individual to hypnotize himself. This, in fact, seems to be the impression which those who employ the term intend to convey. It is, at any rate, the impression which the term conveys to the world, and it is the impression the public in general has obtained.

Self-Hypnotism, or "Auto-Hypnotism," however, is a scientific impossibility.

Those who are responsible for injecting this term into the scientific nomenclature of the age undoubtedly felt themselves justified in so doing. But this does not alter the fact that the term is an improper and misleading one, and is responsible for having introduced into the scientific analysis of hypnotism a fiction pure and simple. It does not obliterate the further fact that this particular term has only served to add to the confusion already existing, and has wholly failed to advance the interests of science or education.

There is no desire nor intention to deny, evade nor ignore any of the facts upon which the writers and authorities have come to feel themselves justified in employing the term. It is, indeed, a well-known fact which has been often demonstrated, long before this particular term was ever employed, that it is possible for an individual to throw himself into a condition of artificial sleep, somewhat analogous to somnambulism. It is this self-induced, artificial sleep that has been improperly designated "Auto-Hypnotism."

This, however, is not hypnotism in any form.

A simple illustration will be sufficient to make the proper distinction clearly apparent. For the purpose of this illustration, let it be supposed that A is the owner and possessor of a magnificent jewel. Its value to him exceeds that of all his other material possessions combined. But it is his, and no matter what its intrinsic value may be, he therefore has the power, if not the right, to risk it or dispose of it as he will. He may even recklessly throw it away, and no one dares interfere.

Following a whim of his nature, he determines to try an experiment with this jewel to determine, in his own mind, whether or not there are burglars in the neighborhood. It is a hazardous experiment, so far as his possession of the jewel is concerned, and one which few men in their right minds would indulge. But it possesses the merit of affording a very effectual and satisfactory test as to the question to be determined.

Before retiring for the night he takes this precious jewel from its safety-deposit vault, unwraps it and places it in a conspicuous place in the middle of the table. He then moves the table near the front door, where it will be the first object seen on entering. He unlocks the door, so that anyone who will may open it, and then retires to a distant part of the house and deliberately goes to sleep.

But what is the meaning of this strange and abnormal proceeding? Only this, that A has simply opened the way to a most easy and successful burglary, nothing more. He has prepared a most tempting situation which will surely induce the first unscrupulous individual who learns of it to enter his home and commit a crime against the laws of the land.

But it is just possible that he may sleep soundly throughout the night and waken to find that his jewel remains undisturbed. If so, he would seem to be justified in assuming that his premises have not been invaded by burglars during the night. At least, no burglary has thus far been committed. His property is still there. This, however, would appear to be the result of his good luck rather than that of his good sense.

But he repeats the experiment the following night, and upon waking the next morning finds that his jewel is gone. During the night, while sleep has encompassed him and shut his consciousness away from the objective plane of the physical world, someone has entered his home and taken unlawful possession of his property. In other words, a crime has been committed. The name by which this particular crime is known to law is "Burglary."

It will be observed that so long as no second party entered upon the scene the crime of burglary could not be committed. That is to say, it is a moral, legal and scientific impossibility for a man to commit this particular crime against himself.

To accomplish the crime of burglary it is necessary-

1.   That there be at least two parties to the transaction.

2.   That one of these enter upon the premises of the other.

3.   That the party so entering take unlawful possession of personal property which does not belong to him, or which belongs to the owner of the invaded premises.

In like manner, the individual who throws himself into the artificial sleep which writers and authorities have erroneously designated "Auto-Hypnotism" has done nothing more than create conditions which make hypnotism an easy possibility.

He may, perchance, put himself in this unnatural condition and waken again without having come in touch with a hypnotist at all. In such case hypnosis, in its proper sense, does not occur. Why? Because no outside party has entered the domain of his individual life and taken possession of that which belongs to the occupant and rightful owner. That is to say, no intruder or trespasser has entered the temple of the soul and deprived the sleeper of his precious jewel— the power of self-control.

But let him repeat the foolish experiment often enough and the inviting conditions will sooner or later attract the attention of some passing hypnotist, who will thereupon enter and complete the process of hypnotism by taking possession and control of his will, voluntary powers and sensory organism.

Reverting once more to the definition of hypnotism, it will be observed that it involves elements and conditions which are strangely and significantly analogous to those involved in the crime of burglary. That is to say:

1. There must be at least two parties to the transaction.

2. One of these must enter the temple of the other, as it were.

3. The one so entering must take unlawful possession of that which of right belongs to the other party.

The interesting analogy between these two processes might, with value and propriety, be carried much further. But it is only intended at this point to suggest the one fundamental fact, that they both involve the commission of a wrong by one person against another. Both, therefore, involve a violation of law, for which offense there are corresponding penalties which must be inflicted upon the culprit.

The individual who thus throws himself into the artificial sleep above referred to invites thereby many results and conditions of which he is generally ignorant. Among others, he makes it easily possible for any one of the following results to obtain:

1. He may, unless interfered with, thus withdraw his consciousness from the objective plane of physical nature and in a perfectly conscious manner—through the medium of his spiritual sensory organs—see, hear and observe whatever may occur upon the spiritual plane within the range of spiritual vision, hearing and observation. His waking memory of all he has thus observed and experienced will be commensurate with the extent to which his consciousness still occupies and continues to register through the third physical brain. If the objective faculties alone are asleep upon the physical plane, all that part of the third brain lying back of and above the organs of perception is awake and active, and the waking memory will be clear and distinct.

2. But he may go still further and withdraw all consciousness from the third physical brain. In this event he brings back to his waking consciousness no remembrance of what he may have seen, heard or observed through the medium of his spiritual sensory organs. To him it has been

but a sound and dreamless sleep, often followed by the most intense nervous headache.

3. In either of the above named conditions the door is wide open to the hypnotist, from either plane of life, who may chance to pass that way. If it be a physically embodied hypnotist, he may enter the domain of the sleeper's soul and take undisputed possession and control of the will, voluntary powers and sensory organism of his subject, without the least possible resistance or opposition. In this event the sleeper becomes a hypnotic subject under the control of his hypnotizer, and can be made to produce such phenomena as the operator would be able to "suggest" or command if he had obtained his control in the ordinary way.

4. But it should never be forgotten that there are physically disembodied hypnotists as well as those yet in the physical body. Those physically disembodied intelligences, commonly known and designated as "spirits," represent all kinds and classes of individuals. The lower the type the more closely they approach the plane of the purely physical. This law of spiritual gravity will be fully developed in Part III of this volume.

The ignorant and the vicious upon the spiritual side of life generally seek to attach themselves to earth's conditions as closely as may be possible. There are perfectly natural reasons for this desire, as well as for the efforts they put forth to accomplish its realization. Such an one as this is ever watchful for an opportunity to fasten itself upon one who is yet in the physical body.

The individual who enters into the artificial and abnormal sleep mistakenly named "Auto-Hypnosis" opens the door of his inmost life to these spiritual intelligences as well as to the hypnotist upon the physical plane. If his abnormal condition is observed and understood by an unscrupulous or ignorant intelligence on the spiritual side of life, such spiritual intelligence may, without the least difficulty, take possession and control of the sleeper's will, voluntary powers and sensory organism, precisely as the hypnotist might do from the physical plane.

In this event the sleeper becomes a "trance medium," in the possession of a "spiritual control."

5.   If such "control" refuse to release its victim, or if he should be unable to do so (which is quite possible among ignorant controls), the case is pronounced "insanity" by physicians of the regular schools.   In this event the "Auto-Hypnotist" is sent to an asylum for the insane, where he is likely to remain until physical death comes to his release.

The conditions which follow physical death under these circumstances will be fully considered in Part III of this volume.

CHAPTER X.

"Suggestion"—A Lexicological Libel.

The term "Suggestion" has been so cruelly and unfairly dealt with in recent years that the spirit of fair play demands its immediate and unconditional vindication.

According to the best lexicological authorities the word means:

1. To introduce indirectly to the thoughts.
2. To propose with diffidence or modesty. To hint. To intimate.
3. To seduce. To tempt, etc.

This last definition is rare, and by some of the authorities is now considered obsolete.

It is safe to say that in its most common acceptation the word is intended to mean "a deferential method of calling the attention of one person to the subject matter in the mind of another and inviting favorable consideration of the same."

For some reason, quite inconceivable at this time, the word has become inseparably connected and associated in thought with the subject of hypnotism. By a sort of tacit agreement or understanding, as it were, among writers and students generally, it has come to include almost, if not quite, all the means and methods by and through which a hypnotist impresses his own thoughts, impulses, desires and will upon the consciousness of his subject.

But it must be borne constantly in mind that in exact proportion to the depth or intensity of the hypnotic state the hypnotist controls the will, voluntary powers and sensory organism of his subject. Under these conditions the subject, to the extent that hypnosis exists, is deprived of the power of independent choice, without which the word "Suggestion" is entirely meaningless to him.

Indeed, every thought, every impression, every impulse of the will projected by a hypnotist upon the consciousness of his subject during the hypnotic relation has, just as far as the hypnotic process is able to carry it, the force and binding effect of a definite and inviolable command. It is not presented to the subject for his consideration as an independent, self-conscious and rational intelligence possessing discretionary powers. It is not submitted to the rational judgment of the subject at all. It is not offered upon the theory that it may possibly be rejected. On the other hand, it is forced upon him under conditions which, according to the laws of Nature, make its rejection an impossibility.

And yet, notwithstanding all this, it is called "Suggestion" by learned men who are wise enough to instantly discover many a less conspicuous error.

It does not require a high degree of intelligence to understand that when one man fires a bullet into the brain of another he does not simply offer it as a "suggestion" to be taken under advisement and possibly returned with thanks. He projects it there to stay, regardless of the desires of the other party, because he has both the power and the will to do so. The law of Nature, bound up in the explosive power of the powder back of it, is inexorable. No matter if he accompany the discharge of the weapon with the most polite and gracious "suggestion" possible, this cannot reduce the force of the charge, slacken the speed of the bullet, reduce its penetrating power, nor lessen its destructive effects. In other words, it cannot modify the results in the slightest degree. Under the conditions named he sets in motion a process by means of a power which, when once applied, produces an inevitable result.

It should not require the mind of a scientist to understand and appreciate the impropriety, as well as the absurdity, of calling this "Suggestion."

And yet, in essence, the term "Suggestion" defines, with as much scientific exactness and literary acuteness, the process by which one man lodges a bullet in the brain of another by the use of a revolver, as it does the process by which a hypnotist lodges an impression in the consciousness of his subject by an impulse of his will. It is therefore just as fitting, proper and scientifically correct to assert that a man may "suggest" a bullet into the brain of his fellow by the aid of a gun as that a hypnotist employs "Suggestion" as any part of the process by and through which he impresses his thoughts, impulses, desires and will upon the consciousness of his subject.

It would seem that the foregoing illustration should be sufficient to make clear the fact that the term "Suggestion" is but another fiction which has found its way into the literature of hypnotism in contravention of all the rules of lexicology and in direct opposition to the interests of science. The consummate skill and subtlety with which the professional hypnotist appropriates and plays upon this word has artfully succeeded in blinding the eyes of the public to the noxious processes and destructive principles which lie back of it.

To thus blacken the reputation of a good, wholesome and altogether useful word by purposely associating it with a process so completely at variance with its true spirit and intent is a character of libel which true science cannot afford to countenance nor encourage. There should be some legitimate method, it would seem, by which this worthy and estimable word might be rescued and restored at once to its original status of respectability and consistency.

This, however, is a difficult undertaking. It is an equally hazardous one. Writers and students have become so familiar with the term in its relation to the hypnotic process that any attempt to introduce a substitute would be deemed an impertinence and an altogether unwarranted interference, even though one might easily be found possessing all the elements of acknowledged consistency and scientific exactness.

For this and other reasons no effort will here be made to eliminate or supplant the term Hypnotic-"Suggestion." On the other hand, with a mental reservation and protest, it will be recognized and accepted as an unpleasant necessity for the present.

Hypnotic-"Suggestion," for the purposes of this work, has therefore been defined as: "A suggestion made by a hypnotist to his subject while the latter is under the hypnotic control of the former."

Let it be distinctly understood, however, that the word

"Suggestion" in this connection, and wherever else it may be connected with the hypnotic process, is always equivalent to "Irresistible Impulse," or "Imperative Command," in just so far as the hypnotic relation exists at the time and under the conditions referred to.

It is anticipated, however, that as science becomes acquainted with the nature and effects of the hypnotic process the term "Command" will naturally supersede the term "Suggestion." And thus a terminology will ultimately be adopted which will convey to the world a definite and accurate understanding of the difference between voluntary and involuntary processes, between independent and subjective states of being, and between responsible and irresponsible conditions of individual intelligence.

CHAPTER XI.

INDEPENDENT SUGGESTION—A FACT.

There is such a thing as true suggestion.

There is a process which, by all the rules of both science and language, is justly entitled to that designation. This, however, is as different from Hypnotic-"Suggestion" as liberty is different from bondage, or as light is different from darkness, or as truth is different from falsehood.

For the important purpose of distinguishing true suggestion from its counterfeit, Hypnotic-"Suggestion," the genuine has been designated as "Independent Suggestion."

Independent Suggestion, accurately defined, may be said to be a suggestion made by one person to another while each is in full and undisputed control of all his independent, self-conscious and rational faculties, capacities and powers. That is to say, while neither is under hypnotic control. In this case each party acts independently of the other, and of his own free will and accord.

It will therefore be observed that Independent Suggestion differs from Hypnotic-"Suggestion" in the following particulars:

1. That neither party is under hypnotic control.

2. That each is in undisputed possession and control of all his own independent, self-conscious and rational faculties, capacities and powers.

3. That each applies his own individual intelligence to the subject matter under consideration and accepts the suggestion or rejects it, as the case may be, in accordance with his own independent judgment, and of his own free choice.

4. That each one is at all times individually responsible for having made his own decision as well as for the results of his own actions in accordance therewith.

But men of science have come to know that there are at least two very different and distinct methods by which an Independent Suggestion may be conveyed by one person to another, viz.:

1. By the usual means and channels of communication upon the purely physical plane, such as the voice, the facial expression, gesticulation, by written or printed words, signs, characters and symbols, as well as by telephone, telegraph and other mechanical means and methods.

2. By mental processes alone.

For the purpose of indicating this important distinction and firmly fixing it in mind, the term "Telepathic Suggestion" has been employed.

Telepathic Suggestion has already been defined as an Independent Suggestion conveyed by one person to another by mental processes alone, without the aid of the usual physical means of communication.

The following illustrations may serve to make the necessary distinctions still more clearly and impressively apparent:

1. HYPNOTIC-"SUGGESTION." Let it be supposed that A undertakes to convey a Hypnotic-"Suggestion" to B. In order to accomplish the desired result he must invoke a process and a power which will first paralyze B's physical sensory organism and deprive him of the power of individual self-control. Through this method A obtains complete control of all the channels by and through which the consciousness of B may be impressed.

In this relation A becomes absolute master, and B becomes a helpless automatic instrument under the operation and control of his will. When this relation of operator and instrument has been fully established between them, A conveys to B what hypnotists are pleased to designate as a "Suggestion," but which, under all the conditions and circumstances, is, in the very nature of things, equivalent to an irresistible impulse or an imperative command. By the law of relationship thus established, B has no alternative but to obey just as far as the hypnotic process is invoked. And this is called Hypnotic-"Suggestion."

2. INDEPENDENT SUGGESTION. Suppose that A, who is friendly to B, discovers what he believes to be an excellent opportunity for B to make a safe and profitable investment. Moved by the impulse of friendship, he goes to B and care-

fully lays before him all the facts at his command bearing upon the subject, and then suggests that B follow up the inquiry and look into the matter for himself.

A, having thus kindly and deferentially called B's attention to the matter and invited his favorable consideration of the same, feels that his mission of friendship has been fully performed. He therefore goes his way and leaves B to investigate the matter for himself and accept or reject his suggestion in accordance with the dictates of his own free and independent judgment.

And this is Independent Suggestion, conveyed by the usual physical means of communication.

3. TELEPATHIC SUGGESTION. Let it be supposed that A desires to acquaint B with the fact that he is perplexed and needs B's counsel and assistance. A desires to communicate the fact to B telepathically. He therefore goes to his room, where everything is quiet and nothing is likely to divert his attention. He places himself in a position and condition of complete physical relaxation, and then intently fixes his mind on B, charging it all the while with the earnest desire that B call and see him at once. At the same instant B obtains the impression that A is in distress and desires to see him. He immediately responds to the impulse and accordingly calls on A.

And this is Telepathic Suggestion. That is to say, it is Independent Suggestion by mental processes alone, without the aid of the usual physical means of communication.

It will now be observed that the various processes involved in the foregoing illustrations mark a radical distinction between what is known as Hypnotic-"Suggestion" and true, or Independent Suggestion. This distinction is of vital importance to a definite understanding of the real principle involved.

The complete failure of modern writers and authorities to appreciate and carefully note this vital distinction is responsible for a very large percentage of the confusion and error which have crept into the recent literature of the subject, and through this channel into the minds of students, investigators and the public in general.

Constant association of the word "Suggestion" with the thought of hypnotism, with hypnotic processes and hypnotic experiments, has invested it with a meaning which, so far as the facts are concerned, is purely fictitious and wholly misleading. Whenever and wherever a hypnotist employs the term "Suggestion" the student is either led or permitted to infer that it means Hypnotic-"Suggestion." In fact, in the language of the hypnotist, the word has come to be but a synonym of hypnotism.

But the distinction between this and Independent Suggestion is fundamental and must be kept constantly in mind. Otherwise the student will inevitably find himself in the midst of a bewildering maze of contradiction and inconsistency. This is more especially true in the department of Suggestive Therapeutics. In this fruitful field of interest and inquiry writers and authorities have either ignored the distinction entirely or have noted it in such manner as to convey the impression that it is of little or no importance.

And yet it is safe to assert that in all the literature of hypnotism wherever the word "Suggestion" appears it should in the very largest number of instances be preceded by the word "Independent." For it is a fact which none but the professional hypnotist and the misinformed proselyte will deny, that the genuine therapeutic results of Suggestion which have been advertised to the world have been the results of Independent Suggestion and not those of Hypnotic-"Suggestion."

Nevertheless, from the fact that those who have charged themselves with the task of reporting the results to the world fail to differentiate between the kinds of Suggestion employed, the credulous inquirer is permitted and even encouraged to attribute the gross results to the alleged or supposed magical power of hypnotism and Hypnotic-"Suggestion."

Under these conditions it is not strange that in the name and under the guise of "Hypnotism" and Hypnotic-"Suggestion" a thousand beneficent results have been wrought which are no more related to hypnotism, in fact, than they are to the Monroe Doctrine or the Clayton-Bulwer Treaty.

No more subtle error could be devised than that which is couched and concealed in the word "Suggestion" as it is employed in connection with Hypnotism and the Hypnotic Process. Upon the basis of this most ingenious device and fascinating fiction even men of science have been misled, just as government experts have often been deceived, for the time being, by artfully designed and skillfully executed counterfeit currency.

But just as there are infallible tests for discovering the most perfect counterfeit coins and currency, so there are unerring and indisputable methods and means of determining counterfeit "Suggestion" from the genuine and true. In like manner there are equally unquestionable methods of determining the exact results of Hypnotic-"Suggestion," as compared with those of Independent Suggestion.

These are subjects which will command further attention.

CHAPTER XII.

Does Hypnotism Cure?

The chief claims which the advocates of hypnotism set up in justification of the hypnotic process are based upon its alleged value as a therapeutic agent. For instance, they claim:

1. That hypnosis may be employed as an anæsthetic in surgery.

2. That through the agency of Hypnotic-"Suggestion" diseases of various kinds may be cured.

3. That by means of the hypnotic process vicious habits may be overcome and evil tendencies counteracted.

4. It has even been claimed by some that through the beneficent action of Hypnotic-"Suggestion" mental and moral powers may be developed.

As evidence in substantiation of these by no means insignificant claims, professional hypnotists throughout the country report a large number of cases such as the following:

1. A sufferer from insomnia has taken treatment from the regular physician and has tried all sorts of remedies in vain. He finally appeals to the hypnotist, who undertakes the case. After a number of trials the patient is placed in the hypnotic trance. While in this state of complete hypnotic control the operator "suggests" that the difficulty will soon pass away and that the patient will immediately begin to grow better. Before awakening him from the hypnotic sleep the hypnotist strongly impresses him with the further "suggestion" that he will sleep soundly all through the following night, and will waken the next morning much refreshed and invigorated. He is then wakened from the hypnotic trance and permitted to go his way, with the injunction to report the following day.

Cases of a similar nature are reported where a single treatment of this nature seems to have relieved the difficulty, for the time being. But if it should prove that a single hypnotic subjection is not sufficient, the operation is repeated, with such variations as the particular operator may deem advisable, until relief is either obtained or the case proves to be one which is beyond the range of the hypnotic process.

2. A clinical case is in course of preparation for the amputation of a limb. The patient is placed upon the operating table. But instead of administering the usual physical anæsthetics of ether and chloroform, a hypnotist is called in. He finally succeeds in placing the patient under complete hypnotic control and inducing the deep, lethargic, trance condition. While in this state the operation is successfully performed. After the surgeon has fully completed his work and everything is in readiness, the hypnotist gives the word of command and the patient wakens from the hypnotic trance without having been conscious of any physical suffering whatsoever. There is not even the usual nausea which so often follows the administration of physical anæsthetics.

3. Through convivial associations an individual acquires the habit of drink. He yields to its seductive influence until the appetite becomes stronger than his desire to overcome it. Various antidotes and substitutes are tried, but without avail. Change of climate and association is suggested and tried with the same result. The habit still remains. It appears to be a hopeless case. But the hypnotist is at last called in. He employs the hypnotic process. Under the influence of Hypnotic-"Suggestion" he finally succeeds in overcoming the craving for drink. The patient goes his way, and it may be that both patient and hypnotist are under the impression that a "cure" has been effected.

In each of these cases the hypnotist flatters himself that he has done a good work. He therefore feels himself entirely justified in recommending hypnotism and Hypnotic-"Suggestion" to all those who suffer from like conditions. The objective facts alone, thus far observed, would appear to sustain his position. He therefore places himself upon the same ethical platform with the regularly schooled physician and challenges the world to successfully refute his claim.

He calls our attention to the admitted fact that the regular physician and surgeon employ physical anæsthetics every day in a wide variety of cases and think nothing of so doing. By this process they also induce what is recognized as an artificial sleep or trance condition, which, in many respects, resembles the condition of hypnotic trance.

Physicians and surgeons justify themselves upon humanitarian grounds, and we do not think of questioning their right nor their wisdom in so doing. To the superficial observer the results of the two methods are identical. He cannot understand why one of these methods should be commended and the other condemned. Nor can it be wondered at that the proposition is one which perplexes him. For indeed it is one which has perplexed the scientist and the metaphysician as well as the casual observer.

In thus basing his justification and advocacy of hypnotism upon its alleged value as a therapeutic agent, the hypnotist has chosen the strongest possible ground upon which to support his claims, and therefore the strongest position in which to entrench himself. He is fortified behind a strong breastwork of objective facts and conditions which, to the average student, would seem to be impregnable.

In order to give him the benefit of every possible doubt which his genius may be able to lodge in the minds of the innocent and the unsophisticated, and thus put into his hands every defensive weapon of which it is possible for him to avail himself, a number of sweeping admissions have already been made a part of this work. By these admissions it is intended to show that in so far as the purely physical facts reported are concerned, there is no material controversy. In other words, it is here intended to admit all the objective facts upon which the professional hypnotist attempts to justify the employment of the hypnotic process for therapeutic purposes.

Having thus admitted the hypnotist's alleged basis of physical facts to be true, for the express purpose of avoiding unnecessary controversy over irrelevant and immaterial matter, it only remains to be determined why his conclusions, based upon these alleged physical facts, are not equally true. If his conclusions are incorrect it is due to him as well as to the public in general that the error be pointed out and the truth made plain. It is the purpose of this work to accomplish this task, if it be possible.

Referring again to the hypothetical cases above outlined, let it be assumed that the facts therein stated are the only facts which appear in each particular case. It is impossible for the average individual to doubt the objective evidences of his own physical senses. The results seem to speak for themselves. Any attempt to discredit them would seem to be gratuitous as well as unwarranted and unjust. In the one case a surgical operation is successfully performed under hypnotic anæsthesia without conscious physical suffering of any kind. In another the debilitated condition of the nervous organism indicated by insomnia is seemingly relieved. In the third a degrading habit is seemingly overcome and a destructive appetite controlled.

These being the specific objects sought to be acomplished, it would appear, from a surface view of the matter at least, that the remedy has proved itself entirely adequate and the process invoked both salutary and commendable. It is quite possible, and even probable, that the physical scientist of the conventional school would so declare.

If these facts which thus appear upon the surface were, indeed, the only facts entitled to the consideration of the inquirer, and the results which appear to the objective vision of the observer from the published reports were truly the only results thereby accomplished, it would then seem quite impossible to find a legitimate excuse for criticising the hypnotist or protesting against the hypnotic process by and through which these seemingly beneficent results were accomplished. In other words, if that which appears upon the surface reports of all these assumed "cures" embodied all the material facts to be considered, it would be difficult to imagine a good and sufficient reason why the hypnotist should not be commended for his work and the hypnotic process fully approved upon its merits.

But it has been strongly intimated that there are other facts than those which appear in the published reports of these experiments. If this be true, then it is manifestly unfair to judge either the hypnotist or the hypnotic process solely upon the objective facts thus reported. No problem can be solved with absolute certainty until all the facts are taken into account. The true scientist never feels himself justified in drawing a final conclusion upon any subject under his consideration, and holding that conclusion to be scientific, until he is certain that all the facts are before him bearing upon that particular question. Even then he must be sure that he has given to each separate fact the full measure of value and importance to which it is entitled before he can hope to reach a just and accurate judgment.

It is indeed true, as above suggested, that there are other material facts concerning hypnotism and the hypnotic process than those which come to the attention of the public, or that of the student through the voluntary and unverified reports of the professional hypnotist who, it will be admitted, has a personal interest to conserve thereby. Such of these additional facts as have been gathered and classified in such manner as to be most readily understood, will be presented for consideration in the following order:

1. It has been found by the School of Natural Science that out of each one hundred reported hypnotic "cures" at least sixty-three are in no sense whatever entitled to be so classified. The subsequent history of these cases discloses the startling fact that the hypnotic process has only succeeded in hoodwinking the patient, and concealing the manifestation of the disease from the objective vision for a brief period.

In due course of time, however (in the majority of instances not exceeding eighteen months), the same disease has "returned" and made its presence fully manifest.

It would seem that the most enthusiastic advocate of the subjective method of treatment, even, unless he be deliberately dishonest, would frankly admit that in all such instances the hypnotic process is in no sense remedial or curative. The most extravagant claim that could be made for it, based upon its therapeutic value, would be to the effect that it is, perhaps, a temporary palliative. But it would scarcely be entitled to even that designation in the accepted meaning of the term as it is used by men of medical science in their reference to disease.   It might, however, very appropriately be considered a "palliative" in the sense that it is a "cover" or "cloak" under which to conceal the true condition of the patient from both himself and the world.

2. Out of the same number of cases it is found that in twenty-four of the sixty-three the same disease "returns" in a more aggravated form than that in which it manifests itself prior to the hypnotic treatment.

This fact would appear to strongly indicate that in all such cases the hypnotic process has acted as an anæsthetic pure and simple.   The sum total of its results is disclosed in the fact that the patient has been made insensible to and unconscious of his true condition for a time.   In other words, he has been deceived or misled for a brief period, during which the disease has been permitted to continue its destructive ravages under the protecting cover of hypnotism, without check or hindrance.

There are many instances where an anæsthetic is desirable, and upon broad, humanitarian grounds would be deemed entirely justifiable.   But certainly this claim cannot be successfully maintained in the cases above referred to.   The physician and the surgeon limit their use of physical anæsthetics to the temporary relief of unendurable pain or suffering.   They at no time employ these agencies for the purpose of concealment or deception.   It is also true that when the physician or the surgeon administers anæsthetics he accompanies their use with remedial agencies intended to correct, restore and cure.   He does not leave the disease to pursue its work of destruction unmolested.

In the cases here referred to it must be apparent to every student who has followed the subject to this point that hypnotism is only a fatal blind that deceives both the patient and the public, as well as the hypnotist himself, concerning the actual conditions.   In all such cases as these it only furnishes disease a convenient cloak under which to complete its deadly work without likelihood of discovery or interruption until it is too late. Certainly this use of hypnotism cannot be justified upon any ground that appeals to human reason, nor upon any which conscience approves.

3. It is also found that in a considerable number of cases, outside of those included in the two classes above referred to, there are equally just grounds for questioning the therapeutic value of the hypnotic process.

For illustration: It is found that other forms of disease than those for which the hypnotic treatment is given soon develop. A case of hysteria is "cured," only to develop epilepsy. A "cure" of stammering is effected, and soon thereafter nervous twitching of the mouth and face develops. A patient is "cured" of the cocaine habit and immediately thereafter develops cancer of the stomach. A case of rheumatism is "cured," and within a short time thereafter blood poison develops.

It would seem that in all such cases the process is one of transformation only. The only change effected is in the form of the disease, and not in its substantial essence. There is certainly no ground here upon which to base a claim of therapeutic value.

4. In a certain number of the last named class of cases the transformation is clearly and unmistakably one of an injurious or detrimental character, and therefore destructive in its effects.

5. There is yet another class of cases not included in any of those above referred to. And here a wholly different element enters into the proposition. It is found, for instance, that insanity seems to be a natural sequel of the hypnotic process. The gravity of this statement is fully appreciated. It is not made lightly, nor without the most unqualified and conclusive evidence back of it.

This subject has been studied quite independently of its relation to the subject of therapeutics. It is found that among hypnotic subjects of all classes, including those who become such for experimental purposes and for entertainment and amusement, as well as for the treatment of disease, a fraction over nine per cent. develop insanity in its various forms and phases. For the sake of perfect fairness it is proper to state that a certain percentage of the cases of this character results from the practice of hypnotism for other than therapeutic purposes.

The record, however, is especially significant and valuable from a therapeutic standpoint, in that it demonstrates beyond all question that hypnotism practiced without destructive intent is nevertheless destructive in its effects. This, perhaps, is as nearly a fair test of its therapeutic value as it is possible to apply upon the plane of its purely physical aspect.

To obtain an adequate understanding of the percentage of insanity from this cause the following illustration may be of value: On the basis of nine per cent. the city of Chicago would furnish about 180,000 insane to be cared for if hypnotism were practiced upon the entire community instead of our recognized systems of medicine. The city of New York would produce about 300,000, and the city of London about 450,000.

The various forms of insanity which follow from this cause also furnish food for much serious reflection. But it is impossible to consider this phase of the subject at sufficient length, in this connection, to develop its specific value and importance. The significance of this phase of the subject will be more fully appreciated as the general theme is further developed.

The foregoing are some of the additional facts of physical nature which must be taken into account in arriving at a correct solution of the problem under consideration. There are yet other purely physical facts which might be added to strongly supplement the position taken in this work. But, viewing the subject now in the light of the facts already in evidence, it would appear that we are justly entitled, upon physical grounds alone, to ask the question in all seriousness, "Does hypnotism cure?"

The data here furnished is such as to fall entirely within the limitations of physical science. They are therefore within the range of actual demonstration whenever physical science shall come to regard the subject as of sufficient importance to command its attention and consideration.

Since the foregoing was written there comes to this country direct from Berlin, Germany, under date of January 29, 1903, the following cable dispatch, which is especially significant and pertinent in this connection:

"The commission of experts in mental diseases appointed by the Ministry of Education to investigate the healing value of hypnotism reports that it is essentially worthless. The commission, which is composed of Professor Mendel and Drs. Gock, Munter and Aschenoorn, was appointed during the faith-healing excitement here a year ago. The report declares hypnotism cannot produce organic changes nor cure epilepsy nor hysteria."

CHAPTER XIII.

A Violation of Natural Law.

On the plane of physical nature there are certain additional facts concerning the hypnotic process which the scientist, the physician, the professional hypnotist and the hypnotic subject all alike recognize and admit.

The value of these additional facts to the individual will depend very largely upon the particular relation in which they are considered. They are essential, however, and therefore should not be overlooked nor ignored by those who are seriously endeavoring to reach a just conclusion as to the real nature and true meaning of hypnosis in all its different bearings.

As briefly and concisely as may be possible a few of these supplementary facts will be presented for consideration in the following order:

1. The advocates of hypnotism, of all grades and schools, find it necessary to admit that the hypnotic relation is "abnormal." It is, in truth, recognized and admitted by all who have given the subject proper consideration to be a relation which Nature does not, of her own accord, establish or maintain between individuals. It is therefore clearly a relation which Nature does not contemplate.

In other words, it is a relation into which the individuals, of their own accord, enter without the sanction of Nature. It would seem that this of itself should be sufficient to condemn its practice either as a therapeutic agent or for any other purpose.

As evidence of the general recognition of this important fact by the established authorities, Webster defines the hypnotic relation as one which is "characterized by *unnatural* or morbid sleep."

According to the Encyclopædia Britannica, "Hypnotism may be regarded as a condition in which the part of the nervous apparatus associated with conscious perception is thrown *out of gear.*"

Foster's Encyclopædic Medical Dictionary informs us that hypnotism is "an *abnormal* state," etc.

Even Prof. John Duncan Quackenbos, of Columbia University, admits that it is an *"artificial* sleep," etc.

Indeed, it is equally true that every acknowledged authority in existence might be quoted in recognition of the fundamental fact that hypnotism and the hypnotic relation are "abnormal" and "unnatural."

The conclusion follows with irresistible logic that whatever is found to be unnatural is necessarily without the sanction or approval of Nature. That which is outside the sanction and approval of Nature is necessarily hostile to Nature's purpose and therefore contrary to natural law. That is to say, it is contrary to Nature's Constructive Principle.

Materia Medica, both prophylactic and therapeutic, is based upon its strict conformity to Nature's Constructive Principle. In its prophylactic aspect it is intended to supplement Nature in her constructive effort to preserve health and prevent disease. In its therapeutic branch the underlying purpose is to supplement Nature's Constructive Process in the restoration of health and the cure of disease.

The true physician bases his entire success in the cure of disease upon his knowledge of natural law and his ability to conform thereto. His study of diagnostics is solely for the purpose of acquiring the ability to accurately distinguish between the "normal" and the "abnormal." Having acquired this knowledge, his success in the practice of his profession is commensurate with his ability to eliminate the "abnormal" and restore the "normal." The basis of all his work, therefore, is the operation of normal or natural constructive processes.

It is, indeed, difficult to understand how it is possible to effect a cure upon any other principle. And yet the hypnotist, by a process which he admits in advance to be "abnormal" or "unnatural," declares his ability to thereby produce a "normal" or "natural" condition or result.

Expressed in a slightly different form, he would lead us to believe that by the application of a process which he admits to be destructive he is able to produce constructive results. By a process which is admitted to be unhealthy he proposes to produce healthy results.

Even if the facts were not all against him, his proposition, stripped of its mysticism, is one which violates all the rules of logic and offends every principle of rational intelligence.

2. Another important fact is with equal unanimity admitted by scientists, professional hypnotists and acknowledged authorities of all the different schools, and is known by the hypnotic subject to be true beyond all possible question. It is this—that Nature has erected certain barriers and safeguards around every individual intelligence which must be broken down or overcome before it is possible to successfully establish the hypnotic relation.

This is evidenced:

(a) By the fact that the hypnotist finds himself unable to hypnotize any and every person he meets. If there were no natural barriers between him and his victim he would be able to enter into the hypnotic relation with every person upon whom he desired to exercise his hypnotic powers. This, however, is not the case. He finds that he is able to exercise his powers upon only such as prove to be susceptible. These are, generally speaking, those who are known as the relatively negative types.

(b) It is evidenced by the further fact that the hypnotist finds himself unable to hypnotize a subject the first time he tries, as a general rule. He finds that even among those who prove to be susceptible to his power, it requires much more time and vastly greater effort on his part the first attempt than it does the second. It requires more time and greater effort the second attempt than it does the third, and so on.

In other words, at each succeeding repetition of the hypnotic subjection the process becomes easier for the hypnotist. And in due time, if the process be repeated sufficiently often upon the same subject, a point is reached where all the barriers and safeguards which Nature has erected are overcome and swept away, and it requires but an impulse of the will to bring his subject under complete hypnotic subjection and control.

In order that these scientific demonstrations may not be mistaken for the mere naked assertions of the writer, the following quotation from the Encyclopædia Britannica, Vol. XV, p. 278, will be of special interest:

"Certain persons are more readily hypnotized than others, and it has been observed that, once the condition has been successfully induced, it can be more easily induced a second time, a third time more easily than a second, and so on until the patient may be so pliant to the will of the operator that a fixed look, or a wave of the hand, may throw him at once into the condition. Such are the general facts," etc.

It will be found that the authorities unanimously agree with the unqualified declarations of the writer just quoted. Further time and space will not be consumed, therefore, upon this particular proposition. It is important, however, to bear in mind the far-reaching significance of all this.

It means that around every individualized intelligent soul Nature, or the great God of the Universe, has erected certain barriers and safeguards to protect him from the unscrupulous encroachments of all those who would otherwise trespass upon his individual rights. It also means that the hypnotist, before he can practice his destructive art upon a fellow creature, must first batter down, overwhelm and destroy this natural fortress of the human soul which stands between him and his intended victim.

3. But there is a natural corollary of all this which is of still more vital importance, because it concerns the status of the subject himself, in whose behalf the best intelligence of the age is earnestly invoked.

It is found that in exact proportion as the hypnotist gains ease and facility in the exercise of his power of control, his subject loses the power of resistance and the power of self-control. At the first sitting the subject finds that he is easily able to withstand the volitional assaults of the operator. It even becomes necessary for him to put himself in a negative or passive attitude of mind and body, and thus become a voluntary accessory or accomplice with the hypnotist in his effort to obtain control.

But the second time he finds that the operator does not seem to require his assistance or co-operation to the same extent. The subject falls into the hypnotic state without any particular effort on his own part. The third attempt he becomes conscious of the fact that he not only enters into the hypnotic relation still more easily than before, but that his power of resistance to the hypnotic influence is being undermined and destroyed. At the fourth experiment he is made to realize the horrible fact that his power of resistance is still more rapidly waning, and that with equal pace he is losing the power of self-control.

This progressive condition continues, with each succeeding subjection, until a point is at last reached where all power of resistance is gone from him. In other words, it is but a matter of time when all the barriers and safeguards which Nature has so carefully and so wisely erected about his individual intelligence as a fortress of defense against the vicious assaults of his fellow men have been overcome and destroyed.

At this point he finds himself uncovered and alone in the presence of the enemy, without means of defense, a helpless victim in the power and under the control of a merciless conqueror. He is bound soul and body by an irresistible bond more relentless and powerful than the felon's shackles. He finds himself at last stripped of every valuable possession of the human soul, and powerless to control a single one of the primary faculties, capacities or powers of his being with which God or Nature originally invested him as an individualized, intelligent entity. He has become but an automaton, a plaything, a bankrupt, a lost soul. He has entered upon THE WAY OF DEATH.

CHAPTER XIV.

True Suggestion and Therapeutic Faith.

The influence of the mind upon the condition of the physical body is one of the most patent, potent and unmistakable pathological and physiological facts of all Nature.

So conspicuously obvious has this become in recent years that it is to-day the primary and fundamental factor in almost if not quite every system which has for its purpose the prevention or the cure of disease.

Of such far-reaching and vital importance to humanity is the principle involved in this proposition that it would seem to be not only expedient but of special value to every individual to have it firmly fixed in memory.

No more available method of accomplishing this desirable result presents itself than that of briefly identifying the principle as it exists and manifests itself in some of the leading systems with which the general public is more or less familiar at the present time. For that purpose the following brief analyses are here presented for thoughtful consideration:

1. Cure by Prayer. Viewed from the standpoint of the patient, the attitude of mind in this case is that of asking a favor with full confidence that it will be granted. In the sense that Faith is the intuitive perception of that which both reason and conscience approve, the basis of this system is Faith.

The act of prayer is but a means to an end. It is the active process by and through which therapeutic Faith, or curative Faith, or a healing Faith (whichever may be deemed the most appropriate name for it), is established in the mind and consciousness of the individual. Prayer is the means. Faith is the end. And it is true that in thousands of cases a cure is the result.

2. Mind Cure. This system is based upon the hypothesis that all diseased conditions of the physical body are but reflex conditions and results of abnormal mental states.

In this view of disease it will be readily understood that its cure is entirely dependent upon a restoration of the mind to its normal status or condition.

Whatever means or methods may be employed to that end are supposed to restore the mind of the patient to its condition or state of normality. The patient is, in this case also, himself a working factor in the process of restoration. He is led to believe that the process invoked is having the desired effect and that his mental state is improving. He grows brighter, happier and more hopeful. Through the subtle alchemy of the soul his unbelief is slowly but surely transmuted into an abounding Faith. He learns to believe that he possesses the power within himself to eradicate disease and establish the harmony of health.

Through the mysterious power of this wonderful therapeutic agent health is finally restored. And thus it is that many cures are wrought. It is not only useless but foolish to deny them. It is far better to frankly admit the fact and then seek to discover the scientific basis or principle upon which it is founded.

3. CHRISTIAN SCIENCE. This system is founded upon the negative proposition that there is no such thing as matter, coupled with the affirmation that mind is the only reality, or that "all is mind." From this basis it is logically held that disease is but a conception of the mind concerning matter which has no existence in fact. It therefore follows that disease itself does not exist in reality. Being but a mental concept of a material untruth, its banishment from the mind is all that is necessary to a condition of perfect health.

The patient is given these fundamental propositions from which to proceed. He is instructed as to the proper formulas by and through which to rid himself of all false mental concepts. He is taught first the formula of negation by which he is to persistently deny the existence of disease. Coupled with this, and as a supplementary process, he learns the formula of affirmation by which he is to bring the mind to a full acquiescence in the proposition that "all is good."

He is instructed as to the necessity of keeping these fundamental propositions constantly in mind and allowing nothing whatever to disturb his confidence in their literal truth. His mind thus becomes active in a process which ultimately brings him to believe in the truth of the formula.

At last his Faith in the soundness of this strange logic is fully established. However remarkable and seemingly "unscientific" may be the process by which this is accomplished, the result is nevertheless achieved. And in all sincerity and truth it can be said that his Faith hath made him whole. It is folly to deny it. It is equally foolish to try to ignore it. The evidences are too many to leave any just ground for doubt in the mind of the unprejudiced. It is a fact with which science must deal if it would discover the principle which underlies the process by which these wonderful results are accomplished.

4. MIRACLE CURES. It is a matter of common report that the Catholic Church has established certain mystic shrines where "miraculous" cures are wrought.

Those who visit these shrines in the hope of relief are led to believe that each shrine is presided over by some saintly intelligence from on high who possesses not only the power but also the will to cure all those who approach in the spirit of humility, piety and unbounded Faith.

The possibilities of the miraculous appeal to the human mind in proportion to its susceptibility to superstitious mysticism. The traditions of the church are filled with wonderful legends of miraculous interventions in behalf of those who unequivocally acknowledge its authority.

Through the instrumentality of these mythological narratives the credulous and the superstitious are led to approach these sacred places with an unbounded Faith that God, or Christ, or the Blessed Virgin, or some saintly, spiritual potentate of the church will take pity on them and relieve them of all their infirmities. Their Faith being thus established, many are indeed and in truth cured, and go their way with praises and thanksgiving and exceeding great joy, fully convinced that a miracle has been wrought.

5. THE BREAD PILL. This is a system or method which,

perhaps, has to its credit a larger number of *bona fide* cures than any other mental or psychic process now employed in common practice. It is often resorted to by the most skilful and intelligent physicians of the regular schools. The results are often truly marvelous. The process may be fully understood and appreciated from the following illustration of the manner in which the good-natured and intelligent country doctor has often employed it, as follows:

He is called to the bedside of a patient who is suffering, let us say, from nervous debility and insomnia. With a dignified bearing and professional air, he feels the pulse, looks at the tongue, inquires into the history of the case, and makes a careful and thorough examination and diagnosis of the case, although his professional eye discovers the true condition at the first glance.

With a wise and knowing nod and an outward manner of perfect assurance and confidence in himself, he gravely informs the sufferer that he must have sleep and perfect relaxation for a number of hours. The patient knows this even better than the physician does, and he therefore feels that the man of medicine understands his business. The first step in the process is thus nicely accomplished. His confidence has been gained. The physician, well knowing the superior value of natural sleep in all such instances, hesitates to administer a narcotic or soporific. But he makes believe that he has a perfectly harmless drug that is a never failing remedy in all such cases. He goes to the cupboard—ostensibly for a spoon—but while there he carefully prepares a good sized bread pill. He then informs his patient, with all the professional unction and emphasis necessary to carry absolute conviction with the statement, that in twenty minutes from the time it enters the stomach this wonderful drug will produce absolute physical and nervous relaxation and natural sleep for twelve hours thereafter, and that he will waken fully refreshed and on the way to rapid and complete recovery.

The innocent bolus of bread, charged with this therapeutic suggestion, is then administered to the credulous patient and with perfect fidelity to its trust, in twenty minutes it brings the promised relaxation and sleep. The wonderful drug has done its work. The good doctor gently steals away into the darkness of the night and reserves a knowing smile until he is out of sight. He pardons himself for this little deception and congratulates himself upon once more having demonstrated the wonderful and mysterious power of mind over matter.

The secret of this formula also is Faith. Every move, every look, every lineament and expression of the physician has betrayed his comprehensive knowledge and understanding of the case and disclosed unlimited confidence in his ability to effect a speedy cure. This all communicates itself to the mind and consciousness of the patient who, in this nervous condition, is intently sensitive to every detail that has a bearing upon the case. This is all rapidly transmuted into confidence and thence into Faith, first, in the physician, and next, in the magical power of his wonderful medicine to bring the desired relief. His "Faith is well founded," for it is the faith which bears upon its wings the healing balm of peace and life.

This is but a single illustration. The same principle, however, is employed in an almost unlimited variety of ways by the intelligent physician. In thousands of instances the medical fraternity daily employ similar means and methods in all kinds of cases, with results which are often almost unbelievable by those who have not actually witnessed them.

As previously suggested, hypnotists throughout the country have so played upon the word "Suggestion" as to convey the idea that the process above outlined is only one of the many forms of Hypnotic-"Suggestion." Even physicians themselves have not always carefully distinguished between this method of suggestion and its counterfeit which is employed in the hypnotic process. The distinction, however, is fundamental. The processes are in no way related and must not be confused.

There are numerous other mental processes by which disease is treated and cures effected. It would seem unnecessary to go into fuller details for the reason that those here outlined are sufficient to develop the principle under consideration. A critical analysis of these five different systems or methods of curing disease cannot fail to establish the substantial and essential fact that in so far as the patient himself becomes an active factor in the curative process the therapeutic agent employed is one and the same. The remedial power in each and every instance is Faith. Not only this, it is literally the same kind of Faith, namely, Faith of the patient himself that a cure will be effected.

The widely divergent methods or formulas employed by the various schools and cults to accomplish the same result, are likely to confuse the mind of the student in the future as they have done in the past, concerning the real curative principle employed. But a careful analysis will disclose the fact that they all work to the same end, namely, the establishment of a therapeutic Faith in the mind of the patient. The only real differences are in the distinctive methods or processes by which this end is accomplished.

A simple illustration will serve to bring the underlying principle more clearly into view:

Let it be supposed, for instance, that the particular thing to be accomplished by a given individual is the lifting of a 2,000 pound stone from the earth a distance of three feet to its intended place upon the foundation wall of a building. The individual charged with the accomplishment of this task may succeed by any one of the following methods:

1. He may employ the services of ten men, each of whom can lift 200 pounds from the ground to the required height. By applying their hands directly to the burden and uniting their strength in a common effort they will thus be able to lift it into place.

2. By the aid of jack-screws he may be able to accomplish the task alone in course of time.

3. Or, he may employ a derrick, and by the application of steam, gas, electricity, or horse power, he may perform the same task in half the time.

In fact, he may, if he is a thoroughly skilled mechanic, accomplish the same result by the application of something like

720 different combinations of the six so-called "Mechanical Powers"—the lever, the inclined plane, the wheel and axle, the screw, the pulley, and the wedge.

If the casual observer, however, were asked to define the principle back of all these various processes, he would very likely be confused. If he were the skilled mechanic and fully acquainted with all the physical means and methods of applying mechanical power he would very likely define the principle from the standpoint of pure mechanics. In this event he would name such of the six mechanical powers as might be employed in each particular method, and would insist that he had thus defined the principle involved.

But in the final analysis there is an active, moving principle back of all these which he has entirely overlooked, namely, the independent, self-conscious and rational volition of the man who utilizes these various processes and so applies them as to accomplish the desired result. All these various mechanical processes and appliances are but so many different instruments, by means of which his intelligence is enabled to produce one and the same result.

In like manner, the first method of cure above named, develops a therapeutic Faith by the lever of prayer. The second accomplishes the same result by the inclined plane of reason. The third employs the wheel of negation and the axle of affirmation. The fourth resorts to the jack-screw of superstition. The fifth relies upon the pulley of suggestion and the wedge of wisdom. But they all accomplish identically the same result, namely, the establishment of an abounding Faith. And this is the therapeutic principle involved, so far as the patient himself is an active factor in the curative process.

As there are some 720 different combinations in which the known mechanical powers may be employed to produce a given result, so it would seem that there is an almost unlimited number of means and methods by which therapeutic Faith may be established in the minds of patients. This suggestion may, perhaps, be of value to those who have allowed themselves to fall into the unfortunate error of assuming that there is but one method of producing conditions which will cure disease.

Inasmuch as one or more of the schools or systems above referred to, as well as numerous other metaphysical systems not here mentioned, profess to represent the Christ Science, or the particular method supposed by them to have been employed by Christ in the cure of disease, it may not be deemed improper to offer a simple suggestion which would seem to have a special relevancy in this connection.

It is reported, for instance, in the book of St. Luke (17, 12 to 19) that as Jesus was on his way to Jerusalem he was met by ten lepers, who lifted up their voices and said: "Jesus, Master, have mercy on us." Jesus directed them to go and show themselves to the priests, and as they went they were cleansed. One of the number, a Samaritan, turned back, fell on his face at Jesus' feet and gave him thanks. Jesus told him to arise and go his way, and then said to him by way of explanation: "Thy faith hath made thee whole."

In the book of St. Mark (6, 25 to 34) is also told the story of the woman who touched his garment and was instantly healed. When she, in like manner, fell down before him, he said to her in exactly the same words: "Daughter, thy faith hath made thee whole."

Again we read (Mark, 10, 46 to 52) of the blind man who besought him that he might receive his sight. When he had been healed Jesus said to him also, in the same significant words: "Thy faith hath made thee whole."

The suggestion which it is here desired to offer for consideration by all those who profess to employ Christ's method in the art of healing disease, is merely this:

Can it be possible that Christ knew what he was talking about when he made these several statements? If so, he either told the truth or a deliberate falsehood when he said to each one of these grateful souls: "Thy faith hath made thee whole." If he told a falsehood in these several instances, then his testimony must be held to be entirely unreliable in all other respects, in which event we have no key whatever by which to unlock the mystery of this man's wonderful power over disease.

On the other hand, if he really knew what he was talking about, and told the truth in each of these several instances, then it is clear that he has stated the facts in unmistakable terms. He said to each of these grateful beneficiaries: "Thy Faith hath made thee whole." If this is the statement of a truth, then Faith is the therapeutic agent by and through which all these particular cures were wrought. More than this, it was the Faith of the patient himself in every case, for he said: "*Thy* Faith," etc.

According to the requirements of this simple method there seems to be nothing which lays upon suffering humanity the impossible burden of thinking matter out of existence as a prerequisite to physical health. It does not appear from the record of these cases that any of these sufferers denied the existence of matter. It does not appear that they even denied the existence of disease. It is not in evidence that they were compelled to affirm that "All is good." In fact, if the reports be true, it would seem that they failed to conform to any of the prescribed formulas which are deemed essential by certain of our modern metaphysical healers who profess to practice Christ's methods. And yet, they were cured. Moreover, they were cured instantly. And in order that each might know the secret by which his marvelous cure was wrought, Christ said again and again: "Thy Faith hath made thee whole."

In the light of all we know today concerning the cure of disease by suggestion, and in view of his own unequivocal statement, does it not seem possible that when the Master said: "Thy faith hath made thee whole," he crystallized into definite form a great fundamental principle which underlies all systems of metaphysical healing wherein the efforts of the patient himself are a potential factor?

Such is indeed the case. It could not be stated more clearly. It cannot be expressed more simply. It will never be declared with greater scientific exactness. It is just possible, however, that our modern method of expressing the same truth will bring it more definitely within the range of our scientific comprehension. With that thought in view, the following statement of the therapeutic principle here referred to may have a possible value:

The relation of the mind to the physical body is such that every mental state or condition has its reflex expression in the physical organism. Just why this is so is a proposition which might lead to endless discussion with fruitless results. But perhaps one of the best known and most frequently demonstrated facts of medical science is comprised in the statement that the state of the patient's mind is a potent factor which must be taken into account in the treatment and cure of disease of all kinds. The regular practitioner who is in daily and hourly touch with the suffering will fully understand the meaning of this proposition, for it embodies a fact with which he is compelled to deal in every case he is called to attend.

He knows that fear, anger, worry, anxiety, sorrow, gloom, doubt, despair, unhappiness and excitement of every kind and degree, are destructive mental conditions which have a tendency to produce disease, and when so produced to aggravate and accelerate its destructive action upon the physical body.

He likewise knows that courage, brightness, cheerfulness, freedom from care, with perseverance, determination, hope and Faith are all mighty factors to supplement Nature's Constructive Principle in the restoration and conservation of health and life.

And again, there are many specific diseases which are unquestionably due entirely to mental causes. Wherever this condition obtains it is entirely within the power of the patient to heal himself by purely mental processes, if he but understand the principle involved and the method of its application.

In just so far as the mental state, condition or attitude of the patient is or may become a salutary factor at all in the therapeutic process, it is based upon three constituent mental elements, viz:

1. The desire to be well.

2. The will to become well.

3. An abounding and unwavering Faith that the agencies employed will make him well.

These are conditions which are practically indispensable to recovery even where the disease or injury may be one which requires the application of other than purely mental or physical remedies. Every physician or surgeon who has given any attention to the psychology of his profession will appreciate the accuracy of this statement.

And here again, it will be observed that Faith is the ultimate condition or state of mind to be attained. All things else are but means to an end, and Faith is that end.

It is now possible to make clear something of the extent to which the term "Suggestion" has been abused and libeled by those who are responsible for having inducted it into the literature of hypnotism and associated it with the hypnotic process.

It will be conceded that in all the various metaphysical processes of healing above referred to suggestion plays an important part. In fact, it may as well be admitted that suggestion constitutes the mechanical device—speaking in terms of physical nature—by means of which the mind of the patient is slowly but surely lifted from the destructive level of fear and distrust to the exalted plane of constructive Faith. It is the lever, so to speak, by which the mind of the patient is lifted out of the dirt of doubt and despair and set in its rightful place in the constructive wall of therapeutic Faith. It is therefore a most potent factor in the curative process.

As already stated, however, the term has become so intimately and inseparably identified and associated with the professional hypnotist and with the language and literature of hypnotism that to the average mind it conveys but one meaning. Wherever it is employed in a therapeutic sense it has come to be understood as Hypnotic-"Suggestion."

Indeed, recent writers have gone so far as to attribute all the results of the various metaphysical systems of healing to Hypnotic-"Suggestion." The injustice and the rank fallacy of this will now be apparent. The character of suggestion by means of which the mental healer, the Christian Scientist, or the good doctor with his harmless bread pill, establishes a therapeutic Faith in the mind of his patient is as far removed from Hypnotic-"Suggestion" as truth is from falsehood.

Thus it is that under the name of "Suggestion" thousands of the most wonderful cures have been accredited to hypnotism which are no more related to the hypnotic process than they are to the tides of the ocean or the Arctic Circle. They are, in fact, the results of true therapeutic suggestion which is always and under all conditions and circumstances "Independent Suggestion" in some form.

While it is not within the province of this particular volume to elaborate the subject of therapeutic suggestion in particular, nor therapeutics in general, it may nevertheless not be amiss to here present the following specific facts, and state that, in Vol. III, of this Series, the subject will be more fully covered:

1. The only true and legitimate therapeutic suggestion is Independent Suggestion.

2. Hypnotic-"Suggestion" is in no legitimate sense therapeutic in its action, but, on the contrary, is destructive in its essential nature.

3. There is not a single result claimed for hypnotism or for Hypnotic-"Suggestion" which cannot be accomplished by legitimate therapeutic agencies that do not in the slightest degree interfere with the patient's unimpaired control of all his independent, self-conscious and rational faculties, capacities and powers. The breadth of this statement is fully understood and appreciated. It is not idly made. Its truth will be made plain to those who follow the subject to its conclusion.

4. While it is true that all the various schools of metaphysical healing employ suggestion as a therapeutic agent, it may be said in all sincerity and truth and without prejudice that not one of them makes use of it in an intelligent and purposeful manner.

By this is meant that the metaphysical healer, generally speaking, does not know that suggestion has anything whatever to do with the process he employs. He attributes his cures to other agencies entirely. Even if told that he employs suggestion as the basic principle of his curative process he would doubtless be offended, for he is not aware of the fact that he employs this agency.

On the other hand, he knows that he does not intend to do so. It is therefore perfectly natural for him to attribute his cures to whatever agency he may have had in mind, even though entirely imaginary on his part. This, however, does not alter the fact that he does employ suggestion, and employs it successfuly as far as he goes.

But it will be observed that inasmuch as he makes use of it unconsciously and unintentionally, this is neither an intelligent nor a purposeful application of the principle involved. It follows that the therapeutic results of all these various metaphysical systems are meager as compared with those which might otherwise obtain if the underlying principle were fully understood by the operator and intelligently applied.

5. The intelligent physician who, by means of suggestion, stimulates the mind of his patient to a therapeutic Faith in the healing properties and powers of his medicines, makes a far more intelligent and purposeful application of suggestion, as far as he goes, than does the metaphysical healer. For it will be seen that the physician understands the principle involved and applies it in such manner as to obtain direct and specific results. In this manner many a drug of indifferent medicinal value has, through the senses of sight, smell, touch and taste, been made by the subtle intelligence of the physician to carry to the consciousness of the patient a powerful suggestion of life and health. Many a cure has thus been wrought by the aid of mental suggestion where physical remedies alone might have failed.

But there is an exact and thoroughly scientific method of applying therapeutic suggestion, with which even the intelligent physician is not yet fully conversant. It is rationally intelligent, entirely purposeful, and thoroughly truthful in every detail, and when fully understood must commend itself to the thoughtful consideration of the medical fraternity as a powerful supplementary factor in the treatment and cure of disease.

The development of this subject, however, lies wholly outside the limitations and purposes of this particular volume, and must therefore be reserved for future consideration.

6. Thus far but a single phase of the subject of true therapeutic suggestion has been considered, namely, that part which the patient himself plays in the therapeutic process. It must not be inferred from this, however, that suggestion is the only curative agency in Nature, nor that it is by any means the most important or salutary in its effects.

It will be remembered that our primary purpose has been to expose to view some of the fallacies of hypnotism and Hypnotic-"Suggestion." To accomplish this result it has been necessary to clearly differentiate between what is rightfully entitled to be known as Hypnotic-"Suggestion" and what has here been defined as true therapeutic suggestion. Having done this, our real task has been accomplished.

Lest there may be some, however, who might otherwise obtain an exaggerated or erroneous impression as to the relative merit and value of true therapeutic suggestion, it would seem proper to here state more explicitly that the therapeutic agencies of Nature are both numerous and potent.

In the order of Nature they divide themselves into three distinct and separate classes according to the planes of their activity. That is to say, they are classified as Physical, Spiritual and Psychical. Those that are purely physical act directly upon the physical organism of man. Those that are spiritual in like manner act directly upon his spiritual organism, and those that are wholly psychical act directly upon the soul or intelligence.

Therapeutic suggestion falls under the third class here named. It is entirely psychic in its nature and action. But it must not be understood that suggestion is the only psychic agency of a therapeutic nature. Neither is it the most potent. It is but one of the many agencies which Nature has placed within the reach of human intelligence by and through which man may establish and maintain harmony in the three-fold relationship of his being. This constitutes health. This means the cure of disease. This is the ultimate goal of therapeutics.

Physical remedies, within the limits of their therapeutic powers, accomplish this result by direct action upon the physical organism. Spiritual remedies accomplish the same result through their action upon the spiritual organism. Psychic remedies, in like manner, reach the same end through their direct action upon man's essential being, the soul, or intelligence.

Thus, it will be observed, there are three distinct and separate keys to the temple of health. One of these unlocks the outer gate which leads to the great broad court of physical Nature. Another unlocks the middle door, which leads to the inner court of spiritual Nature. The third unlocks the secret door to the inner sanctuary, the Holy of Holies.

According to our practical western way of looking at things, the owner of a splendid three-story residence would be considered very foolish, to say the least, if he should lock the doors leading to the second and third stories and then deliberately throw away the keys. By so doing he would only confine himself to the inconveniences and disadvantages of an ordinary flat, and deliberately deny himself and family the facilities, advantages and comforts to which they are of right entitled, and upon which he must still continue to pay taxes.

No less foolish is the man who would lock any of the doors of his being through which the true therapeutic agencies of Nature may enter and come to his relief in the hour of his extremity.

Flooding the basement of a three-story residence will never put out a fire in the garret nor on the roof. Turning a hose on the roof is not likely to stop a fire in the cellar. And yet these are the methods too often employed in the treatment of disease.

The narrow-minded and conventional dogmatist of the purely materialistic schools confines his operations chiefly to the ground floor and basement. In a fair percentage of cases he is successful. Why? Because a very large percentage of disease is of purely physical origin and comes from an over-heated furnace, so to speak.

The spiritual magnetic healer operates almost exclusively in the second story, although he does not always know it. He, too, reports many "put outs." Why is this? Merely because the fires of disease with which he is dealing happen to be of spiritual origin. They therefore yield to spiritual agencies.

The mental healer and the Christian Scientist confine their operations entirely to the third story and the garret. And they also conquer many fires of disease. Lightning and falling embers usually catch in the roof. In all such cases these good people happen to be in exactly the right locality. This is because many diseases are of purely psychic or mental origin. They therefore yield to the higher treatment.

But the ideal fireman is he who is able to quickly and accurately locate a blaze and apply the proper extinguisher, no matter whether the fire be in the basement or on the roof.

In like manner the ideal physician is the man who is able—

1. To quickly and accurately diagnose a disease and determine its exact location, nature and origin.

2. To apply the remedy that will reach the seat of disease most directly, whether it be of physical, spiritual or psychical origin.

The pioneers of the medical profession are to-day approaching this happy consummation. When they shall have fully attained the high position here suggested they will command the unlimited confidence of their fellow-men, but not before. Then and then only will they be entitled to the name of "Great Physicians."

CHAPTER XV.

Post-Mortem Hypnotism.

Up to this point the subject of hypnotism has been viewed from the standpoint of physical Nature entirely. But there is yet another, a higher and more comprehensive position from which to examine it.

If the facts thus far taken into account leave in the mind a possible doubt as to the destructive character of the hypnotic process that doubt will be dissolved by the added light of the higher science.

It has come to be pretty generally conceded, even by men of physical science, that the physical body of man is but an instrument of the intelligent soul which inhabits and operates it. It is, perhaps, not so generally understood and acknowledged that this intelligent entity, the soul, continues to exist independently of the physical body after the transition called death.

Such, however, is the case. This is one of the demonstrated facts of Natural Science, to which reference has already been made. This, therefore, is the primary and fundamental fact which must be taken into account in the final determination of the merits or demerits of hypnosis as a therapeutic agent.

Those who are prepared to accept the fact of a life after physical death, even tentatively, will not hesitate to entertain, upon the same basis, its natural corollary, which is that whatever affects the essential individual, the intelligent entity, the soul, is of vastly greater importance to him than is that which affects only the temporary physical instrument of that intelligent soul, the physical body.

Natural Science has not only demonstrated with absolute certainty the continuity of life after physical death. It has done much more than this. Among other things, it has studied this subject of hypnotism and Hypnotic-"Suggestion" from the same high plane and point of vantage. It has analyzed the process and carefully noted the results trom the planes of spiritual and psychical Nature. The facts of Natural Science, therefore, which bear upon this subject from the plane of man's essential being, the soul, must also be accorded their full measure of value and importance in the final solution of the great problem.

These are the facts which physical science has thus far almost entirely ignored. These are the facts to which the professional hypnotist never refers. These are the essential facts upon which alone the intelligent student must depend in his final analysis. These, in truth, are the facts upon which the cause of hypnotism and the professional hypnotist must ultimately stand or fall.

Strange as the term may sound to the unaccustomed ear, and unsubstantial as the idea may appear to the average reader, the one primary and fundamental fact upon which all other facts depend for their correct reading is, that there is a *"Post-Mortem"* view of this question which cannot be ignored by those who love the truth, nor by those who desire to guard themselves and their loved ones from the insidious dangers which menace them under the seductive guise and fascinating names of "Hypnotism" and Hypnotic-"Suggestion."

For it is a fact that the school of the higher science has followed the hypnotist and his subject into the realm of spiritual life which has been designated by the school of physical science as the "Unknowable." It has there gathered many additional facts of Nature which it is able to definitely formulate and present with unqualified assurance. Among those additional facts which have a specific bearing upon the subject under consideration the following are of particular importance:

1.   Hypnotism, in its essential nature, is a subjective, psychic process.

2.   Its most direct and essential results are related to and registered upon the soul, rather than upon the physical body.

3.   As might readily be anticipated, therefore, physical death does not necessarily break, destroy, counteract nor even

mitigate the hypnotic relation when the same has been fully entered into and established upon the physical plane.

A suggestive hint of this important, underlying fact may be obtained from a simple experiment which is already familiar to both hypnotists and students everywhere.

For instance, it is a well-known fact, fully established by oft-repeated demonstrations, to which hypnotists of all grades, kinds and schools will testify, that a "suggestion" or command given to a subject while he is in a state of profound hypnosis, to be executed or performed at some future time (commonly designated as a post-hypnotic suggestion), will be obeyed with absolute fidelity at the time and place and in the exact manner prescribed.

That is to say, an Hypnotic-"Suggestion" may be given to-day to be executed by the subject a week, a month, a year, or even ten years hence, and when the time comes the command will be executed with perfect fidelity, even though the subject and the operator may at the time be thousands of miles apart, and the hypnotist may have forgotten the incident entirely.

In order that this statement shall not be misinterpreted as an idle or meaningless assertion, the following carefully worded statement is here quoted from the recent work of Prof. De Lawrence, fully sustaining every assertion made. He says:

"Suggest to a subject while he is sound asleep that in eight weeks he will mail you a letter with a blank piece of note paper inside, and during the intervening period you may yourself forget the occurrence, but, in exactly eight weeks, he will carry out the suggestion."

Quoting still further from the same work:

"Suggest to a subject that in ninety days from a given date he will come to your house with his coat on inside out, and he will most certainly do so."

The deep and ominous importance of all this will be better understood and appreciated when the further fact is known that, after a subject in a state of profound hypnosis has thus been given a command to be executed at a future date, and is then awakened, he retains no memory or knowledge of what has occurred during the hypnotic sleep. He has no knowledge that he has been charged with the execution of a command or "suggestion" of any kind. He immediately goes about his own affairs in a manner which would lead the most acute detective or the most learned psychologist to infer that he is entirely free from all hypnotic influence and in a perfectly normal condition. No one, in fact, would ever suspect that his consciousness has been irrevocably impressed with a "suggestion" which he is bound to execute when the time comes. He not only conducts himself after the manner of a free moral agent in full possession of all his rational faculties, capacities and powers, but if questioned on the subject would undoubtedly assert and maintain with strenuous vigor his perfect freedom from all hypnotic influence or control.

Notwithstanding all this, when the appointed time arrives for the execution of the post-Hypnotic-"Suggestion" or command, he goes and does the thing "suggested" or commanded to be done, with absolute obedience and with the utmost fidelity to every detail. Moreover, the perfectly natural manner in which he conducts himself through it all would lead any intelligent observer, who did not know the facts, to infer that he was impelled by his own independent, self-conscious and rational volition. Even the subject himself is under the impression that this is so.

But the fact remains that he is simply executing a "suggestion" or command which was given him weeks, months, or perhaps years before while he was in a profound hypnotic sleep of which he has no knowledge or remembrance whatever. Ask him why he does the particular thing commanded to be done, and in all probability he cannot tell you. Pressed for an explanation of the motive which impelled him, he will tell you that he simply felt an impulse to go and do that particular thing, and that he did it in obedience to the impulse without stopping to reason upon it or anticipate the results which might follow.

Thus it has come to be known as a scientific fact that the hypnotic relation, once established, continues indefinitely. Not only this, it continues even though the hypnotist may have entirely forgotten both the subject and the incident in the meantime. It continues though the subject be wholly unconscious of the fact. It continues regardless of the will, wish, memory or knowledge of either party, or of both. It continues though the parties be separated as far as the opposite poles of the earth. It continues without regard to time, place, distance or physical environment. It continues, in fact, unbroken and unabated until both shall come to recognize the law they have thus violated and shall, of their own volition, unite in a mutual effort to restore themselves to a normal relation. Even then it often becomes a labor of years on the part of both to return again to the condition of independence from which they started.

With these established facts in mind, those who know that there is a life beyond the grave, as well as those who honestly believe that there is such a life, will readily understand and appreciate the horrible truth that even physical death is, of itself, no barrier to the operation of this subtle and mysterious power when once the hypnotic relation has been fully entered into.

For this is but another demonstration of the seemingly universal continuity of natural law. Every law of individual life upon the plane of physical Nature has its correlation upon the spiritual planes of being. They are, indeed, but the same laws running through all the varied phases and conditions of Nature. The laws of spiritual life are but an extension or continuation of the laws of life upon the physical plane. Or, perhaps, more accurately speaking, the laws of physical life are but an extension or continuation of the laws of life upon the spiritual planes.

As a natural sequel of all this, it has been found that in every instance where the hypnotist survives his subject upon the physical plane the disembodied subject is still irrevocably bound by the same immutable and inexorable law which bound him upon earth. He is thus bound regardless of his own will or desire. He is so bound notwithstanding the physically embodied hypnotist may be entirely ignorant of the fact and quite unconscious of the bond. This strange bondage continues throughout the lifetime of the hypnotist, and during this period, however long or short it may be, the subject is known upon the spiritual planes of life as an "earth-bound" soul.

And what could better define his real condition? He is, indeed, "earth-bound," in the most exact and literal meaning of the term. He is compelled by the subtle and overwhelming power of that mysterious force to walk the paths of earth in expiation of his offense against the primary and fundamental law of individual being.

Not only this, in an agony of protest born of suffering and repentance, he is compelled to dog the footsteps of his self-appointed human master through all the varied scenes and experiences of that master's earthly career. He is compelled by this law of association to look upon his hypnotist in all the deformity of his perverted and distorted human nature. Added to all this, he is bound by that mysterious bond to stand in mute and helpless agony and see the chains of abject servitude forged about the souls of other victims.

And so the narration of actual, known results and conditions might be continued, until the brain is weary and the heart is sick, but the cry of the soul rings louder still that the end is not yet.

The final reckoning is reserved for that time which cannot be avoided, when physical nature and human flesh shall no longer conceal the truths of the soul.

In that hour when the hypnotist shall stand face to face with his subject upon the lowest plane of spiritual life and both shall come to recognize the immutable and inexorable law of individual responsibility, this is the real beginning of mutual retribution.

For they stand together upon the path which leads into THE WAY OF DEATH.

CHAPTER XVI.

WHAT OF THE HYPNOTIST?

There are hypnotists and hypnotists.

Their number is rapidly increasing. Hypnotic "Schools," "Institutes" and "Colleges" are springing up on every hand to teach the art of hypnotizing. Their advertisements appear in almost every issue of our leading journals and periodicals all over the world. Their so-called "graduates" are carrying the practice of their art into all the walks of life.

Even our school children, mere boys and girls, have caught the inspiration. In childish innocence and youthful ignorance, they are permitted to amuse themselves with hypnotic experiments, the results of which are wholly unknown to them.

The hypnotist is thus making his impress upon society in such manner as to warrant a definite and searching inquiry into his motives and purposes as well as his status as a member of society.

What, then, of the hypnotist? What of his moral status? In order to arrive at a just conclusion and be able to answer these questions fully and satisfactorily and without prejudice, it is necessary to study the subject from the standpoint of motive and intent. We judge men much more by their motives and intentions than by the actual results of their actions. We prefer to be so judged ourselves, especially when we know that our motives and intentions are just.

We may, indeed, fully intend to do a noble and generous act, only to find when we come to look upon the results that it was a grievous and unhappy mistake. We may even plan a deliberate wrong, only to find that the results are, after all, just and beneficent. From the ethical point of view, however, we must in both instances be judged by the motive and intent by which we were actuated.

In the analysis which follows, therefore, we are not studying results alone. We are, on the contrary, analyzing motives and intentions. The final results of hypnotism upon both the hypnotist and his subject will be more fully considered in Part III of this volume.

Ethically or morally considered, hypnotists naturally divide themselves into three distinct and separate classes, viz.:

1. Those whose motives and intentions are good.
2. Those whose motives and intentions are indifferent.
3. Those whose motives and intentions are bad.

Remembering at all times that the actual results accomplished do not necessarily correspond with nor furnish a proper index of the motives and intentions back of them, a brief consideration of these three classes of hypnotists, in the order suggested, cannot fail to be both interesting and instructive.

In the class with those whose motives and intentions are both good and pure and in every other way commendable we have:

1. The scientist.
2. The physician.

The chief motive which inspires the scientist is the accumulation of exact and definite knowledge. We all admit the value of knowledge. We recognize its transcendent importance in every department of individual life. It is at the very foundation of all our progress. It determines the status of nations as well as that of individuals. Upon it we build our ethical standards. By it we measure the value and the virtue of all religions.

So deeply important, in fact, is exact and definite knowledge to the life and well being of all men, that we are inclined to look with forbearance and toleration upon whatever means or methods men may employ in their pursuit of it.

For instance, we look with horror and righteous indignation upon the wanton cruelty of brutal men toward innocent and helpless animals and birds. But we pause and view with something akin to sympathetic complacency the murderous act of the vivisectionist as he opens the skull of an innocent and helpless dog and removes its sleeping brain. Why? Because we know that he is in search of knowledge. We see him close the opened skull over the now vacant brain cavity and with cold-blooded patience study the actions of his victim in the hope of determining some undiscovered function of the brain. We see him again and again subject the same helpless animal to the relentless tyranny of his will. We watch him cut away section after section of its brain, and after each operation watch without the least indication of sympathy or feeling for some new development which may possibly give him a clue to the mystery of individual being. Why? Because we know that he is in search of knowledge.

We permit him to carry the dead bodies of our fellow men and women into his laboratory and there cut them into a thousand pieces in order that he may study the most complex and wonderful organism that Nature has yet evolved. We permit him to override every sentiment and defy every established convention of society just because we know that he is in search of knowledge. We know that he is searching for that which may be of specific value to us and to all men.

No matter how many or how great are the crimes he commits against the laws of Nature, we are impelled to ignore them, so long as they are committed in the name of science. No matter what individual suffering or sorrow may follow in his footsteps, we are wont to condone his offenses in the name of science and evolution. Whatever may be the cost to individual life, the work of the scientist goes on and we tacitly forgive him for the desolation and the havoc he has wrought, for the laws he has broken, for the crimes he has committed, and for the wrongs he has perpetrated. Why? Because we understand the motive that inspires him and we call it good.

But however lenient we may be, however ready to forgive and forget, there is yet a law that is higher than the caprices of men, a law which is above and beyond their sanctions or their confutations, and to this law the scientist and the sciolist alike must render an individual accounting.

The position of the scientist before this higher law, however, is not the subject of present consideration. We are now concerned only with his ethical or moral status in the sight of men, and we find that, according to their imperfect standards, his motives and intentions are unimpeachable. Although he may practice the processes of hypnotism upon a thousand subjects, and thereby become a party to the violation of a primary and fundamental law of individual being, the law of individual responsibility, yet by the laws and the standards of men he stands acquitted, because his motives and intentions are in accord with our ethical ideas and moral conceptions. He is a hunter for truth and a searcher for knowledge, and therefore, from the standpoint of ethics, we permit him to pass unchallenged.

As with the scientist, so with the physician. His mission is with the suffering. As we see him in his daily battle with the destructive agencies of Nature, and know that his heart is filled with sympathy for those who look to him for help in the hour of their extremity, we are ready to sanction whatever means he may employ in his efforts to heal the sick, relieve the suffering, comfort the sorrowing and stay the hand of death. We know that whatever agencies he may employ his motives and intentions are above and beyond suspicion or reproach from our human understanding.

It is a fact that to-day some of our leading physicians and surgeons are employing hypnotism and Hypnotic-"Suggestion" to some extent as an accompaniment of their *materia medica*. They have found that in certain cases of a neurotic character they have been able to produce temporary anæsthesia. They have not gone beyond this simple fact as a general thing. For their specific and immediate purposes it would seem to be unnecessary. They are chiefly concerned with disease in its purely objective expression upon the physical plane. Whatever will produce a seemingly desirable result is therefore generally deemed both expedient and professionally admissible.

Comparatively few physicians have thus far made a study of hypnotism from its psychological aspect. The few who have done so find that the profession in general is not prepared for its exposition from that standpoint. It is confidently believed, however, that the time is not far distant when *materia medica* and psychology will be recognized as concomitant factors in all true therapeutic processes. When that time shall come, whether it be in the near or remote future, the medical profession will become the most powerful agency in existence for the protection of society against the destructive practice of all subjective psychic processes.

It is the earnest hope of the School of Natural Science that it may be able to so far interest the leading representatives of the medical profession as to lay before them in scientific form a full and complete exposition of its own experiments and demonstrations in this intensely interesting and important field of scientific research. It is believed that if but this much can be accomplished it will undoubtedly open the way for an intelligent, sympathetic and purposeful co-operation in the development of medical science which cannot fail of the most salutary and beneficent results.

It is conceded that the physician who resorts to hypnotism as a final possible agency for the relief of suffering humanity is inspired by a most worthy and noble purpose, entirely regardless of the results accomplished. Measuring his deeds, therefore, not by their results, but by his motives and intentions, all society is ready to accord to him an ethical status above and beyond reproach or criticism.

The actual results of the physician's use of hypnotism in his practice are not under consideration at this time. Our present inquiry is confined entirely to the question of ethics, leaving the scientific analysis and exposition of .the subject for a distinct and separate study.

It is now in order to briefly consider the second general class, namely, those hypnotists whose motives and intentions are neither good nor bad, but are properly classified under the head of "Indifferent." In this general group may be found:

1. The social entertainer.
2. The practical joker.
3. The chronic experimenter.

The first of these, the social entertainer, generally speaking, has in mind nothing more beneficent and commendable than the mere passing of a pleasant hour, and nothing more malevolent than the gratification of his own vanity.

The second, the practical joker, intends neither good nor ill, as a general rule, but seeks only to gratify his sense of amusement at the harmless expense of his friends.

The third, the chronic experimenter, is moved almost entirely by the desire to satisfy his sense of the curious and the mysterious. He has, in reality, neither good nor evil in his mind, and thinks little or nothing of the results in so far as they may affect others. He cares for neither the advancement of science on the one hand nor the alleviation of human suffering on the other.

Judged, therefore, by their motives and intentions alone, and from the purely ethical views of men, there is in the attitude of these three classes of hypnotists little to condemn and practically nothing to commend. Their position is indeed one which may be fittingly designated as morally indifferent.

Passing to the third general class, it is found that those hypnotists whose motives and intentions are unquestionably bad naturally group themselves into three distinct classes, as follows:

1. Those who practice hypnotism as a profession or business, and depend upon such practice for their financial support.

2. Those who employ it as a means of power whereby to achieve their individual ambitions in life and gratify their desire for a personal popularity before the world.

3. Those who use it as a subtle means and method whereby to commit unusual crimes in such manner as to avoid detection and evade the just penalties of the law.

In the first instance the impelling motive is money, in the second power and popularity, and in the third self-gratification and conquest. The first, therefore, represents the gratification of greed, the second means the gratification of vanity, and the third stands for the gratification of the baser appetites, evil passions and criminal desires.

Every student of the subject will be able to call to mind

one or more fitting representatives of the first class, whose ruling motive is money and all that money means to the sordid and avaricious. Such an one may, for a valuable consideration in the form of a ticket to the "show," be seen upon the public platform with his subjects ranged about him. In the presence of the multitudes who have paid their money for the spectator's privileges, he gives a weird and revolting exhibition of all the varied hypnotic "experiments" known to the "profession." He is permitted to subject the minds and mental powers of children, boys and girls, and men and women of all ages and stations of life, to his own hypnotic domination and thus convert them into mere automatic machines, under the autocratic power and control of his will. He thus fulfils his part of the contract by furnishing the promised "entertainment" and in return pockets the gate receipts and passes on to fill other engagements.

We all enjoy entertainment. The more mysterious and uncanny it can be made to appear to most of us the better we enjoy it, and the more liberally we are willing to pay for it. To a large majority of people hypnotic phenomena are sufficiently mysterious and wonderful to afford unusual interest and amusement. For this reason the average professional hypnotist finds the field of hypnotic entertainment a most fruitful one, and he understands the methods of advertising necessary to insure him a rich harvest.

This type of intelligence is the one most generally seen at the heads of the numerous hypnotic "Schools," "Colleges" and "Institutes" throughout the country. These shrewd and enterprising individuals have been quick to analyze the common weaknesses of men and take advantage of the credulity and cupidity of their natures. They have made an exhaustive study of the ways, means and arts by and through which the average man may be induced to part with his money. They have proved themselves to be high-class adepts in the fascinating art of playing upon the sordid and selfish strings of human nature.

As an evidence of the unique and fetching methods employed by them to attract the attention and secure the patronage of the ignorant, the selfish, the vain, the ambitious, the unscrupulous, the conscienceless and the criminal classes of society, by an appeal to all the baser elements of the most vicious side of human nature, the following quotations bear eloquent testimony. They are taken verbatim from books, pamphlets, circulars and other advertising matter but recently scattered broadcast throughout the land.

Such advertisements as these are being distributed daily by these so-called hypnotic schools, colleges and institutes, and by hundreds of individual hypnotists in almost every leading city in the United States, and many such even come to us from European countries. Read them carefully and analyze the motives which inspire them. Study the character of the Muse which could inspire the declarations and promises they contain, and then prophesy the moral character of the men who inspire them and the men and women who most readily respond to them:

Quotation 1.

"Of the large number of students who order my Course of Lessons in Hypnotism I found that very many had a sensible and practical end in view. They wanted to make money. Instead of dabbling in hypnotism for mere pastime, it was their wise resolve to make hypnotism pay, and this by the very speedy and excellent plan of launching out as hypnotic entertainers. . . . I have treated the subject as one would any other money-making enterprise. . . . The more hypnotists there are earning fame and independence, the more people there are who will want to buy my instructions. . . . In other words, IT PAYS ME."

What could better illustrate the spirit of reckless depravity than the cold-blooded manner in which this advertiser offers, for the sum of five dollars, to put into the hands of anyone who applies a course of "Lessons" which will enable him to exercise upon and over his fellow men a power of whose actual results the purchaser is entirely ignorant?

This certainly represents the spirit of commercialism gone mad. Moral considerations do not enter into the proposition at any point. It is a mere matter of money—nothing more, nothing less.

Quotation 2.

"I fully explain my celebrated instantaneous method, by which you can hypnotize as quick as a flash.

"I tell you how to bring your subjects completely under your control.

"I tell you how to compel them to obey your slightest wish.

"I teach you how to fasten the eyes, hands and feet of a subject at the word of command.

"I teach you how your subject's will may be brought in direct subjection to your own.

"I tell you how his will may be placed in abeyance, and how his mental operations may be directed by you.

"I tell you how to control your subjects without speaking to them.

"I expose the vanity of persons who maintain that they cannot be hypnotized.

"I show you how the subject obeys the hypnotist as a locomotive does the manipulations of the driver.

"I tell you how to direct your subject's thoughts into any channel desired, and how to compel him to execute any command.

"I tell you how to hypnotize at a distance.

"I tell you how you can compel a person to be at a certain place at a specified time.

"I tell you how to give your subjects commands and suggestions that they will be obliged to carry out months and even years after the command has been given.

"I tell you how to control your subjects instantly.

"I tell you how it is possible to hypnotize a person who is in a natural sleep, who will waken the next morning without knowing that he has been hypnotized, and will be compelled to carry out any command that has been given him while in the trance.

"I tell you how to walk up to a person anywhere and hypnotize him instantly by a simple wave of the hand or a glance of the eye.

"I explain to you how a hypnotist feels when he begins to taste the sweets of power.

"I teach you how to paralyze a subject as instantly and completely as a knockout blow.

"I give you special hints for impressing the public with your wonderful and mysterious powers.

"I tell you how hypnotism can be used in ordinary business transactions to the great advantage of the operator.

"I give you information that will prevent other people from hypnotizing you. This secret is priceless and should be understood by all hypnotists."

In conclusion, this remarkable genius reminds the credulous public that his "Lessons in Hypnotism" are the only benefits for which he makes any charge. For the altogether insignificant sum of $5 any person who may choose to apply—provided he accompanies his application with the necessary $5—will receive "by return mail" the "Lessons," together with an "Elaborate Diploma " (in advance), fifty "Professional Cards" free of cost, and a few other articles of merchandise supposed to be of enormous value.

To obtain a clear understanding of the true significance of all this, it becomes necessary to study the motives and purposes back of it, and the passions, impulses and desires of human nature to which he appeals. With that end in view the following suggestions are of special importance and should be kept constantly in mind:

1. The advertisement itself is a work of art. It is accompanied by some fifty or more artistic cuts and designs, showing the hypnotist and his subjects in various postures, all of which exhibit the hypnotist as the imperious master and his subjects as the helpless, automatic instruments of his will.

2. This most interesting and attractive advertisement is distributed through the United States Mails to all parts of the country and to all classes of society without regard to age, sex or other condition.

3. No precautions of any kind whatever are taken by the advertiser, nor by the United States Postal authorities, to prevent this literature from going directly into the hands of the most vicious and criminal classes of society.

4. A careful study and analysis of the foregoing quotations will entirely convince any intelligent student that their author has made a deliberate and most powerful appeal to all that is avaricious, base, ignoble, vicious, unprincipled, vile, immoral, unconscionable, infamous and criminal in depraved human nature.

5. Not a single virtuous impulse, moral sentiment, noble purpose nor worthy motive is invoked or inspired.

6. The self-confessed motive in the mind of the hypnotist is money. He makes of his supposed knowledge a matter of merchandise. He offers it for sale to whomsoever he can induce to pay the price. It matters not to him what use may be made of the power he offers to confer upon those who yield to his solicitations. For the sum of $5 he guarantees to invest every purchaser of his "Lessons" with the power to conquer the will and enslave the souls of men, women and children, and suggests to him that he may then gratify his

baser appetites, passions, desires and purposes without the possibility of interference or opposition.

He promises to tell his prospective "students" how to use hypnotism in ordinary business transactions "to the great advantage of the operator." Properly translated, this means that for the small sum of $5 this self-exalted adept in the mystery of Black Magic will invest anyone who applies with the power to hypnotize a business man and take a deliberate and mean advantage of him in a business way, or even pick his pockets without opposition or likelihood of discovery.

A perfectly fair and reasonable interpretation of the great offer this malefactor of the human race places before an innocent and unsuspecting public, by aid of the government postal service, is as follows:

"For the sum of five good and lawful dollars, whenever the same shall be received by me, I hereby covenant and agree with the party of the second part, whoever he may be, and entirely regardless of his motives, purposes, personal reputation or moral character, that I will invest him with a power which will enable him:

"1. To exercise absolute control over the will and voluntary powers of his fellow-men without their power of resistance.

"2. To overcome the rational intelligence of business men and deprive them of their money and their property without due process of law, but in such manner as to overcome all opposition and defy the powers of the most experienced detectives.

"3. To so influence a court and jury as to obtain from them any verdict he may desire, the law and the evidence to the contrary notwithstanding.

"4. To obtain swift and terrible revenge upon his enemies, by the aid of hypnotized subjects, who are obliged to carry out his every command, even to the commission of murder, and who will even suffer the extreme penalties of the law without ever disclosing the real culprit.

"5. To fascinate innocent girls and virtuous women and lead them into paths of wickedness and shame.

"6. To debauch little children without likelihood of discovery by their unsuspecting parents.

"7. To gratify every carnal appetite, passion and desire whenever and with whomsoever he wills, and inspire the commission of every crime known to the laws of God or men, but in such manner as to entirely disarm suspicion, or fasten the guilt upon his helpless subjects."

All this and as much more as the mind can imagine is clearly and forcibly suggested by the inducements held out through this and other equally vicious advertisements to prospective students and would-be hypnotists.

With these simple facts in evidence the ethical quality of the hypnotist's motives and intentions becomes clearly apparent. His purposes are vicious, his intentions are dishonest, his motives are immoral and his actions, which fully conform thereto, are inimical to the rights, duties, privileges, obligations, responsibilities, and best interests of society in general and each and every individual in particular.

All this, and even more, is fully confessed by the last paragraph of the advertisement above quoted. For, this advertiser says, "I give you information that will prevent other people from hypnotizing you. This secret is priceless and should be understood by all hypnotists."

By this one sentence alone the dishonesty and criminality of the scheme stand revealed in all their hideous proportions. Note the declaration that "this secret is priceless and should be understood by all hypnotists." What secret? The secret "that will prevent other people from hypnotizing you." But why is it so vitally important to be able to "prevent other people from hypnotizing you"? If hypnotism is the innocent, harmless and beneficent process claimed, why is it of such vital importance that it should not be used on hypnotists themselves? Why is it that the one "priceless secret" out of the many he offers for sale is that which enables the hypnotist to "prevent other people from hypnotizing you"?

He wisely refrains from taking the public into his confidence on this important point, but this is not because he is ignorant of the answer. He knows full well the vital principle involved. He knows it just as every honest and intelligent student must know it when he has analyzed the subject in the light of the indisputable facts of science and of human experience. He knows that it is because the one "priceless" possession of every honest and intelligent soul is the power of self-control, and the inalienable right of self-consciousness at all times and under all conditions except such as Nature herself has prescribed.

He frankly confesses to his prospective students that the power of self-control is the one power above all others most valuable and important to the individual. And yet, upon the same page he guarantees to instruct his students in the art of grand larceny until they shall be able to successfully steal this one "priceless" possession from their fellow men, women and children wherever they go.

Perhaps the most astounding feature of all this is the fact that the hypnotist accompanies his offer with the autographic recommendation and enthusiastic approval of reputable physicians, surgeons, lawyers, bankers, politicians and business and professional men of education whose acuteness of intelligence would readily detect dishonesty and fraud in any other profession or line of business, and who would not intentionally become parties to deliberate crime.

There is but one natural inference, namely, that this man of mystery and mighty powers has gone about and hypnotized these good people, "with a wave of the hand or a glance of the eye," got their signatures while they were under the spell of his mysterious power, and then permitted them to awaken in blissful ignorance of the fact that their names are now being used as a means of defrauding other equally innocent people all over the country.

The further interesting fact that the United States Government has assisted him in the advertisement of his nefarious business might very reasonably support the theory that even the government of a great nation is not exempt from the hypnotic possibilities of this "Wild and Woolly Wizard of the West." For, it is generally understood that the U. S. Postal authorities intend to exclude from the U. S. Mails all fraudulent and immoral literature, and severely punish all those who violate its laws, rules and regulations in relation thereto.

But this particular man of mysteries and money is not alone in his profession. Indeed, he represents but a type of the professional hypnotist whose motives and inspiration are money and the luxuries money can buy. The writer has before him the literature and advertising matter of so-called schools, institutes and colleges of hypnotism from all parts of the country. Similar advertisements may be found in the leading newspapers and periodicals of all the principal cities throughout the United States.

Most of these offer to instruct their students by correspondence. Their instructions consist, for the most part, of a series of "Lessons by Mail," for which the regular fee in every instance must be paid in advance. The prices for these various courses of lessons range all the way from $5 to $100. Their promises and guaranties are in substance the same, and their "Lessons" cover practically the same subject matter. The only material difference is in the prices charged.

Some of these institutions are incorporated under state laws, and for this reason command a confidence which this implied sanction of the state carries with it. But their underlying motives and purposes are identical with those of the professional hypnotist everywhere. That is to say, they are in the business for money and money alone. The character of their advertisements, assertions, guaranties and promises betrays an utter absence of moral considerations of every kind whatsoever.

Of the three classes of hypnotists whose motives and intentions are bad, consideration has thus far been confined to the first, namely, the professional hypnotist who makes of his profession and practice a mere matter of merchandise. The two remaining classes include:

1. The vainly and unscrupulously ambitious.
2. The criminal.

These require but a passing notice, inasmuch as they are but a natural outgrowth and logical result of the first. Moved only by the base and evil passions of human nature, they naturally seek the shortest, safest and surest road which will lead them to the accomplishment of their wicked and shameless desires.

These are they who are naturally the first to respond to

the alluring promises and tempting guaranties contained in such advertisements as are daily flashed before their depraved imaginations by professional hypnotists of the first class above designated. They find it consistent with their nefarious purposes to obtain their knowledge of hypnotism in the least conspicuous manner possible. For, unlike the first class, their success in the field of hypnotism and hypnotic practice is commensurate with their ability to conceal their knowledge and practice of it from public view. Like their fitting companions in crime—the thief, the burglar, the ravisher and the murderer—they work under cover of darkness as far as possible. Hence it is that they almost entirely escape public attention and are thus enabled to exercise the subtle and irresistible power of Black Magic without even so much as a fear of detection.

This is not a mere fancy picture nor an idle dream. It is a deplorable fact. Not only this, it is a fact which is slowly but surely forcing itself upon the attention of the thoughtful and intelligent students of psychology, and will find ample verification just as soon as the public conscience is fully awakened and adequate methods are adopted for its public demonstration and exposition.

A vital problem with which society must sooner or later deal in this connection is that of locating responsibility for the endless chain of destructive results which are here but dimly and imperfectly suggested.

In the solution of this problem one important fact must not be overlooked nor omitted. This fact is fundamental, namely, that it is the professional hypnotist, moved by the unscrupulous desire for money, who has inspired all these various classes of individuals with the desire for hypnotic power. Through the medium of his artful advertisements he has played upon every vicious passion, propensity and desire of human nature in the hope of touching in each individual the mystic chord of sympathy that will open to him a plethoric purse.

It is here that the initial evil will be found. All others

grow out of it as naturally as vibratory activity is related to the law of motion and number. It is here then that the principle of retributive justice—which is but a limited application of the great universal law of compensation—fixes the primary responsibility for the evil consequences of hypnotism and hypnotic practices.

Spiritual Mediumship

CHAPTER I.

A RISK AND A DUTY.

The writer approaches this branch of his subject with a due appreciation of the unusual, extraordinary and "extra scientific" nature of the facts he is called upon to record.

No man who has been carefully grounded in the facts and methods of physical science and for many years schooled in the principles of law and the rules of evidence, is eager to invoke or invite for himself a reputation for charlatanry, empiricism, falsehood or insanity. And yet, this is the risk every man must assume who approaches the world with a work of any kind which transcends the generally accepted scientific dogmas of his time.

It would seem to be clear, therefore, that no man—however unusual may have been his instruction, study, personal experiences and demonstrations—would voluntarily enter upon so difficult and unpropitious an undertaking unless he were fully persuaded that the knowledge he has acquired is of greater value to the world than his own personal reputation. Even then he might well hesitate lest the world be unprepared to receive the knowledge for the presentation of which he has made the sacrifice.

Indeed, if the following statement of facts were going before a convocation of physical scientists of the present conventional type for final and irrevocable judgment, it is doubtful if it would be either prepared or submitted during the present generation. To do so would certainly be a useless mistake. For, upon the intelligence of such a body of men, recognizing as scientific nothing which transcends the purely physical in Nature, it could produce at the present time but one result. This could afford little comfort or satisfaction to the writer and even less to the thousands of honest, sane and intelligent men and women all over the world who would thereby stand condemned.

Fortunately, however, for the cause of truth, there have come to be in this day and generation many besides the writer who know from their own personal experiences that some, at least, of the statements of fact hereinafter made are true. Indeed, some of these facts have been personally demonstrated by intelligent and honest men and women everywhere. Others have been demonstrated by only the few, but their demonstrations are none the less absolute and conclusive.

Of the many who are today able to demonstrate some one or more of the facts hereinafter stated, very few have deemed it expedient or wise to take the world at large into their confidence. Others who are inclined to be more independent of the judgments and prejudices of their fellow-men have learned from a bitter experience that their reputations for honesty, as well as sanity, depend upon their ability and inclination to conceal the facts from their neighbors, their nearest friends, and oftentimes from members of their own families.

Others who have been strongly moved by the altruistic spirit have defied the established scientific and religious dogmas of the time and have endeavored to give to the world the benefit of their personal experiences and demonstrations. As a penalty for their indiscretion they have been rudely wakened from their altruistic dreams to find themselves carefully labeled and catalogued under the general heading of "Cranks."

To all these, as well as to many other honest and intelligent men and women who have learned the folly of fixing arbitrary limits for the possibilities of human knowledge and achievement, it may be an inspiration of strength and possible comfort to see in cold type an unequivocal statement of such facts as Natural Science has demonstrated with absolute certainty concerning the great problem of individual life and individual destiny.

The following pages are devoted to a presentation of such of these facts as are pertinent to the general subject under consideration.

Fully recognizing in the undertaking both a risk and a duty, the writer has elected to assume the risk and, to the best of his ability, discharge the duty which his knowledge imposes upon him.

CHAPTER II.

OTHER DEFINITIONS.

Perhaps there is no task more difficult for the conscientious scientist to perform than that of accurate publication.

Some one has said that: "Speech is but broken light upon the depths of the unspoken." It is believed that nowhere is the truth of this saying more vividly apparent than in the scientific literature of the age.

When the scientist discovers a fact or a principle of Nature which is new to him he usually experiences little difficulty in properly classifying it and so fixing it in mind as to be able to identify it with facility and certainty thereafter. But when he takes upon himself the labor of giving it to the world he often finds that the language with which the great unscientific world is acquainted does not contain a single term in which it can be accurately expressed. He is then put to the difficult and intricate task of studying words and combinations of words and often, as a last resort, coining new words, until he discovers or formulates some new term or combination that will convey his meaning with all its proper colors and shadings.

But this coloring and shading process is the work of the artist, and it would appear that scientists, as a general rule, are indifferent artists. In no department of scientific labor does this fact appear with greater conspicuity than it does in the literature of psychical research.

The very nature of the subject, and the almost unlimited field it covers, call for the most delicate and subtle distinctions and differentiations. This demands a terminology which is not only free from all ambiguity, but one which cannot, by the most clever devices of resourceful and unprincipled intelligence, be tortured and twisted into meanings at variance with the intentions of the writer.

If the language and literature of Hypnotism are defective in this respect, even more fatally so are the language and literature of modern Spiritualism in general and of "Mediumship" in particular. These subjects have been publicly, expounded by men and women in all the varied walks of life. The learned and the ignorant, the honest and the dishonest, the true and the false, the wise and the foolish, have all given their contributions to the world for what they are worth. They have written from every conceivable standpoint. Their writings are inspired by almost every imaginable motive. It is not strange, therefore, that contradiction and confusion constitute the most prolific result of the vast and almost unlimited energy thus expended.

Among those whose motives are above suspicion the chief difficulty appears to be due to a lack of uniformity in the terminology employed. For instance—one writer seems to regard a "Spiritualist" as something wholly different from a "Spiritist," and then forthwith proceeds to use the terms synonymously. In like manner, he seems to see a vital difference between "Spiritualism" and "Spiritism," and almost before he has finished expounding the difference he is employing the terms interchangeably.

One writer defines a "Spiritualist" to be, "Anyone who believes in a life after physical death." It is plain to be seen that this would include the Methodist, the Presbyterian, the Catholic and all Christians, as well as nearly all mankind, in fact, for there is not a religious sect of any kind but believes in a life after physical death. It is therefore manifestly apparent that such a definition is entirely too broad and comprehensive.

Another defines the "Spiritualist" to be "One who believes that there is not only a life after physical death, but that it is possible for those in the physical body to communicate with those in the spiritual life." But there are a number of religious sects that believe all this. It is therefore clear that the definition is ambiguous.

To avoid this sort of embarrassment and difficulty in the present instance, as far as may be possible, the following additional definitions are here presented as a substantial basis from which to examine the subject of "Spiritual Mediumship" according to the plan and purpose of this work. It is suggested that a careful study of their specific limitations will serve to avoid all cause for misunderstanding or uncertainty as to the particular sense in which the following terms are hereinafter employed:

CONTROL: A spiritually embodied person who voluntarily controls the will, voluntary powers and sensory organism of a person in the physical body.

Special attention is called to the distinction here made between a control and a hypnotist. The hypnotist is in the physical body while the control is in the spiritual only. The one is a human being while the other is a spiritual intelligence. The hypnotist operates from the plane of the earth while the control operates from the spiritual plane. The hypnotist is a physically embodied person while the control is a physically disembodied person. The hypnotist is a human being while the control is an ex-human being.

MEDIUM: A physically embodied person whose will, voluntary powers and sensory organism are subject to the will or domination of a spiritual control.

It will also be observed that the distinctive difference between a medium and a hypnotic subject lies in the fact that the medium is under the control of a spiritual intelligence, while the subject is under the control of a physically embodied intelligence.

MEDIUMSHIP: The process by and through which a spiritual control obtains, holds and exercises control of the will, voluntary powers and sensory organism of a medium. Also the relation which exists between the two intelligences during the mediumistic process.

SPIRITUALIST: One who accepts mediumship as a legitimate and proper method and process by and through which to obtain communications between those in the spiritual life and those in the physical.

SPIRITUALISM: That particular school, cult, religion, philosophy or metaphysical system which is founded upon its acceptance of mediumship as a legitimate and proper method and process by and through which to establish and maintain personal communication between those in the spiritual life and those in the physical.

Special attention is called to the sharply defined limitations of the last two definitions. It will be observed that they purposely exclude all those who do not accept, believe in, and sanction the process and the practice of mediumship.

There are, indeed, coming to be a good many intelligent investigators of psychic phenomena who do not in the least question the fact of spirit communication through mediumistic processes, but who thoroughly disapprove and even condemn the method or process by which these communications are obtained. In other words, while they admit that mediumship is a fact, they do not approve of it as a method or practice.

Such as these are not here classed as "Spiritualists."

Neither is any philosophy, science or religion which condemns mediumship called "Spiritualism."

It is of the utmost importance to fix these distinctions in mind before passing to the consideration of the general subject of Spiritual Mediumship.

SPIRITUAL ORGANISM: The spiritual body of an individual, with all its various organs and organic parts, by and through which the intelligent soul manifests itself upon the spiritual planes of life.

THE SOUL: The intelligent ego, entity, or essential being which inhabits and operates both the physical body and the spiritual body, and manifests itself through them.

It is well understood that from a theosophical as well as from a theological standpoint this definition of the soul is open to criticism. No attempt will be made to defend it against objections from either of these quarters, other than to state the simple fact that neither theosophy nor theology could reasonably be asked or expected to assume any responsibility whatever for the manner in which the term is employed in this work.

In truth, these definitions, like those contained in Part I, of this volume, have been formulated without special reference to any acknowledged exoteric authority. So far as the general public is concerned, therefore, the writer desires to assume all responsibility for their present promulgation.

It would seem quite possible and even probable that there may be learned critics who would be inclined to challenge the accuracy of some or perhaps all of these definitions. If so, it is their privilege to formulate others which will better express their own preconceived ideas whenever they shall feel an irresistible impulse to take the public into their confidence.

All that is claimed for these definitions, at this time, is the simple fact that they are in strict conformity with the knowledge thus far acquired by the writer and his colaborers in the School of Natural Science concerning the subjects covered by them, and that wherever the terms so defined appear in this work and in subsequent works of this Series, they are to be strictly interpreted as here indicated.

CHAPTER III.

SIGNIFICANT ADMISSIONS.

Physical science, broadly speaking, is inclined to challenge the claims of Spiritualism. The substantial basis of this challenge is, that the evidence produced by the spiritualist does not amount to scientific demonstration. Volumes have been written of a controversial nature upon this subject, both pro and con, but the case is still pending in the moot court.

A few eminent specialists such as Alfred Russell Wallace, Sir William Crookes, Dr. Hare, Professor Hodges and others, are notable dissenters from the ranks of physical science. These eminent scientific gentlemen concede that at least two of the most important claims of Spiritualism have been scientifically established, viz.:

1. That there is a life after physical death.

2. That through the process generally known and designated as Spiritual Mediumship, definite lines of communication have been established between those yet in the physical body and those who have passed the crisis known as physical death.

Those who have followed the controversy to any considerable length are doubtless already painfully aware of the fact that it opens to the disputants an almost limitless field of polemics. While the perspective thus afforded is eminently pleasing to the controversialist, it is equally unsatisfactory to the general student of the subject who is in search of definite knowledge.

Inasmuch as this particular work proceeds from the plane of Natural Science, its purpose is didactic rather than discursive or controversial. For the purpose, therefore, of eliminating from the subject as much irrelevant and immaterial matter as may be possible, and thus reaching by the most direct route the real issues under consideration, attention is called to the following significant admissions:

1. It is admitted that Mediumship is a fact.

2. It is admitted that there is a life after what is known as

physical death. That is to say, physical death does not annihilate the essential part of our being, the intelligent soul.

3. It is admitted that after dissolution of the physical body the intelligence, ego, soul or individual entity continues to inhabit a spiritual body.

4. It is admitted that an individual who has passed into the spiritual life may, under certain conditions, come into direct contact with those who are still in the physical body, and may even control the will, voluntary powers and sensory organisms of such physically embodied persons as may be susceptible to such influence, and use them as mediums.

5. It is admitted that by and through such control a medium may be made unconscious, or may be made to produce genuine psychic phenomena of a wide range and variety.

6. It is admitted that as a result of such control genuine communications may be had between individuals in the physical body and those in the spiritual.

7. It is admitted that communications thus obtained have brought comfort to sorrowing men and women whose loved ones have gone before them through the transition called physical death.

8. It is admitted that by and through the process of mediumship a certain amount of information has been communicated by those in the spiritual life to those in the physical, concerning the life beyond the grave.

9. It is admitted that modern Spiritualism is the natural and logical outgrowth of Mediumship, and that it has done something during the last fifty years to open the way to an unprejudiced examination of psychic phenomena, and that such an examination must necessarily result in benefit to those who possess the intelligence to understand and appreciate the results in all their bearings.

10. It is admitted that there are some honest mediums who are conscientiously endeavoring to serve their fellow men and women who are in doubt or perplexity concerning the fact of a life beyond the grave.

11. It is admitted that there are some honest spirit controls who are endeavoring to render a beneficent service to the

world by controlling mediums and using them as instruments by and through which to bring tidings from the spirit life to the friends they have left behind.

12. It is admitted that the mischievous and destructive effects of mediumship do not, as a general rule, begin to manifest themselves at once to the medium nor to the casual observer.

13. It is admitted that much has been written by students, mediums, controls, spiritualists, and investigators generally, concerning the subject of mediumship, at variance with the position taken in this work.

It will be observed that these admissions cover a wide field of hitherto disputed territory. Their purpose is twofold, viz.:

1. To give to Spiritualism and Mediumship the full benefit of every possible doubt which rational and fair-minded intelligence may be able to suggest.

2. Having thus admitted every material claim set up by the most enthusiastic advocate of mediumship, it is designed to remove all these mooted questions from the field of our present consideration.

This course is practicable only for the reason that from the standpoint of Natural Science all these disputed questions are of such secondary and indifferent importance as to be, for the most part, irrelevant and immaterial in the light of the known scientific results.

In other words, the position from which the subject is to be here considered entirely transcends the objective view of all these matters and deals with the principle of Nature which lies back of the factitious phenomena of mediumship.

The general effect of these admissions upon the mind of the reader will depend somewhat upon the position from which he views the subject under consideration.

For instance, if he should be a medium or a spiritualist, or a sympathetic student of spiritualistic philosophy and phenomena, it is not difficult to understand how he might be led to conclude that his claims are not only admitted, but that his position and conclusions are fully approved. If so, however, he is asked to suspend judgment and maintain an open and unbiased mind until he has carefully examined the subject from the position of Natural Science.

If a physical scientist of the school of conventional materialism, it would seem that his most natural impulse might be to close the book at once in a sort of scientific disgust, under the well defined impression that its author is either a knave, a fool, a subject of insanity, or a total stranger to science and to scientific methods and requirements. If so, however, he too is asked to so far master his impulse as to follow the subject to its logical and legitimate conclusion.

If a minister of the Gospel, an honest and conscientious member of any church, or a consistent believer in any of the religious creeds of Christendom, his first impression might reasonably be one of doubt or disapproval as to the effect of such sweeping admissions upon the basis of his religious faith. If so, he is asked to put aside his doubts for the present and withhold his disapproval until he has heard the case through to the end. It would be manifestly unfair for him to draw his conclusions and render his judgment upon but a small percentage of the material facts in the case.

If he should be one who, for any reason, may be bitterly prejudiced against spiritualism or mediumship, he might be inclined to take alarm lest these comprehensive admissions prove fatal to his position and prove that his prejudices are without foundation in fact. If so, he is asked to calm his fears and patiently and carefully analyze the principle which underlies these admissions.

And finally, if, perchance, he should be a broad minded man of intelligence, unfettered by religious, scientific or philosophic dogmatism, free from the blighting influence of conventionalism, bigotry, prejudice and superstition, and sufficiently interested in the subject to give it his thoughtful consideration, he will not need admonitions of any kind. He will patiently follow the exposition through to its conclusion and reserve his judgment until all the facts are before him and the law which underlies them has been made plain.

Prophetic reference has already been made to the possible

attitude of the physical materialist of the conventional type, and it has been suggested that he might be inclined to repudiate the foregoing admissions, or the major part of them at least, upon the scientific ground that the subject matter involved in them has not been proved. From the standpoint of physical science his point would be well taken. This is especially true for the reason that the subject matter covered by these admissions is very largely outside the limitations within which the conventional school of physical science has been and is at the present time operating.

Because of this fact, which common fairness compels us to recognize, it is not to be expected nor even hoped that the physical scientist, generally speaking, will find in a work of this scope and character material for serious consideration or for scientific investigation according to and within the limits of his own conventional school.

Indeed, it will be esteemed an unexpected compliment of the highest character if any acknowledged authority within that splendid aggregation of intelligent and earnest workers shall feel himself justified in devoting the time and thought necessary to a careful and critical reading of this volume.

It is most gratifying, however, to observe that the pioneers of physical science are coming very close to the border line of the psychical in their researches and investigation. A few in the front rank have actually reached it, and it is confidently believed that within a comparatively short time these few will be able to lead the many over into the broader field of Natural Science.

This is a consummation devoutly to be sought. But until that time shall come the less conspicuous intelligences within the body of that school must not be expected to enter with any degree of enthusiasm upon the investigation and study of subjects which are supposed to lie outside the present limitations and legitimate scope and purpose of their empirical system.

For the immediate present, therefore, this department of the work is addressed more especially to the intelligent consideration of spiritualists, mediums, students and investigators of mediumship and psychic phenomena, intelligent Christians of all creeds and sects, and to all those who are likely to fall under the fascinating spell of the seance or fall a victim to the subtle mysticism which surrounds the great and inspiring problem of the continuity of individual life.

CHAPTER IV.

FACTS DEMONSTRATED.

In the preceding chapter certain admissions have been made which, to the minds of many, may appear extraordinary, unscientific, unwarranted, and therefore unfortunate for the cause of truth.

It will be clear that if these admissions should concede that which is false and should thereby introduce falsehood into the record of facts upon which this work is based, there could be no assurance whatever that the results obtained are reliable. In other words, a court cannot be expected to render a correct judgment upon a false statement of facts.

It is an accepted rule of logic that if a premise be false, any conclusion based upon the assumption of its truth must be regarded as unreliable. It should, to say the least, be regarded as unscientific.

The purpose of this chapter, therefore, is briefly and concisely to state the demonstrated facts of Natural Science upon which the admissions referred to are founded. They are as follows:

1. All physical matter, both inorganic and organic, integrates conjointly with a finer ethereal or spiritual pattern, in such manner as to constitute what may properly be termed a double material entity.

No attempt will be made here to account for this phenomenon of Nature. It simply exists as one of the established facts with which Natural Science is compelled to deal. As such it forms an important link in the chain which connects the two correlated worlds of matter, motion, number, life and intelligence.

2. In the kingdom of inorganic matter these two bodies appear to be more equally dependent, one upon the other, than are the duplicate bodies of organic matter. This is more fully explained by the facts which follow .

3. The integration of a physical stone conjointly with its finer ethereal pattern is of such a character that upon the

sudden and forced disintegration and dissolution of the physical stone its finer ethereal body, or duplicate, remains intact for a comparatively brief period of time.

4. In due course of time, however, the ethereal body of the stone also disintegrates, dissolves, and to every appearance returns to its original elements.

5. During the time it remains intact this ethereal body of the stone is visible with perfect distinctness to one whose sense of sight is keen enough to observe it.

6. In the vegetable kingdom the two material bodies do not manifest the same degree of mutual dependence, one upon the other, as in the mineral kingdom. The meaning of this will be more clearly apparent in the light of the following facts.

7. Upon the sudden disintegration and dissolution of the physical body of an oak tree its ethereal duplicate persists intact for a much longer period than does the ethereal body of the stone.

8. But in due course of time the ethereal tree also disintegrates, dissolves, disappears from the spiritual plane of the vegetable kingdom, and to every appearance is resolved back into its original elements.

9. In the animal kingdom the independence of the spiritual body from the physical, in its power of continuity, is very markedly increased. This fact will be more fully explained by the next paragraph.

10. At the period of physical dissolution of an animal it is clear (to one who is able to observe the transition) that the spiritual body carries with it (or accompanies) the animating principle of the animal entity. This is evidenced by the fact that during its existence as a spiritual organism it appears to possess all the natural faculties and intelligent capacities and powers which belong to the animal entity.

11. The animal, however, in due course of time, disappears from the spiritual plane of the animal kingdom.

12. It does not reappear (at least in identical or distinguishable form) upon any of the spiritual planes of life which are distinctively related to this particular planet. What

becomes of it? The answer to this question is reserved for another chapter.

13. In the kingdom of man the transition we call physical death is even more clearly a mere incident in the life of the soul. This seems to be especially emphasized by the further facts hereinafter stated.

14. At the moment of physical dissolution of a man, woman or child, the spiritual body separates from the physical in a manner which appears to be identical with the separation of the two bodies of the animal at its physical death.

15. The animating principle of the double organic entity accompanies (or is accompanied by) the spiritual organism only, when physical death occurs, and in this respect the process of dissolution corresponds, to all appearances, with that of the animal.

16. The spiritual man, woman or child persists intact upon the spiritual planes of life for an indefinite period of time after physical dissolution, as does the animal (with the exceptions hereinafter noted).

17. Men, women and children upon the spiritual planes of life appear to possess all the natural faculties and intelligent capacities and powers with which they were invested at and prior to the time of physical dissolution. In this respect also they appear to acknowledge the same law which governs the animal.

18. But men, women and children, in the course of the ages, disappear from the lowest plane of the kingdom of spiritual man, and yet not always in a manner which is identical with the disappearance of the animal from the spiritual plane of animal life.

19. In other words, man disappears from the lowest plane of his spiritual life in either of two different manners and by two distinctly opposite methods or processes.

20. That is to say, under the constructive principle and process of evolution, growth, development and progress, he disappears from the lowest plane of spiritual life, only to appear upon the next higher, inhabiting a finer spiritual organism, clothed in richer splendor, and in possession of all

the natural faculties and intelligent capacities and powers with which he was invested at the time of the transition, and with the same individuality.   He is fully conscious of the transition and is able at will to reappear upon the lower plane through which he has passed, and manifest himself to those who have known him there.   In an analogous manner he is able to pass on to higher planes of spirituality and life.

21.   But under the operation of the opposite principle and process of destruction, or devolution, man also disappears from the lowest plane of his spiritual life in a manner which corresponds, in every essential particular, with the disappearance of the animal.

22.   In this latter instance he does not reappear (at least in identical or distinguishable form) upon any of the higher planes of spiritual life which are distinctively related to this particular planet.

23.   In the spiritual life man's ability to persist and advance from lower to higher planes of existence is commensurate with his own independent control of all his individual faculties, capacities and powers, and in response to his independent, self-conscious and rational volition and desire to so persist and advance.

24.   He obtains this control of his individual faculties, capacities and powers only in accordance with his own independent, self-conscious and rational desire and will, and through honest, intelligent, courageous and persistent personal effort, in conformity with Nature's Constructive Principle.

25.   But in the spiritual life, as in the physical, man may fail, neglect or refuse to make the effort necessary to obtain or exercise control of his individual faculties, capacities and powers.   Or, once having acquired such control, he may deliberately surrender it to other intelligences, provided he can find those who are willing to assume the responsibility.   Or he may knowingly and intentionally prostitute his powers to dishonest and vicious purposes.

26.   In every such instance he is proceeding in conformity

with Nature's Destructive Principle, and must pay the penalty which Nature exacts therefor. The inevitable result is retrogression, involving a corresponding forfeiture of the power of self-control.

27. This retrograde movement of spiritual life, if persisted in, ultimately leads to man's disappearance from the lowest plane of his spiritual life, in the manner and under the principle and process referred to in paragraphs numbered 21 and 22, above.

In closing this chapter the reader is asked to bear in mind that herein we have been dealing with established facts only. These facts have been demonstrated with as much scientific exactness and certainty as has the physical fact that by the action of electricity light may be produced, power generated and messages transmitted.

Furthermore, it is entirely within the ability of every individual who possesses the necessary Intelligence, Courage and Perseverance to prove the truth of every statement herein contained, provided he also has the necessary time, place and environment for study under proper and efficient instruction.

Let it be also distinctly understood that the process by and through which these demonstrations may be accomplished with perfect safety and the most intense satisfaction to the individual is neither hypnotic nor mediumistic, nor in any other manner of a subjective nature.

It will doubtless be observed that the writer speaks with unqualified assurance as to the facts stated. The question naturally arises, "How does he know these things?"

For the partial satisfaction of those to whom a definite answer would be deemed of special interest or value, the author is at liberty to here state that at a future time and in another volume of this Series he hopes to be able to publish a detailed account of his own personal experiences, studies and demonstrations, together with the nature of his instruction during the twenty years he has been engaged in acquiring the knowledge which enables him to speak with unconditional assurance.

To enter upon the presentation of these matters at the present time would only serve to divert attention from the specific and more important purposes of this volume and entirely transcend its legitimate and proper limitations.

CHAPTER V.

SPIRITUAL MEDIUMSHIP ANALYZED AND CLASSIFIED.

Mediumship is the process by and through which a spiritual intelligence obtains, holds and exercises control of the will, voluntary powers and sensory organism of a medium. It also includes the relation which exists between the two individual intelligences during the continuance of the mediumistic process.

A comparison of this definition with that of hypnotism, in Part I, discloses the fact that mediumship is nothing more and nothing less than spiritual hypnotism. It is, indeed, the hypnotization of a physically embodied individual by a spiritually embodied intelligence.

It is well known that there are a good many mediums who will be inclined, at first thought, to challenge the accuracy of the foregoing definition upon the ground that it does not correspond with their own experiences. If their claim be true, then it is clear that the definition is defective. On the other hand, if the definition be correct, then it is equally clear that those mediums who object to it are simply mistaken in the assumption that it fails to define their particular forms of mediumship. In other words, they are mistaken in the character of their mediumship or in the principle which underlies the mediumistic process.

In either event it becomes necessary to carefully examine and test the accuracy of the definition before proceeding to a consideration of the subject in chief. For this reason it is of the utmost importance to fix in mind clearly and definitely the underlying principle upon which the definition is founded.

This principle may be stated in its simplest and briefest form as follows:

Mediumship is a subjective, psychic process.

Like hypnotism, mediumship involves at least two intelligences. One of these, however, is a spiritual intelligence, while the other is in the physical body. The spiritual intelligence dominates and controls the will, voluntary powers and sensory organism of the medium. The medium, being thus under the domination and control of the outside, spiritual intelligence, is therefore in a subjective condition and relation to the exact extent that such control exists.

That is to say, in just so far as a physically embodied individual is subject to the domination and control of outside spiritual intelligences, in just that far the process involved and the relation thus established are mediumistic and therefore subjective.

The corollary of this proposition is equally true, namely: to the extent that a physically embodied individual is free from the domination and control of outside, spiritual intelligences, to precisely this extent, the relation between them is independent and therefore not mediumistic nor subjective.

It must be remembered that mediumship, like hypnotism, involves all shades and degrees of control, from the mildest form of impressional subjection to the deepest and most profound state of lethargic or trance control. This is a fundamental fact of primary importance. It is a fact well known to all those who have given the subject of mediumship their intelligent consideration. To none is it known more definitely than to mediums themselves.

Notwithstanding this fact, however, this variation in the degree of control undoubtedly constitutes one of the most prolific sources of error and misunderstanding on the part of mediums concerning the real principle involved in mediumship and the mediumistic process. There is a perfectly valid and natural reason for this. The *rationale* of all this error and misunderstanding will become perfectly apparent when the various forms and degrees of mediumship are fully understood. For this purpose the following classification and analysis are of special importance:

I. IMPRESSIONAL MEDIUMSHIP. Under this form of subjection the medium never becomes unconscious of his physical environment to any noticeable degree. On the other hand, he is usually left almost entirely free from what is commonly known and designated as "control." This general form of mediumship may, for convenience, be very properly subdivided into:

1. CONSCIOUS IMPRESSIONAL MEDIUMSHIP. In this case the medium is not only conscious of his physical environment, but is also consciously aware of the fact that he is in touch with outside, spiritual intelligences, although he is unable to either see or hear them. He comes into such close relation to them, in fact, that they are able to control his mental operations to a considerable extent. There are many mediums of this class throughout the country, and every student of the subject who has given this phase of it attention will be able to call to mind a number of such with whom he has come into an acquaintance.

Even where the medium is admitted to be both honest and intelligent, it is found that this form of mediumship cannot be relied upon with any degree of assurance or certainty. This unreliability arises from the fact that mediums of this class are unable to differentiate accurately between their own independent thoughts and those which are impressed upon them from without.

2. UNCONSCIOUS IMPRESSIONAL MEDIUMSHIP. Under this form of subjection the medium is entirely unaware of the fact that he is in touch with outside, spiritual intelligences who are able to control him. Their control over him is of so subtle a character that he does not recognize it as a power independent of himself. Of this class the following may be taken as typical examples:

(a) SO-CALLED "INSPIRATIONAL SPEAKERS." Such an individual as this goes before his audience wholly unprepared. He depends entirely upon "the inspiration of the moment." When he faces his audience he waits an instant for the "inspiration" to take possession of him. When this occurs his whole manner changes. His entire physical body becomes animated. His face takes on an expression of exaltation and rapturous enthusiasm. Although conscious of what is passing about him upon the physical plane, and fully aware, at the moment, of all he is saying, yet the instant his address is finished his manner changes again even more markedly than at the beginning. There comes an expression of lassitude, a depression of spirit, a physical exhaustion, a general inertia of the entire being. In many instances sleep is an immediate necessity. It is not infrequently the case that the substance of the speaker's address, lecture or sermon, as the case may be, soon passes from his memory entirely, or is recalled with great difficulty. Mediums of this character, when not under control, are often exceedingly impulsive, or moody, and are generally of a highly wrought, nervous temperament.

All these symptoms serve to distinguish the impressional medium from the genuine inspirational speaker, who, by the exercise of his own independent powers, rises to the level of his "inspiration."

(b) EMOTIONAL INSANITY. This is the name which the medical fraternity have given to certain phases of unconscious, impressional mediumship. Cases of this nature are found in our insane asylums all over the country. They make up a considerable percentage of the so-called insane all over the world. In such cases the medium may gradually settle into a state of melancholy, or become violently hysterical at times, or obtain the impression that he is going to die, or that he is going to fail in business, or that some terrible disaster is impending.

Such an individual is likely to prophesy all manner of things, fully believing they will surely come true at the appointed time. If he should be of the devoutly religious type, he not infrequently receives the impression that God has commanded him to do some extraordinary thing, such as offer up one of his children as a propitiatory sacrifice, and unless restrained will carry out the command with religious fervor and enthusiasm. Many instances of this nature have occurred in this country within the memory of the present generation. These prophetic and mandatory impressions come to him without his bidding, and, being ignorant of their nature or source, he accepts them as true. If he but knew whence they come, he might be able to guard against them, but in the absence of such knowledge on his part he becomes a victim of these impressions and is locked up with the insane.

Mediums of the sub-classes just named, so long as the process does not carry them beyond the semi-condition here indicated, are quick to deny that they are under the control of outside intelligences. Their position in this regard is perfectly consistent, from their point of view, for they are entirely ignorant of the presence or domination of these outside intelligences. Their ignorance, however, does not alter the facts any more than the ignorance of the Catholic Church in the days of the Spanish Inquisition altered the fact that the earth moves round the sun.

II. MUSCULAR MEDIUMSHIP. This general form of mediumship manifests itself in a wide variety of phenomena. Typical illustrations of this general class are as follows:

1. THE OUIJA BOARD. This consists of a smoothly polished surface from fifteen to eighteen inches wide by twenty to twenty-four inches long, on which the letters of the alphabet are printed in semi-circular arrangement. Upon this smooth surface a small triangular board with three legs is placed. This is known as the "Ouija." Its legs are usually tipped with some kind of soft cloth to facilitate their easy movement over the smooth surface upon which the letters are printed.

The hand of the medium is placed upon the Ouija and allowed to rest lightly upon the tips of the fingers and thumb. The medium then places himself in as negative or passive a condition of mind as possible and awaits developments. Soon the Ouija begins to move about over the smooth surface. It moves from letter to letter of the alphabet, thus spelling out words and sentences with great facility. In this manner authentic messages from spiritual intelligences have been and may be received.

2. AUTOMATIC WRITING. This is but the same process extended. Instead of using the board, a pencil is placed in the fingers of the medium's hand, and the hand is then allowed to rest in a natural position for writing upon a slate or sheet of paper, as the case may be. The same negative or passive condition of mind is then assumed by the medium and his

hand is thus resigned, as it were, to the control of such spiritual intelligences as may be present and able to use it.

It may be of interest to note the fact that Mr. W. T. Stead, editor of the *London Review of Reviews,* informs his readers that his "Letters from Julia" were received in this manner through the automatic control of his own hand.

In both these characters of mediumship the medium almost invariably labors under the impression that he is entirely free from mental domination or control, and that the action of the hand in writing and spelling out the words is wholly automatic. Mr. Stead evidently takes this view of the subject, for in his prefatory explanation he says:

"The hand apparently writes of itself, the person to whom the hand belongs having no knowledge of what it is about to write. It is a very familiar and simple form of mediumship, which in no way impairs the writer's faculties or places his personality under the control of any other intelligence." (Letters from Julia, p. viii.)

It is true that in many instances the hand of such a medium writes words and sentences of which the medium has no anticipatory knowledge whatever, so far as he is consciously aware. He often does not know what his hand has written until he sees the written message or follows mentally the movements of his fingers as they write it out. These facts, which are fully admitted, would seem, upon their face, strongly to bear out the general impression among mediums that this form of mediumship is wholly automatic and does not affect the mind of the medium at all.

Such, however, is not the case. Those who entertain such an idea are cruelly deceived. The demonstration of this fact is scientifically conclusive and will be further considered in a subsequent chapter.

There are many other manifestations of muscular mediumship which might be mentioned, but these illustrations appear sufficient to develop the principle which underlies them all. The principle itself is reserved for consideration further on.

III. NEUROTIC MEDIUMSHIP. The process involved in this general form of mediumship acts more directly upon the nervous organism of the medium. Its phenomena cover a wide range and it manifests itself in many different forms. For the purpose of identification the following illustrations are here presented.

1. CLAIRVOYANCE. Under this form of mediumship spiritual intelligences who understand the process are able to control the nervous organism of the eye through which impressions are conveyed to the consciousness of the medium. By this method of operation they are able to impress upon the consciousness of the medium whatever picture or image they may desire.

Or, they may, in a higher form of clairvoyance, produce a condition which opens, for the time being, a direct channel between the spiritual world and the consciousness of the medium. In this latter case the medium unconsciously employs the spiritual sensory organs of sight. He thus sees whatever there is to be seen upon the spiritual plane within the immediate range of his spiritual vision.

2. CLAIRAUDIENCE. This process is identical with that of clairvoyance, except that it is applied to the nervous organism of the ear instead of the eye. In this case the medium hears whatever the controlling intelligences desire that he shall hear, and nothing else.

Or, if the process be carried far enough, a direct channel may be opened between the spiritual plane and the consciousness of the medium, through the organ of hearing. In this latter case the medium hears whatever there is to be heard upon the spiritual plane within the range of his spiritual hearing.

3. TOUCH, TASTE AND SMELL. In precisely the same manner the remaining senses may be used by spiritual intelligences to convey impressions to the consciousness of the medium. Wherever this occurs he may, for the time being, enjoy the sense of spiritual touch, taste and smell, as well as those of sight and hearing.

4. DELUSIONAL INSANITY. Certain forms of so-called "Delusional Insanity" also fall under this form of neurotic mediumship. Inasmuch as the subject of mediumistic insan-

ity will be fully treated in a separate chapter, further reference to this particular branch of the subject is unnecessary at this time.

IV. TRANCE MEDIUMSHIP. The manifestations of trance mediumship are those which usually attract the largest amount of public attention. This is chiefly because they are of a more exaggerated and mysterious character, and for this reason appeal with added force to our human sense of curiosity. The phenomena of trance mediumship are many and varied. Those, however, which are most familiar to the general public may be designated as follows:

1. SPEAKING MEDIUMSHIP. Under this form of control the medium, generally speaking, is thrown into the deep, lethargic trance. Wherever this occurs he is entirely unconscious of what transpires during the trance condition. The dominating intelligences take complete control of his voluntary physical organism and employ it as an instrument for the expression of their own thoughts and desires. Through this absolute subjection of the will and voluntary powers of the medium the controlling spiritual intelligences are able to use his vocal organs at will. Almost every student or investigator of the subject who reads this volume will be able to recall one or more mediums of this class. There are very many such throughout the country.

2. MATERIALIZING MEDIUMSHIP. Under this form of control the medium is first thrown into a state of profound trance. Spiritual intelligences who understand the process then employ the vital and magnetic properties, forces and energies of the medium's physical and spiritual organisms, in conjunction with outside elemental conditions, in such manner as to produce the phenomena of so-called "Materialization."

A partial understanding of this process may be obtained from the following brief statement:

(a) Every living, human, physical organism is a natural generator of animal magnetism and vital energy. In this respect it is closely analogous to an electric dynamo.

(b) During the physically negative or passive hours of

sleep this human dynamo is constantly engaged in generating the necessary magnetism and vital energy with which to propel the machinery of the physical body during the waking hours of the day. The moment an individual wakens from sleep he begins to draw upon this accumulated supply and continues to do so until sleep once more locks the doors of the storehouse and prevents further escape.

(c) Under proper conditions animal magnetism is faintly visible to the physical eye. This fact may be demonstrated by anyone who will observe the following suggestions:

Arrange a perfectly black background so that an individual may stand in front of it with plenty of margin on all sides of his figure. Then, in the twilight of the evening, have a strong, healthy man take a position within four to six feet in front of this background. Take a position yourself at a distance of twenty to forty feet from him so that his form will be outlined upon the dark background.

Now let your eyes rest steadily upon his form for a few moments, while your attention is directed to the line of its limitations upon the dark background. In a short time you will begin to see a faint radiation of light surrounding the form. The longer you look the more distinct it will become, until the form will appear to be almost illumined with an aura of radiating light. This is animal magnetism and vital energy and is constantly expended in this manner by the physical body during the waking condition of every individual.

(d) It requires but a very small amount of attenuated, physical matter added to this physical magnetism to bring the compound clearly within the range of physical vision.

(e) While the medium is in the deep, lethargic, trance state the physical body is in a negative or passive condition. In this condition it generates animal magnetism very rapidly.

(f) While the physical body of the medium is in this negative condition spiritual forces may be so applied, by those who understand the process, as to draw off its animal magnetism and vital energy as rapidly as they are generated.

(g) The liberated animal magnetism of a medium may

be controlled by the action of the will of one who understands the process by which this is accomplished. This proposition may be doubted by the uninformed, but it is nevertheless true, and may be demonstrated with absolute certainty, as explained in a subsequent chapter.

(h) When the medium is in a state of deep trance the spiritual controls who understand the process of materialization withdraw from the physical body of the medium all the animal magnetism and vital energy possible. To this they are able to add a sufficient amount of attenuated matter drawn from the surrounding elements to bring the whole compound within the range of physical vision. With this magnetic compound they are able to envelop a spiritual form and thus bring it within the physical view of the sitters. This constitutes what is known as "Materialization," as it is usually witnessed in the materializing seance.

There is another process, however, entirely free from subjective conditions, by which a much more perfect materialization is achieved. This, however, has nothing to do with mediumship, and its further consideration is therefore out of place at this time.

Spiritual controls who understand materialization are also able to use the medium's physical body as a "fashion form," so to speak, and invest it with this materializing substance in such manner as to transfigure or transform it into the representation of many different personalities. This sort of impersonation is often practiced by unscrupulous spiritual controls, who find it less difficult than complete materialization.

This is a species of dishonesty, however, which has often resulted in great embarrassment to the medium, as well as to the unscrupulous controls who practice this species of deception. It has resulted in the "expose" of a number of innocent mediums and cast suspicion upon their honesty, as well as upon the authenticity of all materializing phenomena.

3. OBSESSION. This is another well defined form of trance control. It is known to the medical profession and to the public in general as insanity. For this reason it will be further considered under the general head of insanity.

There are other forms of trance mediumship which might be mentioned, but the classes here designated will be sufficient to enable the intelligent student to understand the principle underlying them all, as this principle will be hereinafter developed.

V. INDEPENDENT SLATE WRITING. This form of mediumship is of a composite nature and therefore does not fall entirely under any one of the general classes hereinbefore mentioned. It combines the elements of a number of them.

In this case the medium may be either conscious or unconscious, according to the intelligence of the spiritual controls using him. Two slates are bound together securely, sometimes with a small piece of pencil between them, but quite frequently without. Sometimes the medium touches the top or edge of the upper slate with the tips of his fingers. Other times the slates are left untouched by anyone until the message is completed. While the slates thus lie in full view of the sitter messages are written upon their two inside surfaces, or upon a sheet of paper where paper is placed between the slates before binding them together.

There are numerous variations upon the particular method here outlined, but these variations do not alter the essential process employed in the production of the messages.

VI. TRUMPET SPEAKING. This is another form of mediumship which does not fall entirely under any one of the general classes above defined. It is also of a composite nature, involving elements of two or more of the simpler forms.

In this character of mediumship the medium and the sitters usually sit in darkness around a table or in a circle. A speaking trumpet is placed upon the table or within the circle for the use of the controls. When the conditions are right the spiritual intelligences are able to lift this trumpet from the table, place it to the ear of a sitter and whisper or speak audibly through it so that the sitter may hear with perfect distinctness. Much doubt has been expressed by scientific thinkers as to the possibility of this sort of communication. It is nevertheless a fact that genuine communications are thus received from those upon the spirit side of life.

VII. SPIRITUAL TATTOO WRITING. This is one of the most interesting and unique forms of mediumship thus far developed. It is also, perhaps, about the only one for which physical scientists have thus far found no explanation which is entirely satisfactory to themselves, upon a purely physical basis.

The medium in this case, with rare exceptions, is an infant from one to three months old. The process employed by the controlling spiritual intelligences acts upon the circulatory system of the medium, and to this extent involves a control of the involuntary functions of the physical body.

By this control of the circulation of the medium his skin may be flushed to a deep scarlet or made perfectly white, as the blood is either forced to the surface or withdrawn from it, at the will of the controlling intelligences. By their ability to thus control the circulation of the medium they are able to outline upon its body scarlet pictures or letters upon a white background, or white pictures and letters upon a scarlet background, with great facility.

By this method written messages may be made to appear upon the surface of the medium's body. Messages of this character have been received even explaining the process by which these communications are transmitted. This form of mediumship, however, is rare.

Other methods of applying mediumistic control in the transmission of spiritual messages might be mentioned, but for the most part they are but variations upon those here outlined. It will, indeed, not be difficult, in the light of the foregoing illustrations, to understand that these various forms of mediumship may be combined into an almost unlimited number of composite forms and variations.

While this is true, it will nevertheless be found, upon careful examination, that the principle which underlies these distinct forms of mediumship here outlined covers the entire field of mediumistic control. For the purpose of this work, therefore, it would seem unnecessary to pursue this branch of the subject further.

CHAPTER VI.

THE PRINCIPLE INVOLVED.

The phenomena of mediumship are admitted.

Mediumship is a scientifically demonstrated fact.

The various forms of mediumship outlined in the preceding chapter are also facts which have been demonstrated with absolute certainty. There is no controversy, therefore, between Natural Science and Spiritualism, in so far as the objective facts of mediumship are concerned.

But back of every fact of Nature there is a principle to which that fact is related, and to which it must be referred for its proper interpretation and meaning. Back of mediumship, therefore, is a principle of Nature to which the fact itself must be referred. Back of every form of mediumship there is, with equal certainty, a governing principle which must be considered before science is justified in approving or condemning the practice of mediumship or the process involved.

Ethically considered, there are but two fundamental principles in Nature. In their relation to individual life the one is constructive, or what we are accustomed to regard as "normal," and the other destructive, or "abnormal." Every fact of Nature, whether scientific, philosophic, political, religious or otherwise, aligns itself as a direct result of one or the other of these two fundamental principles in operation.

The great problem of individual life, therefore, is that of identifying these two principles in their relation to the objective facts of Nature, so that we may be able to conform to the one and avoid the other. The degree of accuracy we manifest in the solution of this problem, and in conforming to the Constructive Principle of Nature, measures the potency and value of individual life.

What, then, is the principle at the foundation of mediumship? Is it hypnotic? Does it involve the same character of subjection? In other words, is the process constructive or destructive?

Every individual who is in search of knowledge as a means of individual improvement is entitled not only to ask these searching questions, but also to demand an intelligent and unequivocal answer from whomsoever is in position to speak with authority concerning the principle involved.

Upon this subject, as well as upon that of hypnotism, Natural Science is in position to speak with absolute scientific exactness and certainty. Without equivocation or mental reservation, the answer to each of these pertinent questions is an unqualified affirmative. Mediumship is hypnotic. It involves the same character of subjection as hypnotism. The process is therefore destructive. These facts being established, it follows with irresistible logic that the mediumistic process is inimical to individual life and to the well being of society in general.

But the simple statement of a scientifically demonstrated fact, unfortunately, does not always carry conviction to the mind of the layman nor to that of the student. It is quite possible, and perhaps probable, that among the great multitude of intelligent people who call themselves Spiritualists there may be those who will question the accuracy of the foregoing statements. If so, there is but one ground upon which such a doubt can rest, namely, that in so far as these particular individuals are concerned, the alleged facts have not been personally proved.

In all candor and fairness it is admitted that such a position is not entirely unreasonable. For it is a fact which every scientist is compelled to admit, that absolute scientific demonstration can be made in but two ways, viz.:

1. By the individual himself.

2. By some one else in his presence, under such conditions that he may personally witness and test the demonstration.

But these are conditions which transcend the possibilities of publication in any form. No matter how many or how important are the facts a writer may have personally demonstrated in the field of exact science, it is impossible for him to re-demonstrate them to the world by mere publication alone. When he comes to the task of conveying his knowledge to another in this form he finds that the only instruments at his command are his pen, ink, paper and words. The laboratory, with all its chemicals, essences, materials and appliances, must be put aside. All the instruments of actual demonstration thereby become utterly useless in this branch of his work. The most he can do, and all that he can do, is to state the demonstrated facts of science, as far as he knows them, in as clear and unequivocal terms as possible, and thereby shift the burden of responsibility which his knowledge imposes to the shoulders of his readers.

But the reader occupies a very different position. The problem presented to him does not deprive him of his power of election. It is entirely competent for him to choose his line of action in accordance with any one of the following propositions:

1. He may proceed at once to demonstrate the fact for himself, provided the time, opportunity and facilities for so doing are at his command.

2. He may have the demonstration made for him by one who understands the principle and the process involved, under such conditions as shall satisfy the demands of his own intelligence, and thus dissolve his doubts.

3. He may tentatively accept the fact stated, upon the internal evidences of its truth, without actual demonstration, and shape his life in accordance therewith until such time as actual demonstration may be accomplished.

4. He may reject the fact entirely, and thereupon suffer the penalty which Nature imposes for a violation of the principle which lies back of the fact.

The problem under immediate consideration, therefore, is that of stating as clearly as may be possible the fundamental principle which underlies mediumship and the mediumistic process. This has already been done in the briefest possible manner. It would therefore be entirely admissible to rest the case upon the simple and unqualified statement of facts, and thereby shift the burden of responsibility upon whomsoever may elect to deny them. This is, indeed, the course invariably pursued by science, and it is entirely just.

But the purpose of this particular work is something more than that of the cold scientist. The desire is to accomplish something more than merely to state the facts of science. It is the hope, if possible, to present them so clearly, so explicitly, so earnestly, and withal so simply as to command the thoughtful consideration of every individual whose eyes may chance to rest upon these pages.

It is, in truth, earnestly desired that the principle which lies back of the facts may be so presented as not only to challenge attention and elicit inquiry, but also carry conviction of its unqualified verity to the consciousness of every one who shall follow the subject to its legitimate conclusion.

To that end attention is first called to certain significant facts which are already familiar to those who have given the subject of hypnotism and mediumship more than passing consideration, or who are acquainted with the literature bearing upon these themes.

Some of the facts here referred to are as follows:

1. Hypnotism involves a relationship between at least two individuals. Mediumship does the same thing.

2. A hypnotist controls the will and voluntary powers of his subject. A spiritual control does the same thing to his medium.

3. In the development of hypnosis the subject is required to place himself in a negative or passive condition and surrender himself to the will of his hypnotist. The medium is required to do the same thing and surrender himself to the will of his controls.

4. After hypnotic control is fully established the subject becomes a mere instrument for the execution of the hypnotist's will. After mediumship has been fully established the medium sustains the same relation to his control.

5. In the development of hypnotic control the process becomes easier for the dominating intelligence (the hypnotist) at each succeeding subjection. The same is literally true in the development of mediumship.

6. In exact ratio as a hypnotist gains ease and facility in the establishment of hypnotic control, the subject loses his own power of resistance. A medium loses the power of resistance to the will of his controls under the same conditions and in exactly the same ratio.

7. In the development of hypnotism, where the sittings are frequent and persistent, a point is soon reached where all of Nature's barriers for the protection of individual intelligence are swept away, and the subject becomes a helpless instrument, bound under a bondage of the soul by an irresistible bond which he alone, without the consent and co-operation of his hypnotist, can never break. In the development of mediumship the same conditions obtain on the part of the medium.

8. As far as the phenomena of hypnotism have been thus far developed they are identical with the phenomena of mediumship. It is a notable fact, however, that up to the present time mediumship has produced a greater variety of phenomena than hypnotism, and some which hypnotism has not thus far been able to duplicate.

9. The physiology of mediumship is found to be identical with that of hypnotism. The action of the mediumistic process upon the three brains and nervous organism of the medium is identical with that of the hypnotic process upon those of the hypnotic subject.

(For a more complete exposition of this branch of the subject, see Part I, Chapter VII, et seq.)

There is just one particular and one only in which mediumship and hypnotism may be said to differ. It has been scientifically demonstrated, however, that this difference pertains only to the method of establishing the relation and not to the process involved in the relation after it has been once established. The importance of this distinction will appear more vividly to those who are acquainted with the essential difference between mesmerism and hypnotism.

For the benefit of those who may not be familiar with the subject the following brief explanation will be of value:

1. As far back as the history of civilization carries the

modern intelligence it has been known that every human, physical organism is the generator of a subtle fluid which has come to be known and designated as "animal magnetism."

It has been scientifically demonstrated that this magnetic fluid is susceptible to mental domination and control in, its action. Mesmerism was founded upon a partial understanding of these facts. Mesmer employed animal magnetism as the foundation of all his work. He made it the basis of obtaining control of his subjects, and fully believed that its action was in some way intimately connected with all the phenomena growing out of the relation thereby established. He obtained control of his subjects by making magnetic passes over them from the head downward, and at the same time gazing intently in their eyes until the mesmeric sleep was thus induced.

Mesmer, however, made the mistake of assuming that the somnambulic sleep cannot be induced by any other means or methods.

2. Dr. Braid, who adopted the term "Hypnotism," demonstrated that the somnambulic sleep may be induced without the use of magnetic passes or other means that supported the magnetic theory. He therefore assumed that Mesmer was wholly in error, and that animal magnetism had nothing to do with the process under any circumstances or conditions whatever.

And here Dr. Braid made his fundamental error.

Since the time of these pioneers in the field of psychical research two prominent schools have grown up, each of which has exercised and still exercises a strong influence upon the literature of the subject. Both of these are supposed to be schools of "Hypnotism," as this term is distinguished from "Mesmerism." Both apparently intend to employ non-magnetic methods and processes for inducing the hypnotic state, although they differ very radically in their theories concerning the value and effect of "Suggestion" in the hypnotic process.

One of these two schools was founded by Charcot, and is

known as the Paris School. The other was founded by Lie-
bault, and has come to be known as the Nancy School.

The single point of importance to be noted here is the
fact that mesmerism involves the use of animal magnetism in
the process of obtaining control of a subject, while hypnotism
(strictly speaking) does not.

Mediumship, as will be observed from what follows, is
essentially mesmeric, in that animal magnetism constitutes a
strong and important factor in the process of obtaining control. It is in this particular that it differs from hypnotism
pure and simple, as the latter is distinguished from mesmerism. The one is magnetic in its inception and the other is
non-magnetic.

It must not be understood from this, however, that all so-
called hypnotic processes (as they have been heretofore known
and designated) are non-magnetic. Indeed, much that is now
known as hypnotic is, in truth, mesmeric. The reason for this
confusion will be readily understood in the light of the following illustration:

An operator who calls himself a "hypnotist" (and who
would be very deeply offended with the designation of "mesmerist") assumes that there is no such thing as animal magnetism, and that "suggestion" alone is at the foundation of
the hypnotic process. Acting upon this supposition, he proceeds to its exemplification. To induce the hypnotic sleep he
takes his subject by the hand, looks him squarely in the eyes
with a fixed and steady gaze, all the while strongly "suggest-
ing" the idea of sleep.

Slowly but surely the subject yields to the superior influence and is finally brought under complete subjection and
control. Perchance the operator is a disciple of the Nancy
School of hypnotism. If so, he assumes, and therefore al-
leges, that the results are due solely to the power of "suggestion." And in this assumption lies his error. For it is a
fact that those who are in position to study the action of
animal magnetism and the laws which control it know, that
the eyes and the hands of an operator are Nature's most pow-

erful and open channels for the transmission of the magnetic fluid.

Just as it is impossible to bring the positive and negative poles of a magnetic battery together without thereby generating a current of magnetism, so it is equally impossible for an operator who is in a positive mental attitude to lay his hand upon a subject while the latter is in a negative mental condition without thereby transmitting at once to the subject a strong current of animal magnetism. In like manner it is equally impossible for one who is mentally active to look into the eyes of one who is mentally passive without thereby transmitting to him through the channel of the eyes a strong current of animal magnetism.

In other words, one who employs either hands or eyes in the process of inducing the somnambulic sleep or the subjective condition is in truth much more a mesmerist than a hypnotist, in the strict meanings of those terms.

Natural Science is therefore in position to declare and does so declare upon the basis of actual demonstration that a fundamental error exists in the assumption of the Nancy School. The same error, in a slightly different form, is at the basis of the Paris School. For this reason the data thus far accumulated by the various schools of so-called hypnotism are wholly unreliable, in that they assume to entirely exclude animal magnetism from the process of inducing the state known to them as hypnotic.

Only those who follow literally the method of Dr. Braid, and employ exclusively mechanical means and methods of inducing the subjective condition, are strictly entitled to the designation of "Hypnotists" in the sense here indicated, whereby hypnotism is distinguished from mesmerism. The Paris School undoubtedly intends to do this, but there is much evidence to show that this intent is not carried out in actual practice.

A careful analytical study of the subject from the standpoint of science develops the following interesting and significant facts:

1. As far as hypnotism goes its phenomena are identical

with those of mesmerism. But the phenomena of hypnotism (in the strict sense of that term as here used) are limited to a narrower range than are those of mesmerism.

2. Mesmerism, therefore, includes hypnotism and something more. There are certain manifestations which writers are wont to designate as "The Higher Phenomena"—such, for instance, as clairvoyance, clairaudience and telepathy— quite common to mesmerism, but rarely if ever the results of strictly non-magnetic hypnotism.

3. The phenomena of mediumship are identical with those of hypnotism, as far as hypnotism goes. They are also identical with those of mesmerism, as far as mesmerism goes. But mediumship covers a distinctly wider range of phenomena than both hypnotism and mesmerism combined. For instance, materialization, trumpet speaking, tattoo writing and various other phenomena are common to mediumship, but entirely transcend the limitations of both hypnotism and mesmerism.

4. Mediumship is therefore hypnotism. But it is hypnotism with something added. It is also mesmerism. But it is mesmerism with something added. It is hypnotism plus mesmerism plus something else. The something else is found by science to be the action of independent, spiritual intelligences operating from the spiritual plane of activity.

5. The results of these three schools are also identical in so far as the relation established between operator and subject is concerned. That is to say, hypnotism establishes a relation which enables the hypnotist to control the will, voluntary powers and sensory organism of his subject, within certain limitations. Mesmerism establishes a relation (by a different method only), which enables the mesmerist to do the same thing. Mediumship establishes a relation which enables spiritual intelligences to accomplish precisely the same results.

6. The differences in the range and variety of phenomena under these three systems are due entirely to the varying degrees of knowledge on the part of the operators and to the facilities at their command. That is to say, the mesmerist who employs animal magnetism intelligently from the physical

plane is in possession of an added facility for the production of phenomena, not possessed by the hypnotist who endeavors to exclude animal magnetism from the process. The spiritual intelligences who employ both animal and spiritual magnetism possess added facilities for the production of phenomena over both the hypnotist and the mesmerist. Spiritual intelligences work intelligently from a higher plane of activity.

A broader and more comprehensive view of this subject may be obtained from a critical analysis of the institution known to spiritualists and mediums as the "Developing Circle." The importance of the subject is such that a brief study of the mediumistic process from this standpoint cannot fail to be both interesting and beneficial. To that end the following illustration is here presented:

The proper number of individuals organize themselves into what is known as a "Developing Circle" for the purpose of developing into mediums as many of their number as may be possible. Assuming that they are under the guidance and direction of spiritual intelligences who are familiar with the conduct of such enterprises, they receive, in substance, the following specific instructions from their spiritual guides:

1. Agree upon a regular evening and meet as often as once each week, always on the same evenings of the week. Fix a definite hour for sitting, and begin each sitting promptly at the moment agreed upon. If you ask why this exceeding promptness, it is only necessary to remind you that this is as much for our benefit as it is for yours. We who are upon the spiritual plane are as busy as you who are upon the physical. We have duties to perform and obligations to discharge analogous to your own. The performance of these duties and the discharge of these obligations require both time and labor here as they do there. We upon the spiritual plane must therefore accommodate ourselves to these sittings, just as you upon the physical plane must do. In order that we may so arrange as to be with you and do the developing work, we must know in advance just when the meetings will be held, so that other duties and obligations may not interfere. Inasmuch as we do all the work, while you have only to meet and

give us the opportunity, it is not asking too much to insist that you meet at a definite and regular time and begin your sittings promptly at the moment agreed upon, so as to consume as little of our time unnecessarily as possible.

2. Select a definite room in which to hold your sittings and always meet in the same room. There is a very exact and scientific reason for this instruction, which, briefly explained, is as follows:

Animal magnetism is an important factor in the development of mediumship. In order to accomplish rapid results and waste neither time nor energy, the room in which the sittings are held must become thoroughly magnetized with the animal magnetism of the physical sitters and the spiritual magnetism of the controlling intelligences. This requires time. The first six or seven sittings are often required to create a sufficiently strong magnetic atmosphere in which to work with effect. But a room once thoroughly magnetized remains charged for many days. If the sittings are held in a different room each time all this work of magnetization is lost. The time and energy necessary for the actual developing work must be spent at each sitting in creating a new magnetic atmosphere and environment. Therefore hold your sittings in the same room.

3. Until development is well advanced hold all your sittings as nearly as possible in absolute darkness. Why? Because the development of mediumship is a purely negative process on the part of the medium. Darkness is the negative pole of light. It is a necessary part of the environment and condition in which to work upon a "negative." Just as the photographer must have a "dark room" in which to "develop a negative," so must we have a "dark room" in which to "develop our negative" (the medium). In the midst of darkness physical vision is cut off. In proportion as the objective physical world is removed from the individual consciousness the mind becomes introspective and passive. As the mind becomes passive the whole condition of the individual becomes negative. The object of the sitter should be to attain as nearly as possible a state of absolute negation. In

so doing he assists to "develop a negative" instrument for the accomplishment of our purposes. Darkness strongly contributes to that end. Therefore sit in darkness.

4. Dismiss from your thoughts, while you sit, every disturbing suggestion, and bring your minds into as perfect accord as possible. Nothing contributes to this result more than soft, sweet music. Music is exclusively a vibratory process. Those who sit under the spell of the same music are unconsciously brought into the same state and condition of vibratory activity as far as music may influence them. To obtain the most powerful results, however, the sitters should never be performers. They should take no part in the production of the music. To do so requires a certain amount of thought and effort on the part of the performer. Both thought and effort are active processes, however, and are therefore inimical to the negative condition necessary to the development of mediumistic control. For these reasons, among others, the music should be furnished by those who are not members of the developing circle.

5. When you sit arrange yourselves in a circle in such manner that those of you who are of the negative type or tendency shall alternate with those of you who are of the positive type. Sit with your feet slightly separated and resting squarely on the floor. Join your hands in such manner that the right hand of each sitter shall rest upon the left hand of his next neighbor. When the hands are so joined either rest them upon your knees in an easy position, or lay them upon a circular table, whichever you prefer. The purpose in keeping the feet slightly separated is to throw the full force of the current through the hands and thence into the brains of the sitters, where it must be centered and employed in the developing process.

6. When you have fully conformed to all these instructions then sit quietly, resign yourselves to us without fear, hostility, doubt or protest of any kind, and wait. We will do the rest. But we cannot develop a medium at a single sitting. Give us time. Be patient and wait. Do not ask questions. Do not even think, if you can prevent it, but simply wait.

Assuming that a circle has been completed in conformity to these instructions, a strong current of animal magnetism flows from hand to hand of the sitters, always from right to left about the circle. The law of magnetism is that (except when under control of the will) it flows from the left hand; that is to say, from right to left about the circle. Scarcely a circle is ever thus formed, but one or more of the sitters, and oftentimes all of them, will be able to feel the magnetic current with perfect distinctness.

One who possesses the power of independent, spiritual vision is able under these conditions to observe with wonderful distinctness the strong, luminous current of magnetism as it courses in an endless chain about the circle. And to such an one the following most interesting phenomena are distinctly apparent:

This current of magnetic light makes a complete chain about the circle. But it appears to make the physical nerve centers its depots, relay stations or storehouses of energy. The unbroken stream of magnetic light passes from hand to hand and thence along the arm, forming a great, round, luminous cord. From each armpit this luminous rope spreads out into a fanlike form until it connects with the central nerve cord of the spinal column. Thence it converges at the base of the brain, from which point it illumines the entire skull with an intense brilliancy. Thus each head in the circle becomes a center of magnetic energy and to the eye of the independent clairvoyant appears like a great round ball of radiating light.

In this position and under these conditions the sitters surrender themselves unreservedly to the will of their (to them) invisible controls and await with calm complacency the results of the "developing" process.

It is now the privilege of one who is able to speak from personal observation to explain this "developing" process as it is conducted by spiritual intelligences who are known and aptly designated as "controls."

The "controlling band"—as they designate themselves and are familiarly known to mediums in particular and to spiritualists in general—are generally under the guiding direction and supervision of some one intelligence usually selected by them from among their number for that purpose.

. When the sitters are in proper position and condition for work the controlling band usually arrange themselves in a larger circle, enclosing them in such manner that the joined hands of the controls rest directly upon the heads of the sitters. In this position their hands meet at the several magazines, or depots of magnetic energy, immediately over the nerve centers. This enables the spiritual intelligences to voluntarily control and manipulate the magnetic current with the most perfect facility. In this relation they are able to center the full force of the current upon any one of the sitters they may desire.

They now proceed to their preliminary experimentation. The directing control selects from the sitters the individual who appears to him most likely to become an easy subject. He directs his assistants to turn the magnetic current upon the brain of this particular sitter, in such manner that it shall pass through the three brains in the inverse order of their evolutionary development. That is to say, the current is applied to the sitter's forehead in such manner as to pass directly through the objective organs of the third brain, which lie immediately above and back of the eyes. Thence it is caused to sweep backward and downward through the secondary and primary brains in the order named.

The exact part which this magnetic current plays in the controlling process depends somewhat upon the particular form of mediumship sought to be developed. For instance, let it be supposed that the experiment is for the purpose of developing trance control. In this case the current is surcharged with the "suggestion" of submission and sleep. If the sitter should prove to be a tractable subject the effect upon him will soon become distinctly apparent. A sense of drowsiness creeps into the brain. He begins to lose control of his objective faculties, and then of his nervous and muscular organism. His hands and arms begin to quiver and tremble as if charged with a strong current of electricity. In many instances violent muscular spasms and involuntary contortions follow, as if the sitter were in a death struggle with a powerful and merciless enemy.

This is due to the resistance which Nature interposes as a protecting shield between every individual intelligence and those destructive forces with which individual intelligence is compelled to do battle in its struggle for an independent existence. It represents the natural protest of individual intelligence against the surrender of its inalienable right and power of self-control. Under these conditions, however, Nature's protecting interposition and the individual's intelligent protest are alike unavailing.

Gradually the muscular contortions cease. The tension of the nervous organism relaxes. The head falls upon the breast. The body settles into a reclining position, and profound trance ensues. But the magnetic current is still permitted to course through his already paralyzed brain. Upon this vital current the controlling intelligence is able to ride into the inmost consciousness of the sleeping subject, as it were, and there voluntarily assume control of the will, voluntary powers and sensory organism of the subject.

This relation once established, the imprisoned soul is but an automatic instrument under the will of the intelligent control. By and through this control over the will and voluntary powers of the medium a spiritual intelligence is able to use the physical body of the medium as if it were his own. Every impulse of his will is executed by the physical organism of the medium with absolute fidelity. He may speak, laugh, sing or cry through the vocal organs of the medium, or write through his hand, or perform any other act he may desire, by controlling the medium's will and voluntary powers.

When deep, trance control has been once established it may be passed from one spiritual intelligence to another without in the least disturbing the trance condition. Even those of the sitters who are unable to witness the process from the plane of spiritual vision are nevertheless able to detect from the expression, tone, manner, gesture and language of the medium when these changes occur. A single medium in this condition has been known to pass under the successive control of more than a hundred different spiritual intelligences in a single evening, and in so doing clearly identify to the sitters that number of distinct and recognizable personalities. Hypnotists who understand the process may, in like manner, pass the control of their subjects from one operator to another without disturbing the trance condition.

In one instance which came under the personal observation of the writer a boy of six years was the medium. During a single hour, while under trance control, this infant spoke fluently nine distinct and different languages, with eight of which he was unfamiliar, and six of which he had never heard spoken. The writer was the only person out of the fourteen present on that occasion who, from the physical side, was able to observe the process upon the spiritual plane. He desires to state here, for what it may be worth to the individual reader, that he not only witnessed this process, but that in every instance the spiritual control thus speaking through the medium appeared to him to represent the nationality of the language spoken, with one exception, and that among the parties present on the physical plane but four distinct nationalities were represented.

In order that his position shall not be misunderstood nor his motives misinterpreted, the writer desires to state at this time, in the most explicit terms possible:

That he is not a medium.

That he never has been a medium.

That he never has been hypnotized.

That he never has been mesmerized.

That he never has been a subject of psychic control in any form, degree or manner whatsoever.

That notwithstanding these facts he has developed the ability to exercise his spiritual sensory organism independently, self-consciously and voluntarily, at any time.

That the method by which this power has been acquired and the process involved in its exercise are as different from those of mediumship, mesmerism and hypnotism as the principle of affirmation is different from that of negation, or as construction is different from destruction.

That under competent instruction any man of equal intelligence, courage and perseverance, and a right motive, may accomplish the same results, provided he have the time, opportunity and facilities for carrying on the work.

From this unreserved statement of facts it will be observed that the declarations hereinbefore made concerning the subject of mediumship are not mere idle fancies, nor ingenious theories, nor interesting speculations, nor clever beliefs, nor doubtful hypotheses, nor elaborate arguments; but the results of a definite, personal knowledge of the facts stated.

Briefly summarizing, the mediumistic process is, for all practical purposes, identical with that of mesmerism and hypnotism, with the exceptions noted. This process is, under all conditions and circumstances, a subjective, psychic process. This is true regardless of the form of mediumship established, the character of phenomena presented, or the degree of control exercised.

The principle back of this process is the Destructive Principle of Nature in Individual Life.

CHAPTER VII.

"Automatic, Physical Mediumship" Impossible.

Mediumship without mental domination is a scientific impossibility. Those who comfort themselves with any hope, theory or belief at variance with this fact are cruelly deceived.

It is well known in advance that there are not a few intelligent individuals who hold that certain forms of mediumship do not affect the mind or mental faculties and powers of the medium at all. Strange as it may appear, many of these are mediums.

Let it be distinctly understood that no question is here raised as to the perfect honesty and good faith of those who have heretofore promulgated such a theory. It is respectfully submitted, however, that their perfect integrity is not sufficient to convert an erroneous theory into a fact of science. Neither should they be permitted, out of mere courtesy, to substitute such a theory in lieu of a fact which science has conclusively demonstrated times almost without number. To do so would be deliberately to reverse the process by which intellectual development and moral progress are achieved. Who does this turns his face from the light of truth, and of his own free choice descends from the mountain-side of actual knowledge into the valley and the shadow of ignorance, superstition and dogmatism. But this is not the order of our age.

And yet the honest convictions of every medium are entitled to respectful consideration in all matters wherein he is an interested party. It is also true that no one is more vitally interested in the mediumistic process than the medium himself. Inasmuch as he alone is the individual most deeply and directly concerned, it is not so strange, after all, that he should honestly believe himself in position to know more about the facts than anyone else.

Just here, however, is perhaps the most subtle error with which science has to deal.

To the individual who is not entirely familiar with the

exact process involved in mediumship, the medium appears to be the only party who is qualified to speak with absolute certainty; that is, from the standpoint of personal experience. The great world of unscientific intelligence would undoubtedly be inclined to accept this as a self-evident proposition. But the scientist who understands both the principle and the process back of mediumship knows that the medium, of all men, is the individual least qualified to speak with certainty concerning what actually occurs during the time he is subjected to mediumistic control.

The following illustrations cannot fail to make this fact perfectly apparent:

1. It becomes necessary for a patient to undergo an operation for appendicitis. When everything is in readiness he is placed upon the operating table. But before the surgeon will undertake so delicate and dangerous an operation he insists that the patient submit to the administration of the usual physical anæsthetic. When this has been done and the patient's active consciousness is safely and securely locked in the arms of Morpheus, the skillful surgeon takes his knife, cuts his way to the seat of trouble and deftly removes the diseased organ. When the wound has been properly dressed the patient is removed and the surgeon goes his way. After the effects of the anæsthetic have been dissipated the patient wakens to find himself snugly tucked away in bed with nobody present but the nurse.

To all objective appearances the patient has been through a very intense "personal experience." And herein is where the casual observer who is unacquainted with the nature and effects of a physical anæsthetic would invariably be deceived by objective appearances. Let him but ask the patient and he will find that this was not a "personal experience" at all. The patient, in fact, was wholly unconscious of what occurred, and but for the assurance of those who were present and consciously witnessed the operation, he would never suspect that he had been deprived of that seemingly non-essential organ known as the "appendix."

But suppose the anæsthetic had produced only partial unconsciousness. In that event the degree of his consciousness would measure the degree to which he might be able to render an accurate account of what occurred. In like manner, the degree to which he was under the influence of anæsthetics would measure the degree to which he would be unable to render an accurate report of what occurred. In other words, it is a "personal experience," to the degree of his wakeful consciousness, but no further. To the degree that he is unconscious it is not a "personal experience," and to this degree his statements concerning the occurrence are without value from the standpoint of science.

Again, suppose that instead of administering a physical anæsthetic a hypnotist had been called in and the patient had been placed under hypnotic control in a state of deep, lethargic trance, and the operation had been performed under these conditions. The results would have been identical in so far as the consciousness of the patient is concerned. In the deep lethargic condition obtained he would be wholly unconscious of all that occurred. In this event if he should assume to report upon the case his report would be held entirely valueless for all scientific purposes.

On the other hand, if he were partially conscious during the progress of the operation, he might be able to render a partial report of the case only. The degree of his wakeful consciousness would determine the degree to which it was in reality a "personal experience" to him, and to this degree only could he speak with assurance. Strictly speaking, even this would give to his report greater value than that to which it is properly entitled; for it is a fact that in all semi-conscious conditions of the mind the imagination is more or less active and often produces upon the consciousness impressions even more vivid and substantial than do the actual passing events themselves. In all such cases the individual is more than likely to report his imaginings as actual facts.

In other words, hypnotism is a subjective, psychic process, and it has been scientifically demonstrated that to the degree a subject is under control of his hypnotist he is unconscious of what occurs as a result of the hypnotic process.

And finally, suppose the same patient had been operated on while under trance mediumistic control. The results would have been the same so far as his knowledge of passing events is concerned.

Mediumship is also a subjective, psychic process. To the degree a medium is under control of spiritual intelligences to precisely that degree he is unconscious of that control. For the same reason he is unconscious of the process involved in the mediumistic relation and therefore unable to report accurately upon it from the standpoint of his own independent intelligence.

An excellent illustration of the principle under consideration is to be found in the case of the trance speaking medium. While under trance control he will speak fluently for hours and when restored to consciousness will have no knowledge whatever of anything he has said. Every investigator of this branch of the subject knows with what eagerness such a medium will ask the sitters to repeat to him all that has been said by him while under control, and how it all appears to come to him as entirely new matter.

This brings us to the question over which so many intelligent students have stumbled, namely: Is there any form of mediumship which does not involve mental domination and control? In other words, is there such thing as purely physical mediumship?

The answer to both these questions is an unqualified negative. There are no such forms of mediumship. Whoever undertakes by a personal experience to demonstrate that such forms of mediumship do exist will find, if he persists long enough, the unhappy verification of the truth here declared. Many have already done so, but have learned the truth at a cruel and needless sacrifice, after it was too late to guard themselves from the inevitable results.

Perhaps none of the many forms of mediumship has contributed more to the popular errors concerning this subject than that known as the "Ouija Board," unless perhaps it may be the "Planchette" the "Psychagraph," or "Automatic Writing." Nor is this to be wondered at when the facts are known.   Indeed, some of the brightest minds of both this country and Europe have fallen into error concerning the principle involved in these seemingly simple and harmless processes.

But inasmuch as the facts are definitely known, it would seem possible to so state them as to divest the subject of its mysticism and open the way to an intelligent understanding of the subject from its purely scientific standpoint.

For this purpose a brief analytical study of the process by which so-called "automatic writing" is acomplished will be of special value.

Under this form of mediumship the medium places a pencil in his hand, rests his hand upon a slate or piece of paper in position to write, assumes a negative or passive mental condition or attitude, and then quietly awaits results.   He is conscious of all that is passing about him upon the physical plane, and so far as he knows is in full possession of all his mental faculties and powers.

But while he thus sits with his mind possibly in a contemplative mood, perchance thinking of some subject entirely foreign to that of the mediumistic process, suddenly his hand begins to move.   To his surprise, it may be, he observes it write sentence after sentence upon a subject matter with which he is entirely unfamiliar.   At first the process appears to be slow and labored, but as the sitting progresses the hand moves with greater assurance and facility, just as if the operator were constantly obtaining better control of the instrument.

In the case of a beginner, the following conditions almost invariably obtain:

1.   The medium is absolutely positive that his hand moves automatically.   That is to say, he is not conscious that its movements are in the slightest degree responsive to his own volition.

2.   He has no conscious, anticipatory knowledge of what his hand is going to write.

3.   He may be consciously thinking upon a subject entirely

foreign to that with which the operating intelligence is concerned.

4. The message written by his hand under these conditions may, and often does, contain information clearly beyond the range of his conscious intelligence or knowledge.

All these facts naturally go to convince him that whatever the process may be it is one which does not, in the least, interfere with his own control of all his mental faculties and powers. In other words, he is ready to declare that his mind is entirely free from domination or control of any and every kind. And from the standpoint of his own conscious, personal experience his conclusion would appear to be entirely justified. Herein, however, lies the subtle error.

It must not be forgotten that mediumship, like hypnotism, is a subjective, psychic process. Its primary, motive power is the soul or intelligence of the dominating control. Those intelligent acts of the physical organism of an individual which are the results of the mediumistic process, are but reflex activities resulting from the action of one mind or intelligence upon another.

Nature has constituted each individual intelligence the motive power by which to operate the voluntary processes of his own organism. Through this motive power alone can those organs of the physical body which respond to the will be intelligently set in motion. The intelligence which seeks to control the movements of any voluntary organ of another intelligent individual can do so only by controlling the motive power by which its owner operates it. In other words, the spiritual intelligence which controls the hand of a medium does so only by controlling the motive power by which the medium himself controls it when acting independently, namely, the will.

But the medium insists that such action of the hand is the result of a purely automatic, physical process. He does this because he is not conscious of any act of will on his part. In short, he maintains that it is impossible for him to act voluntarily without being conscious that the act performed is responsive to his own will.

It is just here that the mind becomes diverted from the real principle involved in the mediumistic process. The acts of the medium's hand in what is known as automatic writing, considered from the standpoint of the primary impulse which inspires them, are not the results of his own volition. On the contrary, they are the results of an outside will acting upon his own and through this channel upon the nervous organism which controls the muscles of the hand.

The primary, volitional impulse, therefore, is that of the controlling intelligence and not that of the medium. This is precisely the reason the medium is not conscious of any relation between the acts of his hand and the impulses of his own will. His will acts automatically under the impulse of another will. And because its action is automatic he is unconscious of it.

There is a simple experiment, familiar to many students of psychology, by which the proposition here under consideration may be fully demonstrated. For illustration:

Let it be supposed that half a dozen or more individuals have met for the purpose of experimentation. They select from their number one whom we will designate as "A." This individual retires from the room and beyond the range of sight or hearing, so that he shall have no knowledge of what occurs during his absence. Those who remain agree among themselves that upon his return they will mentally compel him to perform some specific and definite physical act; say, for instance, that of placing his left hand squarely upon the top of his own head.

When all is agreed upon, A is brought into the room blindfolded so that he shall obtain no visible suggestion from anyone as to the act agreed upon. He is asked to assume a negative or passive condition of mind and offer no opposition to whatever impulses may move him. His companions thereupon form a circle about him and fix their minds upon his own. They center all the power of their combined wills upon his own, constantly and intently willing all the while that he shall perform the particular act agreed upon.

In every instance, where the conditions are right, after a

few moments of silent willing, A will slowly raise his left hand and lay it squarely upon his own head.

The most interesting part of this experiment is in the fact that when asked as to the motive or impulse which prompted him to perform that particular act, he will almost invariably say:

1. That he was not conscious of any motive or impulse of his own mind or will whatever.

2. That his hand appeared to him to move of its own accord, just as if impelled by a power entirely independent of himself.

If it were not for the prearranged conditions the subject in this case would almost invariably insist, just as the medium does, that the act of his hand was purely automatic, and that his mind and will were absolutely free from domination or control of any kind. Nevertheless, the facts are all against him, for here is a purely mental process, known to be such by all the parties thereto. Will power alone was the force employed. Furthermore, this is a process which may be verified in many different ways to be the action of mind upon mind.

With this simple illustration clearly in mind, it now becomes possible to state the principle more clearly in the following terms:

1. In proportion as the will of the medium becomes subject to the domination and control of outside, spiritual intelligences it loses the power of self-control.

2. In proportion as a medium loses the power of self-control his own will becomes an automatic instrument under the domination and control of outside, spiritual intelligences.

3. In proportion as the will of a medium becomes automatic in its action under the domination and control of spiritual intelligences, the medium himself becomes unconscious of the relation of his own will to those acts which are the results of the automatic process.

In other words, when the medium's hand writes in the manner above indicated, it is his will that acts automatically, and not his hand. His hand acts only for the reason, and to the extent, that his will responds automatically to the will of his spiritual controls.

The hypnotic subject and the medium are alike unconscious of all automatic impulses of their own wills. To the medium, therefore, his hand seems to act automatically merely because he is not conscious of the action of his automatic will to which it responds. It appears to be moved by an outside, independent impulse or force merely because the automatic action of his own will does not translate itself to his consciousness at all.

At this point, however, the following question obtrudes itself and demands an intelligent and responsive answer:

If it be true that the hand of a medium cannot be moved by psychic process, except by controlling the will of its owner, how is it possible for spiritual controls to move inanimate objects such as chairs, tables, and various other articles of furniture which have no will to be controlled or acted upon?

To one who is not entirely familiar with the nature, action and office of animal magnetism in the economy of the human organism, it would appear that this question is unanswerable. But to one who fully understands the subject from the standpoint of personal demonstration the question almost answers itself.

As stated in a previous chapter, every living, human organism is a natural generator of animal magnetism. The magnetic energy thus generated by it is under the domination and control of the will of the owner and inhabitant of that organism. Just why this is so may, perhaps, never be fully understood until man has fathomed the action and the purposes of Creative Intelligence. All that is known concerning it at the present time is that it is simply a fact which has been often demonstrated with scientific certainty.

This magnetic energy is an important factor in the process by and through which the will of every intelligent, living, human being maintains and exercises control over the voluntary, nervous and muscular organisms. He is able to move his own hand solely because of his ability to control the magnetic forces which play through and upon it. His hand moves in response to his will only because through the control of his own magnetic energy he is able to register the impulses of his will upon the nervous organism which operates the muscles of the hand.

He is unable to control the action of the muscular organism of another individual's hand (by purely mental processes) only because he cannot control the magnetic forces which play through and upon it. And he is unable to control these magnetic forces only because they are already, by the immutable decree of nature, under the control of another will than his, namely, the will of the owner of the organism which generates them.

When spiritual intelligences undertake to control the hand of a human being they find that the only process by which this can be done is by controlling the magnetic forces of that individual's physical organism. But nature, without consulting mankind, has given to each and every intelligent individual, dominion and power over the magnetic forces of his own physical body. They must therefore divest him of that power before they can apply it to the control of his hand, or that of any other organ under his voluntary control. This can be accomplished only by controlling that in the individual which has dominion and power over his magnetic forces, namely, his will.

In the case of inanimate objects, such as chairs and tables, there is no internal will to be considered, and nothing internal to be overcome and conquered. In other words, there is nothing to interfere with the direct application of the magnetic energy of the medium to the object from without. There are no natural barriers to be overcome save those involved in making the necessary magnetic conditions.

The following illustration of an oft repeated demonstration will serve to emphasize the principle under consideration:

When magnetic conditions have been established which enable the controlling, spiritual intelligences to move a table, let a two hundred pound man, who is not a medium nor in the least mediumistically inclined, stand upon it. Then ask the spiritual intelligences to lift both the table and the man, if possible. It will be found that the table with its two hundred pound weight upon it will rise from the floor with as much apparent ease and facility as if the table alone were being lifted.

After this has been done then ask the controlling intelligences to lift the man alone without the table. It will be found that they cannot move him in the least, nor will he be able to feel the slightest impulse of force applied to him.

Now let the same individual sit at the same table. Place a small pencil in his hand and then ask the spiritual intelligences to use his hand in the writing of a message. It will be found that they are entirely unable to move his hand or a single muscle of it, even though they are able to move the table under it weighing many times as much.

Now let him lay the pencil down and then ask the controlling intelligences to use it alone in the writing of the message. Instantly the pencil will get up in obedience to the request and proceed to the acomplishment of its task with perfect apparent ease and facility.

Again the question presents itself: Why can the spiritual intelligences lift the table with a two hundred pound man on it, when they cannot lift the man alone whose weight is much less? The answer will now appear comparatively simple. It is because they are able to apply the magnetic forces of the medium upon which they must depend, to the inanimate substance of the table without having first to overcome an intelligent and independent will within it. But the human body is completely insulated, as it were, with an aura of animal magnetism which is under the control of its owner and inhabitant (so long as he is not under mental domination and control), while this is not the case with the body of the table.

Why can they not lift the non-mediumistic man alone?

The answer to this question also is now simplified. It is because he alone is master of the magnetic forces which act through and upon his own physical body. In order to turn these forces back upon him in such manner as to apply them to the lifting of his physical body they must first neutralize his own control over them. But they cannot control these forces except by controlling that within him which has dominion and power over them, namely, his will. But he is not a medium, nor subject to mediumistic subjection or control. They, therefore, cannot control his will. Hence they cannot control his magnetic forces. Hence they cannot lift his body.

For the same reason they cannot move his hand with the pencil in it, while they can easily move the pencil alone. To move the hand they must be able to control the magnetic forces which play through and upon it. To do this, however, they must control that within him which controls these forces, namely, his will. But he is not a medium. Therefore they cannot control his will. Hence they cannot move his hand.

Again: Try these same experiments, substituting one of the mediums present in place of the non-mediumistic man. It will be found that the spiritual intelligences can lift the table and the medium together, or they can lift the medium alone. They can move the medium's hand with the pencil in it, or they can move the pencil alone.

This is only because they are able to control the will of the medium and through this the magnetic forces and energies of his body. These forces, once under control by them, may be applied to the hand of the medium or to an inanimate object with equal effect. And so it is, that even the moving of a table by psychic means involves the control of some intelligent individual's will to such a degree that his magnetic forces and energies may be diverted to that end.

Experiments of a similar nature almost without number have been made. And every experiment along these lines only serves to emphasize the fact that there is no such thing as automatic, physical mediumship. In other words, there is no form of mediumship which does not act upon the mind of the medium to a greater or less degree. Those who are now or have been cultivating any of these supposedly automatic processes, will be interested to know that there are certain other familiar facts which are both pertinent and full of grave significance in this connection.

For illustration: There is not an instance on record where

a medium has pursued this line of investigation and practice regularly and persistently without sooner or later coming to know for himself that the process is one which does act upon the mind. Those who, at the beginning of their investigations, have most vehemently protested against the fact, have been among the first to demonstrate its truth. These demonstrations, to be sure, have in most instances been of a most unhappy nature, but none the less absolute and convincing on that acount.

By way of illustration, the writer desires to narrate briefly in this connection a few of the many incidents of a similar nature which have come under his personal observation. Some of these have touched very closely the inner circle of his closest personal friendships, and for this reason the names of the parties herein referred to will be omitted. The particular incidents to which reference is here made are as follows:

1. In a small town somewhat west of the city of Chicago, a few years ago, lived a family by the name of C——. This family consisted of father, mother and only son. The father was near sixty years of age, the mother perhaps four years younger, and the son twenty-seven. They were an intelligent and unusually happy family, bound together by the closest ties of affection. They were all consistent and honored members of the Methodist Episcopal church and active workers in the cause of religion, although by no means of the emotional or hysterical type.

The son, who had been the life and the idol of the home, was suddenly stricken with fever and after a short illness died. This came as a heavy blow to the father and mother who remained to mourn his loss. They were indeed disconsolate in their loneliness and grief. Even their religion seemed to have lost its meaning in the presence of such a sorrow.

It so happened that among their nearest neighbors was a family of spiritualists at whose home seances and circles were often held. Under these conditions it will, perhaps, not appear strange that the bereaved father and mother seemed to forget the dogmas and conventionalities of their church and turned, for the time being, to spiritualism in the hope of there finding a way of bridging the gulf between them and their boy.

Here it was that they learned something of the various forms of mediumship. Here they learned of the "Ouija Board." Here it was that through this simple instrument they learned to believe that their son was with them daily and only waiting to talk with them as often as they would give him the opportunity.

The Ouija Board appealed to them because it appeared to be so simple and so entirely harmless. The process appeared to them to be one which in no way affected the mind or intelligence of the medium. Not yet feeling that they cared to be known as spiritualists, they determined to carry on their further investigations alone. To carry out this idea they obtained an Ouija of their own, and began a series of sittings at their own home where they could carry on the investigation without embarrassments of any kind.

Their efforts were rewarded with immediate success, for at the first sitting the instrument worked quite freely and with results which, to them, were far beyond their most sanguine expectations. Messages of affectionate greeting, of assurance, admonition and instruction, were received, from which they seemed to recognize the identity of their son's intelligence, and naturally they were very happy.

The writer, being a personal friend of the family, incidentally learned of these proceedings, and, anticipating the results, made an effort to dissuade them from further sittings and investigations along this particular line. With that purpose in mind he endeavored to present to them the facts and principles involved in the process by which the Ouija Board is operated. Nothing, however, could convince them that the process, whatever it might be, was in the least injurious, or that it acted upon the mind in the slightest possible degree, or that it could under any circumstances involve dangerous, disastrous or unhappy results.

To every such statement or suggestion they replied by simply quoting their own personal experiences. Who could doubt these? They spoke for themselves. No harm had thus far been done. Their minds were entirely free from all domination or control. If the process were one which acted upon the mind, who should know that fact so quickly and so surely as they? Since they could not feel the slightest mental influence, this, to them, was conclusive evidence that none existed and that the process was indeed what it appeared to be, a purely automatic, physical process.

But time passed. As anticipated, in the course of a few short weeks, sitting an hour each evening, they both found that they could begin to anticipate the messages mentally, in advance of the Ouija. This was, to them, a great triumph, for it indicated that in a very short time they would be able to dispense with the clumsy instrument and communicate freely and directly by mental processes alone. And in this they were not deceived, as the sequel will show.

Within a few days thereafter Mr. C—— began to hear voices very distinctly. His wife developed the same experience a few days later. From that time forward rest and peace vanished from their earthly home forever. These voices continued to talk to them at all hours of both day and night. When one ceased another took up the strain and continued until superseded by others still. Life became a torture. Neither rest nor sleep was possible for a moment.

Then it was that the awful truth dawned upon them. The seemingly innocent and harmless process of the Ouija Board was, after all, a process which opens the way to the enslavement of the soul. It had opened a door which they knew not how to close again. They had become helpless victims of their own ignorance and folly.

That which had meant to them the realization of their fondest and happiest dreams had now become a torturing menace to health, to reason and to life itself. The voices which at first had been loving and tender and sweet, and full of comfort, encouragement and hope, now filled their ears with nothing but the most vicious, profane, vulgar and vile epithets known to the English language. Every attempt to silence them or to shut them out or drive them away only increased the torrent of verbal filth beyond the limits of human language to express.

When they could bear the strain no longer Mr. C—— consulted the family physician. He was promptly pronounced insane and was immediately committed to the state insane asylum, where he died inside of eight months from the date of his first sitting with the innocent and harmless Ouija Board.

The wife lived but a few months longer and died an inmate of the same asylum.

Had the attending physician correctly diagnosed these cases and then applied a natural remedy (for there are such remedies within the limits of materia medica) these poor, unfortunate sufferers would have been relieved with absolute certainty. *They were not insane.*

2. During the year 1897, and for several years prior thereto, the writer was closely associated with one of the leading business men of Chicago, who, for the purposes of this narrative, will be referred to as Mr. F.

This gentleman's father had been a prominent figure and influence in the rebuilding of the city after the great fire, and was for a number of years one of its prominent judicial officers. He was undoubtedly a man of superior intelligence and moral character. The son was deeply attached to him by an affection which was as admirable as it is rare among men of strong individuality.

But the father died. His death, coming as it did without warning, was a great shock to the son. This event, perhaps, more than any other in all his experience up to this time, led Mr. F., the son, to seriously contemplate the question of death and the problem of a life beyond the grave. Although a thorough skeptic concerning the question of a future life, he nevertheless followed the course pursued by so many others whom death has separated from loved ones, and began an investigation of spiritualism and mediumship.

After the usual experiences of the intelligent investigator, he succeeded in convincing himself that any form of mediumship which affects the mind of the medium or subjects his mental faculties and powers to the domination and control of outside intelligences is, to say the least, undesirable. He could not harmonize this idea of mental domination and control with those of independence and individual responsibility. He therefore consistently refused to sit for development along these lines.

But in the course of his investigations he learned to know something of the Ouija Board. After studying its action as best he could, he finally became convinced that the process is purely physical and entirely automatic. Having reached this conclusion he at once began a series of sittings with the instrument, and to his great satisfaction, found that it would write for him quite readily. Through this process he was soon convinced that he was in direct touch and communication with his father. This was, for the time being, a great comfort to him.

But one evening during the progress of these sittings, after having received a number of messages purporting to come from his father and other intelligences he had come to know by other names, his sister, who usually sat with him, was called away for a moment and left him sitting alone with his hand upon the Ouija. Suddenly, and without an instant's warning, a great, horrifying wave of mysterious influence swept over him. So intense, so horrible, and yet so irresistible was it that he found himself rapidly sinking into a state of unconsciousness.

Dimly realizing that he was under the spell of some evil influence, he summoned all his powers of resistance and by one mighty effort succeeded in throwing the Ouija across the room and springing to his feet. For the instant this act appeared to free him from the dreadful influence and he began rapidly walking the floor. But soon thereafter the same experience was repeated. As he walked he felt himself again slipping from his mental moorings into a state of unconsciousness. By another heroic effort he succeeded in again throwing off the spell for a little time.

By this time he was fully aware that, whatever the process employed might be, it was an attempt on the part of some evil influence to obtain complete control of his intelligence. Seizing his hat he rushed from the room and into the street, hoping thereby to break the line of connection which had enabled such an influence to approach him. This also failed. Again and again the attack was renewed. Fortunately, however, he is a man of strong will and splendid courage, and although many times carried almost to the verge of complete unconsciousness, he continued to defend himself with all the power and intelligence at his command.

It was indeed a battle royal while it lasted and Mr. F. finally triumphed. But the disastrous effects were plainly visible in every lineament of his features when he appeared at the office ready for work the following day.

Fortunately for Mr. F. this experience proved of great value. It completely shattered all his theories concerning the process involved in the operation of the Ouija Board, and cured him of all desire to experiment further along that line. So far as the writer knows he has entirely abandoned all subjective methods of inquiry and accepted his experience at its true value.

But the sequel of this incident is of peculiar interest. It has been ascertained since that this vicious and determined attack was made by one who, in physical life, had conceived the idea that Mr. F. was responsible for some fancied injury which had never been condoned. The attack, therefore, was made in the spirit of revenge, and had it been entirely successful would have sent its victim to the state insane asylum, where he would, in all human probability, have spent the balance of his life.

This one experience of itself is full of valuable suggestions, and to those who are not hopelessly bound in the chains of mental slavery it contains many important lessons.

Other experiences of a similar nature, almost without number, might be presented covering every phase of so-called automatic, physical mediumship. But these would merely serve as cumulative evidence of the law of mediumship which is so clearly disclosed by the illustrations already submitted.

Further time and space will therefore not be consumed on this branch of the subject.

It only remains to close this chapter with a restatement of the fundamental fact that there is no such thing as mediumship free from mental domination and control. Whoever may be induced to undertake the development of any form of mediumship whatsoever, upon the theory that it does not affect the mind, is cruelly deceived. *Caveat!*

CHAPTER VIII.

Neither a "Gift" nor a "Power."

To the popular mind there is no fallacy so subtle or so difficult of detection as that which is carelessly concealed beneath the noble exterior of an innocent and gracious word misapplied.

Hypnotists have misapplied the otherwise harmless word "Suggestion," and by so doing have filled the popular mind with the impression that hypnosis is nothing more harmful than a sort of patent process by which one individual may pump valuable thoughts and ideas into the mind of another.

It will, in all probability, require at least a generation to fully expose this fallacy and in its stead fix in the public mind a clear understanding of the fact that the word "suggestion," wherever and whenever it is employed in connection with the hypnotic process, is a misnomer. It will doubtless require another to repair the injury that has already followed and is yet to follow as a direct result of this simple but subtle fallacy.

And all this is merely because the word "suggestion" is, in itself, a good, gracious and virtuous word whose excellent qualities stand out in such bold relief as to overshadow all things else and entirely conceal from the unsuspecting intelligence the destructive principle of nature which underlies the hypnotic process.

In like manner there are, perhaps, no three words in the English language which, in themselves, are more entirely harmless and free from obloquy, when properly employed, than those which follow, viz.:

1. "Gift." This word, when properly employed, is defined as "Anything given or bestowed," or "A special talent," etc. Its most usual synonyms are, "Present, donation, benefaction, boon, endowment, talent, faculty," etc. From these it will be seen at once that the term carries with it a distinct suggestion of good and nothing but good.

2. "Power." A proper definition of this word, when correctly employed, would be, "Ability to act. The exercise

of a faculty. The employment of strength. The exercise
of any kind of control, influence, domination or sway. Mental or moral ability to act," etc. Its usual and acknowledged
synonyms are "Potency, might, force, strength, ability, capacity, capability," etc. When applied to the individual who is
supposed to possess it, therefore, it conveys the distinct idea
of merit, worth, desirability, value and individual power, all
of which are good.

3. "DEVELOPMENT." In its common acceptation this
word means "A gradual unfolding. A formative process by
natural growth. Improvement by natural processes," etc.
The word carries with it in its general use the unmistakable
suggestion of progression and improvement by natural processes. In other words, it is associated with the constructive
side of nature's evolutionary processes.

So numerously and conspicuously do these excellent qualities cluster about and so tenaciously do they cling to the mere
words themselves that it seems almost impossible to understand how they could ever be employed to conceal a fallacy
or befog the intelligence.

Such, however, is the case. To these simple, innocent,
worthy and meritorious words misapplied, more, perhaps,
than to any other single cause, the public is indebted for its
widespread misconception of the fundamental principle at
the basis of mediumship.

When the medium honestly and conscientiously speaks of
his mediumship as a "gift," the credulous, the unthinking and
the unscientific take for granted that he uses the word in its
usual and legitimate sense. They, therefore, are led to assume that he is the possessor of "a special talent," or that
he has been the recipient of a "beneficent endowment" which
God or Nature bestows upon only a select and favored few.
There are doubtless many mediums who honestly look upon
their mediumship in precisely this light. The writer has met
a number who maintain that attitude.

But what are the facts? Mediumship is a subjective process on the part of the medium, and is so admitted. There
are no exceptions. It is a dominating process on the part of

his controls, and is so admitted. There are no exceptions. Any process which establishes a different relation than this is not mediumistic. Mediumship, in fact, is possible only in proportion as the medium becomes an instrument under the domination and control of outside, spiritual intelligences. But he becomes such an instrument only in just so far as he surrenders himself, body and soul, to the domination of his controls. That is to say, in exact proportion as outside intelligences control him and convert him into a medium they rob him of his power of self-control.

From the standpoint of the recipient, therefore, mediumship represents nothing whatever in the nature of a "gift" to the medium. On the contrary, it represents only a loss of individual power. Instead of being the recipient of a valuable "gift," the medium is robbed of his most valuable possession, the power of independent, self-conscious and rational volition upon which the power of self-control depends. Mediumship from the standpoint of the medium is, in fact, a purely negative proposition. It is a self-surrender and not a "gift." If gift in any sense, it is a gift *from* the medium instead of a gift to him.

It is true that the negative quality of mind and soul which forms the basis of mediumship may be and often is transmitted by heredity to some extent. In so far as this is true, in any given case, it may be said to represent a natural condition. In other words, to that extent it comes to the individual without effort on his part. And it is just possible that this is the reason mediums themselves have come to regard their mediumistic tendencies as "gifts of nature."

However this may be, it must not be forgotten that insanity is also very often a "gift" in precisely the same sense. In like manner drunkenness and licentiousness may become "gifts." In precisely the same sense rheumatism, scrofula, cancer, consumption and various other ills and misfortunes are very often "gifts of nature." In the sense that these things are "gifts," however, they are those of which no man is proud, and they do not fall within the accepted meaning of the term at all. They are in no sense benefactions. They are not generous gratuities. They are not valuable endowments. On the other hand, they represent only human frailties and natural weaknesses. They stand for the absence of health, strength, virtue and individual power. We therefore do not call them "gifts." They are, in truth, but robberies.

When it comes to be generally known among the people that mediumship is only a negative quality as well as a negative quantity, and that it represents the absence of all that is desirable in individual life, mediums will cease to call it a "gift." It will then be given a name in accord with the facts. It will come to be known for what it is in reality—a deprivation, a robbery, a weakness, a detriment, a deterioration, a retrogression, a degeneracy, a devolution.

In like manner, mediums are wont to speak of their mediumistic "powers." Although this is done honestly in many instances and without intent to deceive, nevertheless it is misleading. It conveys to the casual student, the credulous and the unsophisticated, the unmistakable impression that mediumship really gives to the medium added powers. It conveys the idea that it makes him stronger in himself, gives him independent control over new forces and processes in Nature, and adds to his individual ability, efficiency and strength. It conveys all this, whereas, the exact reverse is true.

Every medium of intelligence knows and admits that in exact proportion as he becomes a medium he surrenders the power of self-control. In precisely the same proportion he becomes subject to the domination and control of outside intelligences. It is true that in one view of the subject the mediumistic process involves the development of "powers," but not those on the part of the medium. All the "power" it develops is on the part of the dominating, spiritual controls. Moreover, the power which the controls thus acquire is that power which enables them to rob the medium of his own natural and rightful power of self-control.

The truth of all this is demonstrated in every phase of mediumship. From the beginning to the end the mediumistic process involves a continued loss of power on the part of the medium, and a corresponding acquisition of power on the part of his controls.

This strange and ingenious misuse of terms which is so apparent in spiritualistic literature involves an error so subtle that even mediums themselves appear to have become confused as to the principle back of the mediumistic process.

As an illustration, they often speak of clairvoyance as if it were a definite power possessed by the medium, whereas the exact reverse is true. The fallacy is so patent to those who understand the subjective process back of mediumship that to them it needs no explanation. But the great multitude who have relied upon the accuracy of the terminology employed, rather than upon a demonstration of the principle at the foundation of the mediumistic process, have been in the past and will continue to be in the future, grievously misled. It is especially important that they too should understand the true principle for the purpose of self-protection.

For the benefit of those who may not have personally demonstrated the error for themselves, the following facts, which are familiar to every medium, are here presented for careful consideration:

1. An individual who has become clairvoyant through the subjective process of mediumship does not see clairvoyantly whenever he so desires any more than does the hypnotic subject.

2. He is not able, as many suppose, to open his spiritual eyes at will and see whatever there is to be seen upon the spiritual plane about him.

3. On the contrary, he sees clairvoyantly, just as the hypnotic subject does, only when conditions are made for him by his controls.

4. Moreover, he sees only those things which his controls desire him to see and which they actually place before his spiritual vision.

5. His spiritual vision comes to him without his knowledge of the process involved. It comes without an effort on his part. It comes and goes regardless of his own efforts or his own will. It is something over which he has no control

whatever. He may desire with all his soul to see. He may exert every power at his command to accomplish that desire. But his own volition unaided is without avail. His spiritual vision, so long as subjective methods and processes are employed, will remain closed until it is opened for him by his controlling, spiritual intelligences.

A vision is flashed before his eyes. He sees it for an instant and it is gone. The more he tries to see it the more quickly it evades him. Let him exert every power of his being to follow it. He cannot do it. In spite of all his individual efforts it passes from him. In other words, his psychic vision opens and closes regardless of his individual will or wish. It takes possession of him and departs from him in defiance of all his own powers. He is its plaything and not its master. It controls him. He does not control it. All the powers involved in the process are upon him and not within him.

The very attitude he assumes betrays the fact that his clairvoyance is anything but a "power" of his own. When he desires to see things upon the spiritual plane he places himself in a negative or passive condition of both body and mind, and then what does he do? Simply waits. For what? For his controls to do the rest. Without their co-operation he is helpless. He can no more open his spiritual vision of his own volition than he can change the course of the stars. He must await the pleasure of his controls. Unless they choose to make conditions for him he will remain spiritually blind until death shall remove the scales from his eyes.

And yet, he calls his clairvoyance a "power," thereby projecting the suggestion that it is a power which he controls, whereas, it is a power which controls him and to which he is only a subject. By this gross misapplication of the word he inevitably conveys to the uninformed the mistaken impression that it is something over which he has perfect command and individual control. He thus erroneously leads them to believe that it is something which he can exercise at will. And thus they are deceived. In like manner the world in general has been deceived and is still deceived concerning many of the most important facts of mediumship and the mediumistic process.

With precisely the same degree of consistency it may be said that insanity is a "power," or that paralysis and impotency are "powers," or that weakness, helplessness and bondage are "powers."

Mediumistic "development" is often spoken of in the same manner. The word is used in such manner as to convey the impression that mediumship is the result of a process of individual self-development. It is, however, the exact reverse of this. The medium does not develop himself. He is developed. That is to say, all the developing work is done by his controls and not by the medium himself. He is developed in precisely the same sense that a patient is developed under the influence of an anaesthetic. That is to say, he is "developed" into a condition of subjectivity which, to precisely the degree it exists, marks the surrender of his individual and independent powers.

Attention is here called to an exceedingly important distinction, viz.: While mediumship is at all times and under all conditions and circumstances a subjective process and invariably results in a surrender and sacrifice of individual powers on the part of the medium, this does not mean that all psychical development is mediumistic. On the contrary, quite the reverse is true.

There is, in fact, a method of development which, when once accomplished, enables the individual to come into as conscious relation to his spiritual environment as he is to his physical environment. He sees clairvoyantly whenever he desires to do so, and when he opens his spiritual eyes he sees whatever there is to be seen upon the spiritual planes within the range of his vision. He hears clairaudiently whenever he wills to do so, and when he thus exercises his spiritual sense of hearing he hears whatever there is to be heard upon the spiritual planes within the range of his hearing. He is able to communicate with those upon the spiritual side of life as freely and as voluntarily as he does with those upon the physical plane.

Spiritual intelligences have no control over him whatever, nor any of his faculties, capacities or voluntary powers. He is absolutely independent in the exercise of his sensory organism. In other words, he is an independent psychic in every sense of the term. He is in every sense a natural "development," and at every progressive step along the way he acquires definite and specific "powers."

He occupies the position of a Master, while the medium occupies that of the subject or slave. The one is independent, the other dependent. The one possesses specific and definite "powers," the other is robbed of the powers with which Nature originally invested him. The one is an active, intelligent factor, the other a passive instrument. The one is a responsible, individual intelligence, the other an irresponsible automaton to the extent he becomes a subject of mediumistic processes.

The purpose and limitations of this volume forbid any presentation at this time of the rational method of independent, spiritual self-development here referred to. This subject, however, will be fully covered in another volume of this series.

Briefly recapitulating:

1. Mediumship, from the position of the medium, is neither a "gift" nor a "power." It is the antithesis of both.

2. From the standpoint of the medium, it is not a "development." It is a progressive suppression, retrogression and degeneracy.

3. In the light of the known facts of science the words "gift," "power" and "development," whenever and wherever applied to the state or condition of the medium, are misnomers.

4. To the inversion and misuse of these terms in their relation to the mediumistic process is due a very large proportion of the confusion and misunderstanding on the part of the public in general concerning the principle back of mediumship and the subjective process.

CHAPTER IX.

THE DESTRUCTIVE PRINCIPLE IN MEDIUMSHIP.

Perhaps the one error most difficult to dislodge from the human mind and consciousness is that which is bound up in a comforting belief.

It needs but a glance at the pages of history to discover that throughout the ages the great body of humanity has expended vastly more energy in hugging its delusions and cherishing its beliefs than in its search for truth.

The cause of this interesting phenomenon of the human intellect lies deeply imbedded in the very texture of our essential nature. The pathway of the soul which leads to human happiness, or to the goal of human ambitions, is both steep and rugged and beset with many dangers. Each individual who travels this way is forever in search of congenial fellowship. He is ready to accept as a friend and cherish as a companion whatever brings to him courage, faith, hope or comfort. He is ever ready to let down the outer gates and open wide the inner doors of the soul to admit even a delusion, if it be but a friendly one, or a mere belief, if it brings comfort; and when once admitted he stands ready to defend it against all the world, truth included.

Human intelligence does not confine itself to the study of logic, nor to the art of reasoning from acknowledged premises to legitimate conclusions. If it did so it would discover many things in Nature of which it has thus far never dared to even dream. Consistency is a jewel so precious and so rare that it is possessed by only the few. While we all know and freely acknowledge that truth is better than falsehood or error, nevertheless, when we have once come into possession of that which to us is a comfort or an inspiration to faith, hope or happiness, even though it be a delusion or a fallacy, it is a part of our human nature to cling to it with all our strength and all our might lest some one shall wrest it from us and deprive us of the pleasure it has afforded.

To many a lonely and anxious soul spiritual mediumship

has been the open door through which the dove of peace has entered with its olive leaf of glad tidings from beyond the dark and troubled waters. It is not strange, therefore, that those who, through this open door, have watched for the coming of the winged messenger of hope, should bar the approach of those who would forever close it against them.

For such as these, however, there is a greater comfort than the mere leaf of hope in the beak of a fleeting dove. There is yet another and a higher door from which you your-self may pass beyond the restless tide and for yourself behold the tree of life from which that leaf was plucked.

The purpose of this work, therefore, is not to condemn those who have sought knowledge of the life that lies beyond the dark shadow of physical death, nor yet to inveigh against mediums as the instruments by and through which this knowledge has been transmitted.

Let it be remembered that all the material claims of spir-itualism are admitted in advance. Not only this, they have been fully verified by scientific demonstration. The question before us, therefore, is not as to the fact of mediumship it-self, nor the genuineness of its phenomena. It is solely and entirely a question of principle.

Those who view this subject from the standpoint of personal interest appear to take for granted that merely because mediumship has given to the world that which the world has desired, that is, definite assurance of a future life, the principle and the process involved in mediumship are therefore necessarily right. At first view this assumption would appear to be justified.

If mediumship involved no other results than that of giving to the world knowledge of a life beyond the grave, this volume never would have been written. But such is not the case. It involves vastly more than the mere question of another life. Its results are therefore complex. Its merits must be determined by all the results which flow from it, and not by a single or isolated result which may represent but a mere fraction of the great aggregate of which it is but a part.

It will help to clear the mind for a more perfect understanding of the subject if we first arrive at a satisfactory solution of the following question, viz.:

Is it possible for any given result which, in itself, is desirable and beneficent, to follow, as the natural sequence of a process which is indefensibly wrong, immoral and injurious?

A complete answer will be found in the following illustrations:

1. A gentleman desires to educate his son for the ministry. This is a desire which is admittedly worthy. To accomplish this worthy result requires money. He knows that upon the death of his own mother he will fall heir to a fortune which would enable him to accomplish the fulfillment of his worthy desire. He therefore plans and successfully accomplishes his mother's death. The fortune is received. His son is educated. The ministry receives a worthy and valued brother. The world is greatly benefited as the result of his ministry.

Here is an instance in which the father's desire is in every way commendable. The results to both the son and the world are, in themselves, desirable and beneficent. But the method by which those results were accomplished is not only indefensibly wrong, immoral and injurious, but criminal to the last degree.

It will be observed that the primary result sought in this case, namely, the son's education, constitutes but a part of the aggregate results which flowed from the method and the process by which it was accomplished. Herein lies the mystery. There were other results, and these are they that stamp the process as injurious and wrong.

2. A scientist desires to obtain certain geological data from a cave which he has reason to believe is inhabited by venomous reptiles and ravenous beasts. He is afraid to enter the cave himself. He therefore sends his innocent and trusting child in the hope that he may perhaps be able to bring back the desired information. At his command the child enters the cave and is stung by a venomous serpent. He brings back the desired information but dies as a result.

The desire for knowledge in this case may have been entirely commendable.   The knowledge obtained may have been of special value to the world.   But the method or process by which it was obtained was cruel, inhuman, cowardly and criminally unjust.

3.   A physician desires to know the physiological action of a certain drug.   He therefore feeds it to his innocent child. The child dies.   The physician thereby obtains the desired knowledge.   This knowledge, in itself, is both desirable and commendable.   It may be of great value to the rest of humanity.   It may result in a beneficent discovery.   But who shall say that the method or process by which it was obtained is right?

4.   A psychologist desires to obtain definite knowledge concerning the great problem of a life beyond the grave.   He nas already learned from the professional observations of physicians that those who slowly bleed to death almost invariably fall into a psychic state during the closing moments of life in which they often see, hear and talk with those who are known to have passed to the other shore of life.

For the purpose of obtaining more light upon this most fascinating of all subjects, he takes one after the other of the members of his own family into his laboratory and there slowly bleeds them to death in order that he may hear their last words and question them concerning those whom they see and hear and speak with as they descend into the valley of the shadow.   Through this method he obtains authentic messages from his own mother, perhaps, and from other relatives and friends who have gone before, and he is thereby satisfied that death does not end all.

The knowledge he has thus acquired is that which all the world is seeking.   It is the knowledge which would bring comfort and strength and courage and hope to many a troubled soul.

But what shall we say of the method or process by which he obtained this knowledge?   What of the instruments by and through which he accomplished his purpose?   These were his "mediums."   These he sacrificed for his own selfish purposes. Every impulse of the human soul protests against such a sacrifice. Every element of justice condemns the process as indefensibly wrong, immoral and unjust. Far better to have left the problem unsolved than to have obtained his knowledge at such a sacrifice.

These illustrations furnish a complete and unequivocal answer to the question under consideration. It will now be seen that it is quite possible for a given result which, in itself, may be desirable and beneficent, to follow as the natural sequence of a method or process which is indefensibly wrong, immoral and injurious. Not only is this possible, but it is one of the commonest facts of Nature and confronts us at almost every turn in the pathway of life.

There are two well defined reasons for this, viz.:

1. A complex process often produces mixed results.

2. Whenever a given process produces mixed results some of these results may be good while others may be bad.

In all such instances it is impossible to determine the real merit or demerit of the method or process without taking into account all the known results which it produces. When this is done, and only then, is it possible to determine with certainty the exact nature and quality of the process.

A study of the foregoing illustrations will develop the further fact that the desired result in each instance might have been achieved by other methods than those employed. This suggests the further important fact that from the standpoint of the individual almost every desired result may be accomplished by at least two different methods or processes, one of which is ethically right and the other wrong.

And so it is with the great question of another life. We all admit that knowledge concerning this great and profound problem is desirable. To most men and women it would seem to be an inexpressible comfort, joy and benefit. There are at least two distinct and radically different methods or processes by which the individual may obtain that definite and specific knowledge. One of these is ethically right and the other is ethically wrong. One is subjective. The other is independent. One is constructive in its effects upon the individual. The other is destructive.

One of the processes is known to the world as "Spiritual mediumship." Is it the right one, or the wrong one? Is it constructive, or destructive?

The correct answer to these questions will be found only through a careful study of all the known results of the mediumistic process.

In the analysis of this subject there are two general classes of results which must be taken into account, viz.:

1. Those which affect the medium.
2. Those which do not affect the medium.

Those results of the mediumistic process which do not affect the medium may, for convenience, be subdivided as follows:

(a) Those results which affect such of the sitters, in a spiritualistic seance or circle, as are not in the least mediumistic.

For the sake of avoiding all questions of controversy it will be admitted that a fair proportionate number of this class have been convinced by mediumistic phenomena that there is a life after physical death. These have come to believe that through mediumship it is possible to communicate with and receive communications from those on the spiritual side of life. Thus they are given a belief, and their faith is established.

The nature of the messages received and the phenomena witnessed, however, has produced upon them very different results. On the one hand, where the communications have been intelligent and of a sufficiently high moral tone, the results have been, to all appearances, of a beneficial character. They have, at least, brought to the recipients a certain amount of hope and a comforting assurance that death does not end all.

On the other hand, in quite as many instances, the nature of the messages received and the character of the phenomena witnessed have been so entirely devoid of intellectual merit, moral quality and common honesty as to convey the impres-

sion that the spiritual world is exclusively inhabited by im-
beciles, fools, liars and knaves.   In all such instances the results have been of the most unfortunate character.   They
have brought neither comfort nor hope nor an inspiration to
better living.

Then again, many of this class have spent years investigat-
ing the subject only to turn from it all, weary and heart-sick
and disgusted, with the firm and unalterable conviction that
it is all a fraud from beginning to end.   If skeptical at the
beginning, their skepticism has been thereby many times intensified.   If religiously inclined, their faith in both God and
man has been completely shattered.   Their hope of a future
life and their inspiration to higher ideals have been taken from
them.   To all such as these mediumship has brought nothing
but disappointment and direct personal injury.

(b)   The results of mediumship which affect those sitters
who are not yet mediums, but who are of the negative types
and more or less susceptible to spiritual influences.

With comparatively few exceptions, the result is that individuals of this class are ultimately overwhelmed by the spiritual influences and either become mediums of the various
forms and in the varying degrees hereinbefore outlined, or
they are adjudged insane and committed to the various institutions for the insane throughout the country.

(c)   The results of the mediumistic process upon the spiritual controls who participate in the work of developing mediums.

Inasmuch as this branch of the subject will be fully considered in Part III, of this volume, it is only necessary at this
time to state that the results upon this class are, without exception, of the most harmful and destructive character.

This brings us to a consideration of the results of mediumship which affect the medium himself.   This is by far the most
important branch of the subject under consideration.   It
therefore demands the most careful study and analysis from
the standpoint of the accumulated and verified facts of science.

A critical study of mediumship from the standpoint of the
medium himself involves three distinct and separate lines of

inquiry by which to determine the possible merits or demerits of the mediumistic process, viz.:

I.   Its physical effects upon the medium.

II.   Its mental effects upon the medium.

III.   Its moral effects upon the medium.

In the order named our present inquiry is concerned with:

I.   The purely physical effects of the mediumistic process upon the medium himself.

A complete exposition of this subject would demand an exhaustive inquiry into the physiology and pathology of mediumship.   But in all their essential features these are identical with those of hypnotism.   The physiology and pathology of hypnotism, however, have been sufficiently outlined in Part I, Chapter VIII, of this volume, to which the reader is referred for the specific data necessary to a complete understanding of the subject here under consideration.   It would seem but needless repetition to cover the same subject again in this connection.   A brief summary of the most salient facts there presented would appear to be all that is necessary at this time.

These naturally divide themselves into two general classes, viz.:

1.   Immediate results.

2.   Subsequent results.

The immediate physical results of the mediumistic process upon the medium may be briefly summarized as follows:

(a)   The mediumistic process acts directly upon the physical brain of the medium in the reverse order of its evolutionary development.

(b)   Its primary physiological action, therefore, is upon the objective and perceptive organs of the brain which lie immediately above and back of the eyes.

(c)   Thence, as the subjective state deepens, its effects sweep backward through the intellectual brain, downward through the middle brain, and in its most profound state of catalepsy or lethargic, trance control, it acts upon the primary brain.

(d)   The direct and specific effect of the mediumistic

process, from its inception to its conclusion, is paralysis of the physical brain and physical sensory organism of the medium.

(e) The degree of paralysis at any given stage of the process is measured by the degree of mediumistic control attained.

(f) The varying degrees of paralysis, therefore, range all the way from the first faint mediumistic impulse of subjection through all its deepening stages to the state of complete catalepsy or lethargic, trance control.

The subsequent results of the mediumistic process upon the physical organism of the medium, briefly summarized, are as follows:

(a) As the mediumistic state or condition is developed through a series of sittings the nervous organism of the medium becomes more and more acutely sensitive to the pressure of its environment. This at first manifests itself in what is often defined as simple nervousness. As the process of mediumistic subjection progresses this state of nervous sensibility to environment usually leads to insomnia and thence to intense nervous irritability.

(b) Long continued or oft repeated subjection of the medium to the mediumistic process almost invariably results in complete nervous prostration.

(c) If the process be carried far enough the physical brain tissues become impaired, from which condition brain diseases of various kinds and degrees follow as a natural consequence.

(d) Wherever mediumistic control becomes continuous insanity follows as a natural result. This subject will be more fully considered in a subsequent chapter.

(e) The very nature of the mediumistic process is such that in the production of mediumistic phenomena it is necessary for the spiritual controls to appropriate and expend the medium's animal magetism and vital energy as rapidly as the same are generated by his physical organism.

This is illustrated by the fact that wherever the medium voluntarily submits to control (under the mutual agreement that the spiritual intelligences are to have the use of the medium's physical organism at stated intervals without opposition), they seldom hold the medium under complete and continuous subjection longer than from one to two hours at any one time.

Mediums themselves invariably recognize this condition of magnetic and vital depletion after each mediumistic subjection. Oftentimes it is so marked as to result in complete physical exhaustion.

(f)   The amount of magnetic and vital energy thus appropriated and expended by the controls depends somewhat on the form of mediumship employed.

For instance, it is a fact well known to every one who has given the subject consideration that the process of materialization calls for the largest expenditure of magnetic and vital energy within a given period of time. Other forms of complete trance control follow next in regular order, and so on down through all the other forms of partial control.

(g)   It is found that this depletion of magnetic and vital energy is, with very rare exceptions, commensurate with the degree and continuity of the control exercised.

(h)   The power possessed by every human, physical organism to resist the encroachments of disease is measured by the volume of its magnetic and vital energy in stock at any given time. The literal truth of this statement is known to every practicing physician throughout the country. It will therefore be observed that the inevitable depletion which follows from the mediumistic process leaves the physical organism of the medium, for the time being, practically defenseless against the arch enemy of mankind in the form of physical disease.

This is also fully verified by the most recent and reliable statistics, which show that the average life of the medium, dating from the development of the mediumistic condition, is only a fraction over seven years. This includes mediums of both sexes and all ages who have given themselves up to the practice of mediumship either regularly or as a business.

It is true that there are a few very remarkable exceptions

where mediumistic subjection has followed with reasonable regularity over a period of years. These cases, however, are the rare exceptions and only serve to prove more fully the general rule. It is found that in every such exception there is a specific cause, which only serves to verify more fully the principle above stated.

For illustration: A certain well known medium of international reputation has been giving public seances and delivering public sermons under complete trance control for something like twenty-five years, and possibly longer. The question very naturally arises as to how this is possible, when the mediumistic process, under all ordinary conditions, is known to be so extremely enervating and paralyzing to the physical organism of the medium.

It is known that in this particular instance the magnetic and vital energies of the medium, appropriated by her controls, are immediately resupplied to her from the negative and mediumistic members of her audience. In this event the largest ultimate draft is upon the audience instead of the medium. The audience, therefore, is the sufferer in this instance without knowing it. Certain members of her regular audience are so completely enervated by this draft upon them that for hours after each regular service they are seriously affected. They have not yet located the cause. If they will hereafter carefully note the effects they will be able to fully verify the statements here made.

Let this same medium be subjected to the same character of control under conditions which preclude the possibility of such draft upon her audience and she will break under the strain in a very short time.

II. This brings us to the second general line of inquiry as to the results of the mediumistic process upon the mental condition of the medium.

These, in like manner, naturally, divide themselves into two distinct classes, viz.:

1. Immediate and more or less transitory results.
2. Subsequent and more enduring results.

The immediate and more or less transitory results of the

mediumistic process upon the mind of the medium are as follows:

(a) During the continuance of the mediumistic process the will, voluntary powers and sensory organism of the medium are under the domination and control of spiritual intelligences to the exact degree that the mediumistic relation is established.

(b) In proportion to the degree of mediumistic control established, at any given time, the medium is deprived of the independent power to exercise his own will.

(c) In the same proportion he loses his independent control of the voluntary organs of his own physical body.

(d) In exactly the same proportion his physical sensory organism fails to report to his own consciousness accurate impressions as to passing events upon the physical plane.

(e) To the extent that the mediumistic process interferes with the normal action of his physical sensory organism the medium's judgment concerning the ordinary affairs of life is impaired.

(f) In proportion as the medium loses the power of independent volition under the mediumistic process his will becomes an automatic instrument under the domination of his controls.

(g) In all forms of trance mediumship the medium is deprived of the independent exercise of all his mental faculties, capacities and powers, during the continuance of the mediumistic process.

(h) In all the lighter forms of mediumship his loss of the independent power of self-control is exactly commensurate with the degree of mediumistic control to which he is thereby subjected.

These results upon the mind of the medium are all immediate. They are also of a more or less transitory nature, except to the extent that injury follows therefrom.

The subsequent and more enduring results of the mediumistic process upon the mind of the medium are, in part, as follows:

(a) As the process of mediumistic subjugation progresses the dominating spiritual intelligences obtain a constantly increasing power and control over all the mental faculties, capacities and powers of the medium. As a natural result at each succeeding sitting the complete subjection of the medium becomes less and less difficult for them. This is a progressive and permanent condition.

(b) The natural corollary of this demonstrated proposition is equally true. That is to say, in exact proportion as the spiritual intelligences attain ease and facility in the process of obtaining control of the medium, the medium himself loses the independent power of resistance. This condition, therefore, also involves a progressive and permanent loss to the medium.

(c) The mediumistic process involves no independent, self-conscious and rational activity on the part of the medium. On the other hand, it calls for the exact reverse of this. That is to say, to the exact degree that the mediumistic relation obtains, the mind of the medium is in a negative or passive condition, and therefore inactive.

A high state of mediumistic development, therefore, means a correspondingly low state of mental activity on the part of the medium. Continuous mediumistic practice means continuous mental inaction or stagnation on the part of the medium. This means a corresponding inactivity of the physical brain through which his mind operates.

But it is an immutable law of physical nature, with which medical science is already thoroughly familiar, that the inaction of any organ of the physical body soon results in its atrophy and decay, in the loss of its natural powers and the suspension of its natural functions. This is a fact of Nature, the complete verification and demonstration of which is within the power of every individual who desires to test it.

For illustration: Let him completely suspend the muscular activity of the arm. In a very short time its muscles become flabby and soft and its powers wane in exact proportion to its atrophied condition. To the same degree its natural functions are suspended.

The passive condition of the mind in mediumship and the

consequent inactivity of the physical brain, through which the mind operates, soon result in atrophy of the brain tissues, degeneracy of the mental powers and suspension of the mental functions.

No fact of Nature is more conclusively demonstrated than is this particular result of the mediumistic process. It is the common experience of every medium who has ever reached the degree of mediumistic subjection here referred to. To a proportionate degree it is the experience of every other medium, whether he is able to measure it or not. It is a condition which may be observed by every individual who is in position to study the effects of mediumship upon the mental powers of a medium.

An instance or two out of the many that have come under the personal observation of the writer will be sufficient to fully illustrate the principle under consideration. For instance:

1. In 1895 the writer, through a business transaction, came into a personal acquaintance with a Mr. W., of Chicago, a gentleman of exceptional mental powers and qualifications, and the highest type of intellectual and moral manhood. This gentleman was, at that time, at the zenith of his mental vigor and intellectual power, and a man whom it was a rare pleasure to know and to hold as a personal friend.

It so happened, however, that just prior to the inception of the acquaintance he had become interested in the subject of mediumship and had commenced the developing process. During the first year of his mediumistic development the writer saw him frequently, and often endeavored to dissuade him from his mediumistic pursuits, but without avail.

In less than two years he had become an old man, broken in both body and mind, and but a pitiful suggestion of the splendid and manly intelligence of two short years before. The operations of his mind, when not under control, were a complete index of the atrophied condition of the brain tissues. He was a complete mental wreck, the utter ruin of a splendid intelligence.

2. Mrs. L., one of the brightest journalists of the coun-

try at one time, and the widow of a well-known newspaper correspondent, became interested in mediumship. She sat for development and soon became a very remarkable trance-speaking medium.

From the day she became fully convinced that she was under the guidance and direction of spiritual intelligences she appeared to surrender herself, body and soul, to the domination and control of her "spiritual band."

In less than two years she passed from a state of splendid mental equipment, intellectual power and womanly grace to that of a maundering, mental wreck, more pitiful than language can picture.

It would be manifestly unfair and equally untrue to assert that this is the inevitable fate of every medium, for it is not. But it is a fact beyond dispute that in exact proportion as a medium surrenders his power of self-control and becomes an instrument under the domination and control of spiritual intelligences, he just that far approaches the mental condition here indicated.

Every student of mediumistic phenomena who will put himself in position to observe the results of the subjective process upon the mind of a medium will be able to note some, and oftentimes all, of the following significant peculiarities and symptoms:

1. One of the invariable signs of a subjective, mental state on the part of a medium is a certain far-away, hazy, abstract, introspective or glassy stare of the eyes.

2. A gradual and progressive loss of memory of things present.

3. A growing inability to hold the mind intently, for any length of time, upon any subject which demands thoughtful study.

4. A growing inability to think consecutively or logically upon any subject which calls for analytical thought.

5. A growing inability to give undivided attention to an ordinary conversation.

6. An increasing tendency to lapse into a state of mental abstraction and introspection.

7. A gradual and progressive loss of will power and energy to perform hard mental labor of any kind.

8. A growing suspicion concerning the motives and intentions of those with whom he comes in contact.

9. An increasing sensitiveness to unimportant things.

10. A growing irritability of temperament.

11. Increasing nervousness.

12. A growing childishness and vanity concerning little things.

13. Increasing egotism and selfishness in almost everything that concerns the individual.

14. And finally, a gradual decrease of the purely intellectual activities of the mind, accompanied by a corresponding increase of emotionalism and of the physical appetites, passions and desires.

CHAPTER X.

MEDIUMSHIP AND MORALITY.

III. The third general line of inquiry brings us to a consideration of the moral results of mediumship upon the medium himself.

The discoveries and demonstrations of Natural Science in this particular field of inquiry are of the most significant character and the most vital importance. They should command the instant attention and the most thoughtful consideration of every intelligent individual who has at heart either his own personal interests or the well-being of society. To no individual or class of individuals are the known facts of science of such transcendent importance as to the medium himself, and to those who are liable to become such.

But herein serious difficulties arise. Human nature is so curiously and wonderfully made that the particular knowledge each individual most needs is very often that which he does not appreciate, does not want, or does not care for. Even when we recognize our need of definite knowledge we often refuse to accept it unless it comes to us from exactly the source we expect it and in the identical manner and form we demand it.

For illustration: A minister of the gospel is apt to assume that he knows more about theology than a blacksmith does, and sometimes he is correct. For this reason he refuses to accept theological suggestions from such a source. It is just possible, however, that the blacksmith may know the very thing the minister most needs and desires to know, but he will never be able to convey his knowledge for the simple reason that the minister will not receive it. The presumption of ignorance, in this case, is against the blacksmith.

On the other hand, the blacksmith would very likely feel the same way toward the minister if the conditions were reversed. However much he might be in need of definite knowledge concerning the welding of metals, he would never receive it from the minister, even though the latter possessed it and were perfectly willing to impart it. In this case the presumption of ignorance is against the minister.

Then again, suppose a learned scientist should offer to instruct the minister in the field of theology. The same presumption would bar his way. But in this case there is yet another difficulty to be met and overcome. By reason of the relation which has existed between them in the past, theology has come to look upon science rather as an enemy than a friend. Men do not, as a general rule, accept favors from those whom they regard as their enemies. Here, then, the additional presumption of hostility or enmity would also bar the way of the scientist, no matter how profound a theologian he may be.

Mediumship is not only a profession, but an experience, to the full measure of the medium's wakeful consciousness. To the same extent it is a deeply personal matter with every medium. It enters into his life as a vital and essential factor. It gives form and color to his entire world of thought, feeling and action. He therefore assumes to know more about it than anyone else. In this case the presumption of ignorance is against whomsoever shall venture to cross the threshold of his own convictions.

Not only this. His mediumship is the one thing which distinguishes the medium from ordinary mortals. It leads many of his fellows to regard him with a certain degree of awe or reverence as a mysterious being quite out of the ordinary. Many even come to look upon him as an oracle of wonderful wisdom. This flatters him. It naturally increases his estimate of himself and his own importance, and correspondingly stimulates his pride in his mediumship. It develops, in many instances, the honest though unfortunate conviction that the balance of humanity are intellectual infants in comparison with himself. In all such instances pride of intelligence also bars the way of every one whomsoever having definite knowledge to impart.

Then again, in proportion as mediumship brings to the medium fame, notoriety or money, it becomes to him a thing of value. It is natural that he should prize it accordingly.

It could not well be otherwise, for it is a part of human nature to prize whatever gratifies our vanities or our selfish desires.   Whatever would come between us and the thing we value is, to us, an enemy and not a friend.

These, then, are the chief obstacles which stand between the medium and the definite knowledge he most needs:

1.   The presumption in his mind that he alone, of all men, knows most about mediumship and the mediumistic process.

2.   The presumption in his own mind that any one and every one who is not a medium is necessarily, by reason of that fact alone, ignorant concerning the principle and the process involved.

3.   The pride of intelligence which prevents him from mentally stooping to those whom he conscientiously believes to be his intellectual inferiors.

4.   The honest conviction that those who would condemn his mediumship, for any cause whatsoever, thereby necessarily condemn him also.

The sincere desire and earnest hope of the writer is that his work may reach the intelligence and win the confidence of every medium or student of mediumship who shall honor this volume with a careful and critical reading.   Then, and then only, will it be possible to lay before him, in acceptable form, the demonstrated facts of science touching the moral phases of mediumship and the mediumistic process.

To that end the following brief statement may, perhaps, be of value:

The writer holds himself to be the friend of every honest medium, spiritualist and student of psychic phenomena, no matter what his attitude toward this particular work may be.   For more than thirty years he has been a close student of psychic phenomena in all their various phases, under the most favorable conditions possible for the acquisition of exact and definite knowledge; and as such, during that time, he has personally witnessed perhaps every important phase of both mediumship and hypnotism, as well as many other psychic manifestations and phenomena which are entirely independent of these processes.

His study of the subject has been pursued in the spirit of sympathy and good faith. His mind has at all times been as free from prejudice or bias as possible to one whose central motive has been the acquisition of exact and definite knowledge concerning the most fascinating and absorbing problems of human life.

Most of his immediate relatives and many of his most intimate personal friends are known as active and leading spiritualists within the circle of their acquaintance. Some of them are mediums through whom a wide range of mediumistic phenomena has been produced. Not one of these, however, so far as he knows, has ever given public seances or practiced mediumship for money or for any other valuable consideration.

Their motives and purposes are in every respect above suspicion or reproach, and their perfect integrity and good faith are beyond all possible question among those who know them. The same, it is believed, can be said with equal truth concerning a very large number of earnest and conscientious believers in mediumship and spiritualism all over the world.

For these and other good and sufficient reasons, the writer accords to all such the most friendly and courteous consideration. He only asks in return that his present message, which is largely intended for mediums, spiritualists and students of psychic phenomena, be received by them in the same spirit of friendly courtesy and freedom from prejudice or hostility.

With this personal pledge of sympathy and good faith, let us proceed at once to the subject under consideration.

Individual responsibility is the basis of morality. This is a fact that is universally recognized among civilized people. It is acknowledged by men and women of all schools, cults, philosophies, creeds and religions. It is the fundamental principle at the basis of every form of government. It is at the foundation of every social and moral structure. It is the central principle about which cluster all our laws and codes, civil and criminal, as well as moral.

So long as man is held to be a responsible, individual intelligence, he is accountable to his fellow-man and to society for all his acts, influence and conduct which in any way affect them. Just so long he is held accountable to the moral law. Just so long he has a moral status.

The moment he becomes an irresponsible, individual intelligence, no matter from what cause or by what process, his accountability to his fellow-man and to society, as well as to the moral law, ceases. He is at all times accountable to the degree of his individual responsibility only. He is exempt only to the degree of his individual irresponsibility. Man's entire value as a member of society, in fact, depends upon the extent to which he is held to be a responsible, individual intelligence.

But when, or under what conditions, is an individual responsible? When, or under what conditions, is he not responsible? In other words, upon what does individual responsibility depend?

This is one of the most important questions ever propounded to mankind. Its full and complete analysis will be found in Part III of this volume. To avoid repetition, therefore, the simple answer will be given at this point without elaboration.

Individual responsibility depends at all times upon the ability of the individual to exercise his volition independently, self-consciously and rationally.

That is to say, every individual is morally responsible for such of his acts and such only as he performs independently (*i. e.*, of his own free will and accord), self-consciously (*i. e.*, knowingly and intentionally), and rationally (*i. e.*, anticipating the results).

The several elements, therefore, upon which individual responsibility depends are:

1. Self-consciousness.
2. Independent choice.
3. Reason.
4. Volition.

The degree to which the individual is in possession of all

these faculties, capacities and powers marks the degree of his individual responsibility at any given time. The degree to which he is not in possession of any or all these, marks the degree of his irresponsibility at any given time.

It now becomes possible for us to understand and appreciate the moral status of the medium. It is well known that the mediumistic process deprives the medium of his ability to exercise each and every one of these faculties, capacities and powers, to the exact degree that the mediumistic relation is established.

Mediumship, it will be remembered, is a subjective, psychic process. It is, in fact, that process by and through which spiritual intelligences obtain, hold and exercise control of the will, voluntary powers and sensory organism of a medium.

To the degree that mediumship exists at any given time it deprives the medium of the use and exercise of his own sensory organism. But his sensory organism includes all the channels through which his consciousness may be reached and impressed. He is therefore robbed of his self-consciousness in just so far as he is deprived of the use of his sensory organism. That is to say, he sacrifices his self-consciousness to exactly the degree that he surrenders himself to mediumistic control.

Again, his will or power of volition, passes from his own control in exact proportion and to the exact degree that he becomes a subject of mediumistic control. But his ability to reason is also dependent upon his power of will or volition. Therefore, in just so far as he is at any time a subject of mediumistic control he is deprived of the power of reason.

And again, the power of independent choice is also dependent upon his will, or volition. This, therefore, also passes from him in exactly the same ratio.

It now becomes possible to clearly state the following demonstrated facts of Natural Science which bear directly upon the question under consideration:

1. In just so far as mediumship exists, at any given time, it deprives the medium of the ability to exercise each and

every one of the faculties, capacities and powers of the mind and soul upon which his individual responsibility depends.

2. In proportion as he forfeits his individual responsibility, he violates the moral law, and thereby becomes a menace to society.

3. His moral status of accountability is at all times commensurate with the degree of his individual responsibility.

4. At no time does his moral status as an individual intelligence rise above the level of his individual responsibility.

5. His individual, moral nature may, and often does, sink very far below that level.

6. Mediumship, inasmuch as it divests the medium of his individual responsibility, is a direct violation of the moral law, and to the same degree and for the same reason is inimical to the rights and interests of both the individual and society.

Up to this point we have considered the subject from the standpoint of the moral principle alone which is involved in the mediumistic process. We have clearly defined the moral status of mediumship and the degree to which the medium is at all times morally accountable.

It now becomes necessary to examine the subject from the standpoint of the actual results of mediumship as they translate themselves into the inspirations, emotions, impulses, desires, appetites, passions, actions and life of the medium himself. This is both a delicate and a difficult task and demands the utmost care in order to avoid the possibility of misunderstanding, misinterpretation or offense.

The chief psychological distinction between man and the animal is in the fundamental fact that the animal does not rise to the level of moral accountability, while man does. In other words, the animal has no moral status, while man has. The animal, therefore, is exempt from the obligations of individual responsibility, while man is not.

But why is the animal not a responsible, individual intelligence? Why has he not risen to the level of moral accountability?

There is but one answer. It is because the animal nature and development are devoid of the soul attributes—those faculties, capacities and powers—upon which individual responsibility depends. If the animal possessed these attributes of the soul he would be both individually responsible and morally accountable under the law of his being. Without them, however, he is neither individually responsible nor morally accountable.

Indeed, it would almost appear that in the stupendous scheme of evolution Nature, or Universal Intelligence, has been engaged in a process of evolving an order of intelligence upon which it could shift the burden of individual responsibility for its acts and conduct beyond that point. In man it has achieved that end.

In other words, at man's evolutionary estate it would appear that Nature, or Universal Intelligence, weans the individual, as it were, and then, putting into his hands the key to his own destiny, charges him with the burden of individual responsibility and thereby confers upon him a moral status. That is to say, man, as a responsible individual, is charged with the burden of self-control. The animal is not.

Man possesses those peculiar attributes of the soul—self-consciousness, independent choice, reason and volition—which, acting together, give him dominion and power over that part of his nature we differentiate as animal, and, accordingly, he is thereby charged with the individual responsibility of regulating and controlling all his animal appetites, passions, emotions, desires and propensities. By such self-control, and such alone, he lifts himself forever higher and higher above the level of animal life and nature.

The animal, on the other hand, being devoid of those attributes of the soul which charge it with the duty of self-control, lives out its animal nature without check or hindrance. Living thus upon the plane of physical nature, it lives only in the physical appetites, passions, impulses, emotions and desires, and lives solely to gratify them to the fullest extent possible under its environment.

The man who continually fails, neglects or refuses to discharge his individual responsibility by the exercise of self-control of all the elements of his nature, inevitably sinks to the level of animal life. There is no other destiny for him. And in exact proportion as he fails, neglects or refuses to discharge this duty or obligation which God or Nature has fixed upon him, just because he is a man, in like proportion he approaches the level of animal nature. There is no escape from this result.

Mediumship deprives the medium of the ability to exercise each and every one of those attributes of the soul upon which his individual responsibility depends, in just so far as he is affected by the mediumistic process at any given time. In equal measure, therefore, as this becomes a fixed and permanent result of mediumship, the medium is deprived of the power of self-control, and necessarily sinks toward the level of his animal nature. This is the law of spiritual gravity.

In exact proportion as the individual loses the power of self-control, or voluntarily suspends its exercise, the check upon his animal nature is relaxed and the restraint upon his animal appetites, passions, emotions, desires and propensities is removed. This is inevitable. Every man and every woman living has no doubt demonstrated a thousand times over the operation of this law of Nature.

Harsh and unlovely and revolting as the thought may be when set out in cold, unsympathetic type, it is nevertheless a fact which we must all face, whether we be mediums or not, and from which there is no escape.

Inasmuch as mediumship slowly but surely destroys the individual power of self-control, its inevitable tendency is toward animalism. The law is inexorable.

This is neither an idle fancy, an unhappy theory nor a troubled dream which waking intelligence may dispel or disprove. It is an uncompromising fact of Nature, as patent as that an apple severed from the limb on which it grows will fall to the ground. The force which carries the apple down we name gravity.

When its natural sustaining power, the power of self-control, is neutralized, suspended or destroyed, the gravity of the soul, like that of the apple, carries it downward toward the plane of the earthly animal.

It needs but an intimate acquaintance with the daily lives and practices of those who follow mediumship as a profession or business to find the unanswerable demonstration of this melancholy fact.

It will be observed that this statement has special reference to professional mediums only. There are very definite reasons for this particular limitation, viz.:

1. There are thousands of non-professional mediums all over the world, known only among their friends and acquaintances as such, who devote little or no time, thought or attention to the mediumistic process. Their development, therefore, has not been carried to a point where its results may be clearly and unmistakably formulated and defined with accuracy.

2. The professional medium, with sufficiently rare exceptions to clearly establish the rule, devotes enough of his time and energy to the active practice of mediumship to reach, in time, a state of more or less complete psychic subjectivity. The effects of the process upon his life and character are observable in proportion as he yields himself to its domination and control.

But what of the statistical facts? Do they verify or disprove the principle here declared? Let us see.

From the class of mediums whose development has been sufficient to establish definite and unqualified results, science has gathered and is able to formulate and present the following verified results of the mediumistic process upon the medium, viz.:

1. Seventy-three per cent. of the professional mediums referred to sooner or later develop abnormally increased and uncontrollable sexual passions, while as high as ninety-two per cent. show marked increase of the sexual appetite or desire.

2. A fraction over sixty per cent. develop hysterical or ungovernable temper, while as high as eighty-five per cent. show marked increase of nervous irritability.

3. Fifty-eight per cent. develop dishonesty and fraud,

while ninety-five per cent. show lack of moral discrimination and courage.

4. A fraction over seventy per cent. develop inordinate vanity, while ninety-two per cent. become more or less egotistical.

5. As high as ninety-eight per cent. develop some discoverable form of selfishness, sensuous desire, emotional weakness or degrading physical appetite.

6. In no instance does the process develop marked individual improvement from a moral standpoint.

In order that no injustice may be done the individual medium, it is proper to explain that the results here given arise from two distinct and separate causes, viz.:

1. Natural degeneracy of the medium as a direct result of the mediumistic process.

2. The direct and overwhelming domination of vicious controls.

No attempt has been made to determine the percentage of results separately due to each of these causes. In fact, it has not been deemed necessary, inasmuch as both classes of results are directly referable to the mediumistic process, and both find their expression in the life and conduct of the medium.

From whatever point these facts may be viewed, their meaning is perfectly plain. They speak for themselves in tones which should be heard by all the children of earth, both now and throughout all the generations yet to come. They clearly and unmistakably identify the principle back of the mediumistic process as *The Destructive Principle of Nature in Individual Life.*

RECAPITULATION.

Briefly recapitulating the last two chapters, there are two general classes of results which flow from the mediumistic process, viz.:

I. Those which do not affect the medium. These are:

1. Those which affect such of the sitters as are not in

the least mediumistically inclined. Three classes fall under this head, viz.:

(a) Those whose faith in another life is thereby established, and who appear to be happier therefor. Results, seemingly good.

(b) Those who are convinced of another life, but who are wholly misled as to the character of intelligence which inhabits the spiritual world. Results, bad.

(c) Those who are convinced that the whole thing is a fraud from beginning to end. Results, bad.

2. Results of the mediumistic process which affect those sitters who are not developed mediums, but who are more or less sensitive to mediumistic influence. Results, very bad.

3. Those which affect the spiritual controls who participate in the mediumistic process. Results, all bad.

II. Those results of the mediumistic process upon the medium himself. These divide themselves into three distinct classes, as follows:

1. The purely physical results, which are:

(a) Immediate. All bad.

(b) Subsequent. All bad.

2. The purely mental results, which are:

(a) Immediate. All bad.

(b) Subsequent. All bad.

3. The purely moral results. All bad.

CHAPTER XI.

MEDIUMSHIP AND MARTYRDOM.

Mediumship is a martyrdom. Moreover, it is a martyrdom which is both cruel and unnecessary. The cause which it is supposed to represent neither needs nor demands martyrdom of anyone.

Perhaps among all the varied classes and conditions of society no individual man or woman upon the physical plane of life is more cruelly imposed upon than is the honest and conscientious medium.

Indeed, the pitiless deceptions and relentless brutalities practiced upon these honest, simple-minded and credulous souls by unscrupulous, selfish and vicious spiritual controls, in order to insure their willing and continued submission to the mediumistic process, should command the generous sympathy and unfeigned pity of every honest lover of fair play. It should also stimulate an indignant protest in the mind of every one who has even the most limited appreciation of what we know as common decency and honor.

In order to understand and appreciate this phase of the subject as it deserves, it is necessary to call specific attention to the following facts of spiritual nature which have been demonstrated by Natural Science. Some of these facts are also fully verified by spiritualists and mediums themselves as well as by the spiritual intelligences who speak through them:

1. The mere putting off or dispensing with the physical body at physical death does not in the least alter the essential nature or character of the individual himself. He is exactly the same, minus the encumbrance of the physical body. He is neither essentially better nor essentially worse. He is neither wiser nor more honest. He enters that life precisely as he leaves this. His moral status is neither higher nor lower. He carries with him into that life all the predominating habits, appetites, passions, desires, propensities and ambitions which have governed him in this.

2.   There are known to be thirteen distinct spheres or conditions of life connected with this planet, through which the individual man and woman must pass in their evolutionary flight from the lowest to the highest.   These different states or conditions of life have come to be known, through spiritualistic philosophy and terminology, as "spheres."   The term is perhaps as appropriate as any that could be employed, and because of its familiarity to most students will be used in this connection.   .

3.   These spheres represent definite locality in their relation to the planet, as well as a definite state of being in relation to those who inhabit them.

That is to say, denominating this present physical environment, condition and state of being as the first sphere, the second immediately surrounds and encloses the first, the third encloses the second, the fourth encloses the third, and so on through to the thirteenth, which in like manner encloses the other twelve.   Thus, in point of relative location, an ascent of the individual from the first sphere to the thirteenth takes him with each advance further and further outward (or upward, as we are accustomed to say) from the earth's surface.

These spheres, in like manner, represent an ever increasing degree of material refinement and vibratory activity, as well as an intellectual achievement, a spiritual refinement, a mental attainment and a moral power.

4.   The first seven spheres of life are known to Natural Science as "Terrestrial Spheres," and the remaining six (numbering from the eighth to the thirteenth, inclusive) are known as "Celestial Spheres."

The specific reason for this distinction is most interesting and important, but not within the scope and purpose of this volume.   It is sufficient to note the fact at this point that through mediumship spiritualists have learned to accept, in a vague and indefinite way, the fact that there are at least seven spheres of life connected with this planet.   The information filtered through the mediumistic process concerning them, however, has been so meager,   uncertain and contradictory as to convey but a dim and indistinct impression as to their real existence, their nature, their relation or their meaning.

It is undoubtedly true, however, that the seven spheres of spiritualism represent a very incomplete and imperfect conception of the seven terrestrial spheres of Natural Science.

A vast store of exact and definite knowledge concerning these several spheres of life and activity has been accumulated. The subject is also one of absorbing interest and of the most vital importance, but inasmuch as it does not fall within the limitations of this work, it must be reserved for another volume of this series.

5. The individual man or woman who attains to these several spheres does so by and through his or her individual effort, and in accordance with the natural law of individual development and evolutionary progress. There is absolutely no other means or method of advancement. It is the law of life. Nature, in this respect at least, appears to have no favorites. Individual advancement means always and everywhere individual effort in right lines. Individual laziness or indolence, as well as individual effort in wrong directions, means retrogression, always. There are no exceptions.

This would seem to indicate that our individual faculties, capacities and powers were given us for a very specific and definite purpose. If we would reach the mountain top we must climb. We cannot ride upon the shoulders of our fellows. We cannot furnish a proxy to do the climbing while we use the field glass and enjoy the scenery.

Each of these several spheres of life, therefore, may be said to measure very accurately the amount of individual effort necessary to achieve that particular level of progressive development. It is needless to say that the attainment of each successive sphere of life brings to the individual its own peculiar reward. God, or Nature, seems to have made each particular sphere of life a treasure-house to which each individual is given a key at entrance.

Each sphere, therefore, is inhabited by those and those only who, by individual effort, have climbed to its level and earned the right to enter and share its rewards. Thus, under the natural law of spiritual gravity, each individual of the spiritual world inevitably finds the exact level to which his particular development corresponds.

6.   Under this law of spiritual gravity the **first** spiritural sphere (the first beyond the physical) is the natural abiding place of those who represent the lowest degrees of spiritual development.   This does not necessarily mean the lowest in point of intelligence.   The distinction here suggested is of the utmost importance, and would seem to justify the following brief explanation:

Spiritual development does not consist of intellectual development alone, although intelligence is a primary and fundamental element of it.   Neither does it consist of moral development alone, although morality is a basic and necessary principle involved in it.   Nor does it consist in the acquisition of knowledge alone, although knowledge is an important and indispensable ingredient of it.

The fact is that it involves all these elements with something added.   The spiritual development of an individual is, in truth, measured by the intelligence with which he applies his knowledge to the accomplishment of moral purposes.

An individual may, therefore, possess a wealth of knowledge which he does not intelligently apply to any purpose whatever.   Or he may possess the same knowledge and intelligently apply but a mere fraction of it to the accomplishment of moral purposes.   He may, in like manner, possess vast knowledge and intelligently apply the whole of it to the accomplishment of vicious and immoral purposes.   In each of these cases, even though he possesses great knowledge and fine intelligence, he would nevertheless represent a low order of spiritual development, and would gravitate to the spiritual sphere corresponding thereto.

Thus, it will be seen that while intelligence, morality and knowledge are all essential elements of spiritual growth and development, it requires the three in relative combination in the life of an individual to determine his spiritual gravity.

This will explain why it is that powerful intelligences, through the degrading influence of vicious habits and evil practices, may and often do gravitate to the lowest plane of spiritual life. It will also suggest why it is that ignorance on the one hand and indolence on the other serve as "sinkers" to prevent many an otherwise qualified individual from rising to higher and more exalted planes of spiritual life and being.

We are now in position to understand and appreciate the fact above stated that the first sphere beyond that of the physical is the natural and inevitable abiding place of the ignorant, the indolent, the selfishly ambitious, the immoral, the vicious and the depraved who have passed from this life.

But this, it will be remembered, is the sphere which lies closest to earth and therefore nearest the plane of physical life. This is a most important fact, for it means that in point of locality, at least, man in the physical body is more closely in touch with the spiritual world of ignorance, indolence, immorality and vice than he is with that of wisdom, virtue and truth.

This is the great fundamental fact which mediums and spiritualists generally appear to overlook and ignore. And yet, it is the one fact of all facts which should stand as a perpetual warning to all mankind against the practice of hypnotism, mediumship and all other subjective psychic processes.

The experience of mediums themselves and the observations of every honest and intelligent student and investigator of mediumistic phenomena all bear eloquent testimony concerning the intellectual and moral status or level of the average spiritual control.

Indeed, the question has often been asked by intelligent students of psychic phenomena why it is that the "departed spirits" of American Indians constitute so large and important a percentage of mediumistic controls. Neither mediums nor spiritualists generally have thus far returned a satisfactory answer. The problem, however, is a simple one to those who understand the law of spiritual gravity above referred to.

The American Indian is essentially a "child of earth." His intelligence, habits of life and standard of morality are such that when he passes to the "Happy Hunting-Ground" the law of spiritual gravity binds him very closely to the plane of physical nature. He finds himself among that vast and innumerable multitude known to science as "earth-bound" souls. He is thus, by the very law of his being, brought into close touch and intimate relationship with men and women upon the physical side of life.

He enters the spiritual life just as he leaves this life. He is neither better nor worse for the change. He is neither wiser nor more honest. He carries with him the same habits of life, the same appetites, passions, desires, impulses, emotions, ambitions and proclivities, with the same unrestrained will to indulge them. Many of these he finds himself unable to gratify upon the spiritual plane, because he is deprived of the physical organism to which they were related and to which alone they respond.

But he is not slow in learning the important fact that through the power of hypnotism he may, by the exercise of his indomitable will, gain control of the physical organism of some physically embodied individual and through this as an instrument find the means of partially gratifying the grosser appetites, passions and desires of his nature. He therefore finds him a "medium," to whom he attaches himself, and by the power of his imperious will subjects to his domination and control. Through the physical organism of his medium he thus finds the channels through which to partially gratify his lower nature. By means of a subtle fiction he appoints himself as his medium's "spiritual guardian," and thus establishes a relation which is satisfactory to him, only in so far as it enables him to gratify his own personal desires.

Again, the question is often asked by intelligent students, why it is that the standard of intelligence and morality among mediumistic controls is, on the average, so much lower than that of the medium, and why they practice so much wilful deception and deliberate dishonesty.

The answer (usually given by the controls themselves through the lips of their mediums) is to the effect that they are unable to use the organism of the medium with perfect facility. Thus, they claim that the mind of the medium often asserts itself, to a certain degree, and says things, or causes them to say things, which they do not intend to say.

While this would appear to have an element of plausibility in it, and seems to be acceptable to spiritualists generally, it is nevertheless an ingenious falsehood invented for the express purpose of covering a deliberate fraud which the medium would not tolerate if he knew it.

A significant fact bearing upon this phase of the subject is that the controls never attempt to correct these falsehoods of their own accord. They invariably wait until they are caught in them and then attempt to shift the blame upon the innocent and helpless medium who is entirely irresponsible. This is both cowardly and unjust.

The correct answer to these important and searching questions is doubtless already anticipated. The coarse, the vulgar, the licentious, the dishonest, the ignorant, the vicious, the vainly ambitious and the immoral in general who pass from this life, under the operation of the law of spiritual gravity, find their immediate abiding place in the first spiritual sphere. They are therefore closely bound to the plane of physical nature for the time being.

They find themselves still possessed of the same appetites, passions, desires, habits, selfish ambitions and propensities in which they were most intently absorbed while in the physical body. Many of these they are unable to gratify from spiritual nature alone. They find, however, that through the hypnotic process they are able to attach themselves to those yet in the flesh. By so doing they are able to obtain partial gratification of their evil passions and vicious habits through the physical organisms of their subjects. For this purpose, and this alone, they adopt the profession of spiritual controls. They then proceed to locate mediums whom they can control, and through these they educate others. By the aid of the mediumistic process they are able to find partial gratification of their grosser appetites, passions and desires.

But in order that they shall not unwittingly disclose their real designs and thereby incur the hostility of their mediums, they adopt the cunning pretense of unselfish devotion to the cause of spiritualism. By this means they beguile their mediums into a willing submission and a ready co-operation. It is not infrequently the case that more than one hundred spiritual controls thus use the same medium regularly to obtain gratification of their various evil passions and selfish desires. The world in general knows nothing whatever of this phase of mediumship, save as the results are registered upon the life of the medium. Even the medium himself is often deceived as to the purpose, though fully aware of the harmful results to himself. Like the patient martyr that he is, he accepts his degradation as a duty in the mistaken belief that it is for the benefit of humanity.

A definite illustration will serve to develop the principle more clearly:

A few years ago there lived in one of our western cities a man well known to the writer, whom we will designate as Col. B. He was a confirmed drunkard and likewise afflicted with nearly all the vices that usually accompany that particular habit. He died, and the medical certificate read, "Chronic Alcoholism."

At the time of his death, and for some years thereafter, there lived in the same town a rising young merchant, who will be designated as Mr. H. The latter knew Col. B. well during his lifetime and had a great sympathy for him in his depravity, although up to that time Mr. H. had never tasted liquor in his life. Neither of these men knew anything about mediumship and had no interest whatever in the lines of psychical inquiry.

About three months after Col. B.'s death Mr. H. started out from his place of business one morning, went directly to one of the leading saloons of the city and began drinking and carousing like a man who had been addicted to the habit for years. After three days of debauchery he appeared at his store and took up the line of his duties as if nothing had happened.

His friends who expostulated with him found, to their great surprise, that he had no remembrance of the incident whatever. The only thing he could recall was the fact that while he stood behind the counter of his store on the morning of his alleged fall, there suddenly appeared before him the form of Col. B., whom he knew to be dead.

A few days later he started out in the same manner and repeated his former three days' carouse. During this time the writer saw him a number of times and questioned him closely. He declared that he was not Mr. H. at all, but was Col. B., and that he was back among the boys having a good time, and did not care to be bothered with silly questions.

These periodical relapses continued for several months, during which time the writer obtained the following statement, in substance, from Col. B. concerning his experiences upon the spiritual side of life:

When he first wakened upon the spiritual plane he did not know what had happened. He could not understand that he was in another world. It took him some time to realize that he was a spirit instead of a human being. This was all the more difficult because he felt all the old appetites, passions and desires of the flesh as keenly as before the transition.

When he came to know that there is no process by which these purely physical demands can be satisfied by purely spiritual means, he began his search for some other method by which to accomplish that result. He visited saloon after saloon and there mingled as closely as possible with those who were drinking and carousing. He found that the atmosphere and magnetic conditions of the saloon and the drunkard had a satisfying effect upon his condition. The more closely he could approach the drunken man in the flesh the more directly he was able to absorb from him the stimulating effect of the liquor he had drank.

This fact led him to the study and practice of mediumistic control, in order that he might thereby be able to approach more closely the plane of physical nature and obtain more directly the desired results.

He then began his search for some one whom he could control and use as an instrument through which to gratify his insatiable craving for drink. Mr. H. proved to be that individual. He had compelled him to drink in order that through the channels of his physical organism he might absorb some of the effects of liquor and thereby obtain partial satisfaction of his craving appetite. He thus used him as long as his physical organism would stand the strain. When he had reached the limit of physical endurance he would release his victim for a time in order that he might regain his physical vigor and thus be able again to undergo the same ordeal.

Through a course of education and medical treatment both parties were made to understand the principle involved and the chain of relationship was ultimately broken. This was a case of periodical obsession. Although an extreme case of its kind, it nevertheless represents the principle and the process involved in the largest number of cases of periodical drunkenness. Such cases can be cured very readily when properly understood. The treatment, however, is not covered by the materia medica of the recognized schools of medicine.

In the largest number of instances the individual is at no time so far controlled as to become entirely unconscious of his environment or of his own acts. He is simply impelled by a power which he cannot resist.

Whenever this semi-condition obtains it is just so much more difficult for the spiritual intelligences to command the forces necessary to effect the desired result.

Unless a medium is in full sympathy with the purposes of his controls it becomes necessary for them to invent a cunning fiction of some kind which shall overcome all opposition on the part of the medium and if possible win his active co-operation. The artfulness with which this is often accomplished is suggested by the following incident which came under the writer's personal observation:

In 1892 a personal acquaintance of the writer, a Mr. W., was a successful business man of Chicago. He was a man of fine intelligence, finished education, unimpeachable moral character and a devoutly religious nature. Through the practice of asceticism and the introspective tendencies of an emotional religious devotion, he gradually fell into a negative condition of both mind and body. As a result he became extremely sensitive to his spiritual environment.

As often occurs under similar conditions, he at length began to hear a voice "from out the silence." It spoke to him, called him by name, and told him that the voice he heard was indeed the voice of the Son of God, the Lord Jesus Christ. To him who had prayed to the Master daily for many years, this seemed the most natural thing in the world. It came as if it were a direct answer to prayer. It appealed to his religious sense and satisfied his emotional desires.

But after the voice of the "Master" came other voices. Those of Moses, Aaron, Elijah, Paul, Peter, John, Thomas, Luke, Matthew, Mark, Joshua and many others of the prophets, apostles, disciples and wise men of religious history became familiar to him and conversed with him daily.

This all appealed to his sense of the "eternal fitness of things," and was therefore accepted by him with absolute sincerity and good faith as the truth and nothing but the truth. He was thus taught to believe with all his heart that he was the specially chosen instrument of God the Omnipotent for the re-establishment of His kingdom upon earth.

He therefore left his business, gave up everything else and submitted himself in perfect faith to the guidance of the "Master," as he verily believed. Day and night he spent in what to him was sacred communion with the mighty men of old, as well as with God Himself. They told him many wonderful things (concerning matters and things which were quite beyond the possibility of his verification or disproof). They unrolled to him the scroll of the heavens, as it were, named the stars and the inhabited planets and gave him the names of all the planetary rulers of the universe, with all of which he became as familiar as with the names of his nearest earthly friends and acquaintances. They opened to his fevered imagination the great book of divine mysteries, and thus kept his attention riveted and his interest transfixed.

But at length the strain began to tell upon him. He grew physically weak and nervous and debilitated. He realized that he was breaking under the continued tension. This was the moment for which his controls had patiently waited. They told him the work they had for him to do was more than his physical body could endure without stimulants. He must therefore have liquor. He must drink and drink freely in order that he might be able to endure the strain of the mighty work before him. In the name of the "Master" he was commanded to drink, but with the assurance that it was only a sacramental service required of him in order that he might do his appointed work, and thereby become worthy to receive still more important secrets from the great storehouse of universal wisdom. To him this was law. He began the use of liquors as a sacramental stimulant. For three years he did nothing but drink "to the glory of God" and listen to the wonderful teachings of the "Master" and His chosen people.

At the end of this time he was as pitiful an object as human eyes ever beheld. Bloated to almost double his normal size, skin parched and fiery red with the fever of alcoholic fire, eyes bloodshot, bleared and wild with an unnatural agony, and yet with a faith unshaken and a soul ready for the tortures of even a more terrible hell, if but the voice of the "Master" should demand it.

Was this man insane? No. He was as far from insanity as is the average physical scientist who denies the existence of another life, or who, admitting the possibility of another life, denies that the establishment of such a relation is a possibility. He was simply deceived as to the identity of the intelligences with whom he had come into personal communication, just as the scientist is deceived as to the possibility of such an experience, or as the unsophisticated farmer is deceived by the confidence man.

But why are this intelligent man and the physical scientist both deceived concerning that which lies beyond the veil of physical nature? Merely because neither is able to see behind that veil. The spiritual sense of sight would enable both to apprehend the truth and thus avoid deceptions.

But what of the eternal justice of all this? Why is an innocent individual not protected against such horrible impositions? Are there not forces for good sufficiently potent to prevent such seeming fraud and injustice?

There are perfectly consistent and scientific answers to all these questions, as well as to all others which arise out of the same subject matter. To enter upon their consideration here, however, would take us far out of the line of this specific volume and only tend to obscure its vital purpose. This is a subject, therefore, which is reserved for future consideration.

Particular attention is called to the following special points in this most interesting and pitiful case:

1. It will be observed that his controls approached him through the spiritual sense of hearing alone. They did not develop his spiritual sense of sight. Why? Because this would have enabled him to detect the fraud they desired to practice upon him. Those who are sufficiently interested in the subject to follow the suggestion will find that this is one of the most common as well as the most cunning tricks employed by mediumistic controls to deceive the medium and avoid detection.

Had Mr. W. been able to see his controls, as the writer was able to see them, he would have known at once that the voice of the "Master" was, in fact, but the voice of an ex-drunkard, who upon the physical plane of life had been a prominent and brilliant lawyer, but who had fallen a victim to the habit of drink, and had died in a delirium of drunkenness. In the voice of "St. John" he would in like manner have recognized that of an ex-physician of some note who had died from the same cause. And the various prophets, apostles, disciples and wise men would have been disclosed to him as so many other like individuals who had passed to the spirit life burdened with the weight of evil passions, appetites, desires, habits, ambitions and propensities which they had permitted to control them during their earthly lives. For this reason the spiritual eyes of their victim were kept carefully and securely closed.

2. It will also be noted that they approached him along the lines of least resistance, namely, his religious convictions

the natural law of spiritual gravity, each individual of the spiritual world inevitably finds the exact level to which his particular development corresponds.

6. Under this law of spiritual gravity the first spiritural sphere (the first beyond the physical) is the natural abiding place of those who represent the lowest degrees of spiritual development. This does not necessarily mean the lowest in point of intelligence. The distinction here suggested is of the utmost importance, and would seem to justify the following brief explanation:

Spiritual development does not consist of intellectual development alone, although intelligence is a primary and fundamental element of it. Neither does it consist of moral development alone, although morality is a basic and necessary principle involved in it. Nor does it consist in the acquisition of knowledge alone, although knowledge is an important and indispensable ingredient of it.

The fact is that it involves all these elements with something added. The spiritual development of an individual is, in truth, measured by the intelligence with which he applies his knowledge to the accomplishment of moral purposes.

An individual may, therefore, possess a wealth of knowledge which he does not intelligently apply to any purpose whatever. Or he may possess the same knowledge and intelligently apply but a mere fraction of it to the accomplishment of moral purposes. He may, in like manner, possess vast knowledge and intelligently apply the whole of it to the accomplishment of vicious and immoral purposes. In each of these cases, even though he possesses great knowledge and fine intelligence, he would nevertheless represent a low order of spiritual development, and would gravitate to the spiritual sphere corresponding thereto.

Thus, it will be seen that while intelligence, morality and knowledge are all essential elements of spiritual growth and development, it requires the three in relative combination in the life of an individual to determine his spiritual gravity.

This will explain why it is that powerful intelligences, through the degrading influence of vicious habits and evil practices, may and often do gravitate to the lowest plane of spiritual life. It will also suggest why it is that ignorance on the one hand and indolence on the other serve as "sinkers" to prevent many an otherwise qualified individual from rising to higher and more exalted planes of spiritual life and being.

We are now in position to understand and appreciate the fact above stated that the first sphere beyond that of the physical is the natural and inevitable abiding place of the ignorant, the indolent, the selfishly ambitious, the immoral, the vicious and the depraved who have passed from this life.

But this, it will be remembered, is the sphere which lies closest to earth and therefore nearest the plane of physical life. This is a most important fact, for it means that in point of locality, at least, man in the physical body is more closely in touch with the spiritual world of ignorance, indolence, immorality and vice than he is with that of wisdom, virtue and truth.

This is the great fundamental fact which mediums and spiritualists generally appear to overlook and ignore. And yet, it is the one fact of all facts which should stand as a perpetual warning to all mankind against the practice of hypnotism, mediumship and all other subjective psychic processes.

The experience of mediums themselves and the observations of every honest and intelligent student and investigator of mediumistic phenomena all bear eloquent testimony concerning the intellectual and moral status or level of the average spiritual control.

Indeed, the question has often been asked by intelligent students of psychic phenomena why it is that the "departed spirits" of American Indians constitute so large and important a percentage of mediumistic controls. Neither mediums nor spiritualists generally have thus far returned a satisfactory answer. The problem, however, is a simple one to those who understand the law of spiritual gravity above referred to.

The American Indian is essentially a "child of earth." His intelligence, habits of life and standard of morality are such that when he passes to the "Happy Hunting-Ground" the destructive nature of the mediumistic process, but they do not understand the remedy for it.

Moreover, to them the sacrifice of a few thousand mediums annually seems a small thing as compared with the supposed benefits to accrue to humanity in general therefrom. They know that thousands of missionaries of earth are annually suffering martyrdom to carry the cross of Christ into heathendom. Why, then, should anyone seriously object if they add a few more individuals to the number of candidates for canonization? This reasoning isn't bad. It is, in fact, fully up to the logical level of much of the philosophy and religion by which mankind is governed to-day all over the world. But it is nevertheless all wrong just the same.

The unreasonableness of the medium's position will be apparent if the matter is presented in a slightly different form.

Suppose, for instance, a band of Sioux Indians were living upon a near-by reservation where they were perfectly free to give expression to all the savagery and depravity of their Indian natures. And suppose they were all professional hypnotists, how many of the men and women who are to-day practicing mediumship would be willing to submit themselves to the domination and control of such a band, or of any single member of it? It is safe to say, not one. Why? Because they understand enough of human nature to know that any individual is in a much safer, healthier and altogether better and more respectable condition and state of being while in his own right mind and in the rightful possession of his natural faculties, capacities and powers than he could possibly hope to be in the hands and under the absolute mental domination and control of the wisest and best Indian on earth.

But an Indian upon the spiritual plane is only an ex-human Indian. He is identically the same intelligence, neither better nor worse, neither wiser nor more honest. Why, then, should we permit him to control us from the spiritual plane when we would only run from such a proposition on earth?

Again, suppose an adjacent room is filled with people,

some of whom are known to be of the most depraved and vicious character. The proposition comes from the room in a general way that among the number therein are several individuals who will undertake to hypnotize anyone who will submit himself to them for that purpose. How many people now living would accept the invitation without first knowing something of the character of the individual who is to do the hypnotizing? It would be strange if one sane individual in all the world could be found.

And yet this is precisely what every individual does who sits for mediumistic development. He knows absolutely nothing concerning the character, individuality, knowledge, virtue, honesty, morality or purpose of a single intelligence to whom he is submitting himself as a subject. He is offering himself, body and soul, to the veriest strangers without even so much as an introduction, an inquiry or a credential of any kind. And the most degrading part of it all is in the fact that perhaps ninety-nine out of every one hundred of those who would control him, if they could, are those with whom upon earth he would have deemed it a lasting disgrace to associate upon terms of equality, to say nothing of becoming their pliant and willing subject and tool.

It would seem almost inexplicable that this phase of mediumship, which is so apparent to every one who thinks, should have made so slight and so indifferent an impression upon the minds of those who are in position to understand something of the nature of the mediumistic process and of the subjective principle involved.

It may be accepted as an axiom of spiritual life that no spiritual intelligence, to whatever sphere he may have attained, from the first to the thirteenth, who has learned the meaning and the results of the mediumistic process, and who is honest, will ever subject any individual of earth to the blighting influence of mediumistic control.

Whoever does so thereby convicts himself of either gross ignorance, deliberate dishonesty or unconscionable immorality. For whoever understands the true character of the mediumistic process and the nature of its inevitable results knows that it is but an expression of *The Destructive Principle of Nature in Individual Life,* and that it leads ever and always to THE WAY OF DEATH.

CHAPTER XII.

MEDIUMSHIP AND "AFFINITY."

Almost from the foundation of modern Spiritualism the organization has been placed under the ban of suspicion because of its alleged or supposed advocacy of the doctrine of "Freelove."

However unjust this charge may be when broadly applied to the strict intent of the spiritualistic philosophy or to the practices of those who represent the best intelligence among progressive spiritualists, there is nevertheless a logical cause for this cloud upon the moral status of spiritualism.

In the higher science and philosophy of life it is known that there is a principle in Nature which impels every entity to seek vibratory correspondence with another like entity of opposite polarity. This principle has been known and recognized under many different names. For instance, it is known as the Law of Motion and Number, the Law of Vibration, the Law of Polarity, the Law of Correspondences, the Law of Natural Selection, the Law of Affinity, etc.

In Volume I of this Series, entitled "Harmonics of Evolution," this principle of Nature is fully developed. It is there traced from its lowest form of expression in the chemical affinities of inorganic matter through the involuntary and non-intelligent affinities of the vegetable kingdom upward through the natural selections of the animal kingdom to the Law of Individual Completion in the human kingdom. From the atom to man it runs like an unbroken thread of purest gold through all the evolutionary ascent of Nature. In the kingdom of man it finds its highest and most perfect expression in the indissoluble monogamic union of man and woman in the perfect marriage relation.

This indissoluble monogamic union of man and woman is at the farthest possible point of difference from the principle involved in "Freelove." The two, in fact, represent as diametrically opposite principles of life and conduct as it is possible for the human mind to conceive. It would therefore seem impossible that the one should ever be mistaken for the other, or that human intelligence should be led into confusion or uncertainty concerning their respective meanings. Such, however, is the case.

Among the most powerful intelligences of the first spiritual sphere who are bound to earth by the weight of their evil appetites, passions and desires, the law of affinity is known far more generally than it is upon the physical plane. Through the mouths of their innocent mediums so much of the law is declared and so much of it suppressed or misrepresented as may be necessary to serve their evil purposes. And thus the most sacred and beautiful law of life is often tortured into a cunning and cruel sophistry which translates itself to the world as moral laxity, promiscuity or "Freelove." Why? In order that the medium may be thereby furnished a reason and a motive for overruling his conscience and surrendering his physical body to the lustful demands of his controls.

The following illustration will serve to make the application more apparent:

Some years ago an acquaintance of the writer, a lady of unquestioned intelligence and moral character, became interested in the study of spiritualism. She was finally developed into an excellent trance-speaking medium. Her controls, however, encouraged her to believe that under their domination she might become a world-renowned "magnetic healer." They held up before her the two most powerful motives or incentives possible in her case—the love of humanity and the gratification of vanity. She was led to believe that in the capacity of a great "healer" she would be a blessing to humanity and at the same time be able to gratify her vanity through the lavish expenditure of unlimited wealth.

These proved sufficient motives and inspirations to command her willing and active co-operation. She advertised herself to the world of suffering humanity according to the usual methods, and soon succeeded in the establishment of a large and lucrative practice. At first both men and women were her patients, among whom a number of remarkable cures were soon reported. It shortly developed, however, that her methods of treatment were offensive to her lady patients. This became so pronounced that under the guidance of her controls she ultimately confined her practice to "gentlemen only." This was but the prelude to her complete ruin.

Step by step she was led onward and downward by her controls until her "magnetic treatments" became only another name for the indulgence of the most depraved passions of human nature. While under complete trance control she delivered learned lectures to her patients on the subject of the great law of "magnetic exchange," which her controls alleged was at the basis of all therapeutic processes.

Cunningly and with consummate skill it was developed that the patient needed and must have the magnetism of his medium, and the medium in turn needed and must have the magnetism of the patient to sustain her in her work. This was but an even exchange, and was demanded by the great law of the "equilibrium of forces." Thence it was but a natural step to develop the sophistry that the sex relation was God's divinely appointed institution by and through which to effect this "magnetic exchange."

As might be anticipated, the natural sequel of all this was an abandoned exemplification of the doctrine of "Freelove." By both precept and practice this medium, under the domination of her controls, became an exponent of that blighting and destroying fallacy. As a perfectly natural result, spiritualism in general and spiritualists in particular were compelled to share the burden of moral turpitude for which her depraved and degenerate controls alone were responsible.

Leading spiritualists defended themselves against the charge of "Freelove" upon the ground that the entire organization of spiritualism could not justly be held responsible for the sophistries or the deliberate wickedness and depravity of a few "bad mediums." Here again the innocent and defenseless medium is made the scapegoat to carry the sins of her false and vicious controls into the wilderness.

But there are all shades and degrees of control, and

therefore all shades and degrees of individual responsibility and moral accountability on the part of the medium. It will not be difficult, therefore, to understand that there are many instances wherein the medium is *particeps criminis* and should be held equally accountable with those who exert an influence upon him from the spiritual plane.

This is usually the case wherever the medium is constitutionally of a strongly preponderating physical nature. In proportion as this is true he surrenders himself to the mediumistic process, more especially to its degrading suggestions, with diminished reluctance. In like proportion he loses not only the power of self-control, but the desire to exercise it, and as a result sinks to the level of his animal nature. The check upon his physical appetites, passions and desires is relaxed. His unbridled physical nature is thus permitted to run riot, and as a result spiritualism is made to carry the burden of his moral obliquity.

The natural tendency of the mediumistic process is toward animalism. A considerable number of the more intelligent advocates of modern spiritualism already recognize this fact. Inasmuch, however, as they are unable to suggest a remedy, they have become more or less inclined to accept the fact as a "necessary evil."

The large amount of attention given by spiritualists to the idea and the theme of "affinities" is the most natural thing in the world. Love and the individual love relation of man and woman are, after all, the very basis of life and living. They are fundamental principles of Nature. They are of universal interest. The individual relation of man and woman is, in fact, the secret spring of individual action. It is the very foundation of individual happiness as well as of individual misery.

Very naturally, then, among the first results of "spirit communication" are inquiry on one side and explanations from the other concerning this most important relation and principle. Very naturally, also, those who are alone, unhappy, mismated and miserable seek for some hope of ultimate release and ultimate satisfaction. It is therefore but natural that the dissatisfied and the unhappy, as well as the weak, the foolish and the vicious, are misled by the confused reports and deliberate misrepresentations of their "spirit guides." Under all the conditions which obtain the matter of surprise is not that so many but rather that so few have been thus misled.

So long as spiritualism gives its sanction to the mediumistic process as the corner-stone of its superstructure, just so long will it be compelled to defend itself against the charge of promiscuity, moral laxity and "Freelove."

Whenever, if at all, it shall abandon the subjective process of mediumship and plant itself squarely, firmly and unequivocally upon the fundamental principle of independent, spiritual self-development, the day of its trials shall cease, but not before.

Have leading spiritualists the intelligence and the courage to take this step and the perseverance to maintain it?

CHAPTER XIII.

Mediumship and Emotionalism.

Emotionalism is an open door to mediumship.

Intense emotion produces paralysis of the will.

Paralysis of the will, from whatever cause, involves a psychically negative state or condition of the intelligence.

Whatever produces in the individual a psychically negative state or condition opens the door to mediumistic control.

The rationale of this proposition is easily understood in the light of our present knowledge of the nature and results of the mediumistic process and the operations of our emotional natures.

For the sake of clearness, however, it may be well to understand in advance what is an emotion and what are the principal elements of which it is composed.

Webster defines the term as "A state of excited feeling of any kind," or "The excited action of some inward susceptibility or feeling."

While these definitions do not give us a final analysis of the metaphysical process involved, they are nevertheless sufficiently accurate and lucid, as far as they go, to develop the central principle with which we are chiefly concerned at this time.

As indicated by the authority quoted, the fundamental basis of all emotion is "feeling." That is to say, the emotion itself is in no sense an intellectual process, although experienced by an intelligent being. We unconsciously recognize the truth of this by the manner in which we verbally express our emotions. For instance, it is perfectly natural as well as accurate to say, "I feel angry. I feel sorry. I feel happy. I feel glad. I feel a sense of fear or dread," etc.

That is to say, we *feel* all these various emotions. They translate themselves to our intelligence as feeling and not as intellection. And thus it is that the emotional nature of man is within the realm of individual feeling. Emotionalism is therefore confined entirely to the sensuous plane of individual life. It lies upon a plane entirely distinct from that of the purely intellectual or rational processes.

We feel things whether we will or not. In other words, our emotional natures act quite independently of our intelligence or reason. It is true that after an emotion has been excited or set in motion we may by the exercise of will control it, but the exciting cause is entirely involuntary. When an emotion has been once brought into existence it is then a contest between it and the intelligent will of the individual for supremacy. If the will succeeds in controlling the emotion the intelligence maintains its positive status or condition. If the emotion controls the will the intelligence thereby falls into a negative or passive state. The extent to which our emotions control us at any given time determines the measure to which they produce in us a psychically negative or passive condition.

An illustration will serve to bring the principle more clearly to view. Let us suppose, for instance, that a mother is informed of the death of her child. Instantly the emotion of deepest sorrow takes possession of her. If she but yield to its power it will overcome and completely master her. If, on the other hand, she exercise her power of will upon it, she may control its violence and ultimately master it.

In this instance it is clear that the excitant or cause of her emotion is wholly involuntary on her part. The emotion of sorrow takes possession of her without even so much as consulting her intelligence, will or desire. But after it has come into active existence within her emotional nature, it is then possible for her to apply to it the power of her will and intelligence and thus control it. On the other hand, she may fail or refuse to exercise her will upon it, in which event the emotion will completely master her.

It is a frequent occurrence in medical practice to find an individual in a state of hysteria as the result of unrestrained or uncontrolled emotions. It may be the result of sorrow, or anger, or fear, or excessive joy. It matters not what the particular emotion may be, whether of the most exalting or the most debasing character, if the individual but yield to its influence it will ultimately control every faculty, capacity and power of the soul, including the power of will.

On the other hand, we have all seen both men and women in the midst of deepest sorrow and affliction who, by the intelligent exercise of the power of will alone, have passed through the trying ordeal with a self-control which never fails to command our unlimited admiration and respect.

In the latter case the individual controls his emotions; in the former he is controlled by them.

It is now possible to understand that while an emotion is the result of an active state of feeling, it does not necessarily mean an active state of intelligence. Indeed, it is possible to understand that it may involve an inactive or passive condition of the mind or intelligence. This is suggested by the well-known fact that animals experience all the simple emotions common to mankind.

In its final analysis emotionalism is the result of sensuous activity and intellectual passivity. The intensity of the emotion measures the degree of sensuous activity. In proportion as the sensuous activity increases the intelligence becomes passive.

It is a fact of Natural Science which every individual has already demonstrated many times and may do so again as often as he so desires, that in proportion as we permit our emotions to control us we thereby surrender the power of self-control. And, on the other hand, in proportion as we control our emotions we preserve intact the power of self-control.

The specific point of first importance to be observed and held in mind is the fact that emotionalism paralyzes the will and thereby the power of self-control. Emotionalism therefore removes from the pathway of both the hypnotist and the spiritual control the one most important obstacle in the way of their success, namely, the active and intelligent power of will. By so doing it opens the way to either hypnotic or mediumistic control.

Inasmuch as the power of self-control is at the basis of individual responsibility, it is of the most serious importance to understand and appreciate the fact that in proportion as we are under the control of our emotional natures at any given time we are to that extent in a state or condition of irresponsibility.

But individual responsibility is the basis of morality. That which deprives us of our individual responsibility is therefore inimical to the moral status of both the individual and society. It follows with irresistible logic that emotionalism is not only a question of science, but that it is an ethical problem as well.

This brings us naturally to the specific subject of religious emotionalism. Almost from the time of John Wesley, the founder of what is known as Wesleyan Methodism, this has been a mooted question within the body of the Methodist Episcopal Church. With comparatively few exceptions, other religious organizations, especially those denominated Christian, seem to recognize the fact that ultra emotionalism in religious work and service is inimical to the best interests of both the individual and the church.

It is true that their reasons do not always appear to be very well or clearly defined. In many instances, in fact, the opposition to ultra religious emotionalism appears to be much more a matter of intuition than that of reason. To such, however, as view the subject from this standpoint it may be of interest and possible value to know that science fully sustains their objections to that form of emotionalism in religious service specifically covered by the term "Revivalism."

Lest there be some whose understanding of this term differs from the meaning here attached to it, the following brief account of a "religious revival" will serve to more clearly define the term as it is here employed.

Some years ago the writer attended a revival service of the character here referred to. It was conducted by one of the most eloquent and enthusiastic revivalists of the country. From the results of his work it would appear that he possessed the ability to play upon all the strings of emotional human nature at will. His stock of pathetic stories seemed inexhaustible, and the manner in which he employed them as fuel to warm up the emotional sympathies of his hearers was both dramatic and artistic as well as highly entertaining.

A "mourners' bench" was provided in the foreground, where "sinsick" souls were urged to go and kneel for prayer. Those who went were supposed to be "under conviction." These constituted the specific storm center of interest and effort. The special purpose was to carry them to the point of "conversion." This was the goal toward which all effort tended.

A choir of sympathetic voices sang and chanted pathetic hymns, and all things combined to excite religious enthusiasm and emotional fervor.

The revivalist preached, then prayed, then exhorted, then told pathetic stories. The choir sang. Then followed more preaching, praying and exhortation, with more pathetic stories and songs. This continued with an ever-increasing enthusiasm, until the atmosphere seemed to vibrate with intense emotion.

Gradually men and women began to give way to their emotions. One after another they found their way to the "mourners' bench," where they knelt to pray and mourn over their sins. In the midst of prayers and songs and exhortations and agonizing groans and ecstatic shouts they worked themselves and each other, and were worked, into a state of emotional frenzy.

When, through the effects of emotional subjectivity, an individual felt himself distinctly in touch with the spiritual plane of intelligence, he sprang to his feet and proclaimed in ecstatic shouts that he was "saved." Or, in some instances, the individual fell prostrate upon the floor in a condition of trance. In this event he was removed and cared for by those whose intelligence was still intact.

Through the process of emotional subjectivity many were thus brought into direct contact with the spiritual plane. They were thus conscious of definite spiritual experiences. For the time being they felt that they were in the atmosphere of another world, and so they were. This to them meant "salvation." All their effort had been to receive some "sign" which should be to them a token that their sins had been forgiven. This touch with the spiritual world answered to them as the "sign" for which they had labored and suffered. It therefore had but one meaning. It was the tangible and therefore unmistakable evidence of "salvation." It could mean nothing else. And thus, "many were brought to Christ," and the revival was deemed a great success.

Those who assume to assert that the experiences of these good people are but the results of imagination are grievously mistaken. Their experiences are genuine. Not only this, they are spiritual experiences. The fact that they are interpreted by the individuals as direct communications from God is not to be wondered at. This is precisely what anyone else would do under the same conditions. Many are thus "converted," and many more receive what to them is "sanctification" or the "second blessing."

Now and then during these emotional cataclysms an individual is subjected to complete trance control. Such cases, however, are usually pronounced "emotional insanity" or "religious insanity" or "religious mania," and the individual is sent to an asylum for the insane. It is a matter of astonishment to those who have followed the subject to know how few of this class ever fully recover.

Within the last few months an authentic instance is reported from a neighboring state where almost an entire community was thrown into a state of emotional religious frenzy as a result of just such a revival as above referred to. Three of the leaders were officially pronounced insane and committed to the asylum, while many others were temporarily *non compos*.

A contemporaneous report also comes from a neighboring country to the effect that an entire colony, numbering into the thousands, has very recently fallen under the spell of a peculiar religious emotionalism which has resulted in a practical dethronement of reason.

Religious revivalism of the character here referred to is but an Americanized version of the Indian Sun Dance. Those who participate in this religious dance pursue but a slightly different method of reaching the same result. They follow their own peculiar method of working themselves into a state of emotional subjectivity. While in this state many a savage Indian has come into direct and conscious touch with the great braves of the tribe who have gone to the "Happy Hunting Ground." To such it is a spiritual reunion. It means to them all that the religious revival means to those who participate in it.

The dance of the Dervishes is but the same thing in a still more primitive and barbaric form. This dance only illustrates their own peculiar method of reaching the same state of emotional subjectivity.

It was the writer's privilege recently to spend a week in the company of a prominent Methodist revivalist of the East, who is well-known from one end of the country to the other as a man who possesses "the power" to an unusual degree. During the course of the acquaintance, in response to a line of inquiry, he stated that he seldom made any definite or special preparation for his meetings. He had found that he seemed to do better work when he trusted entirely to "the inspiration of the moment." It was his custom to enter upon a revival meeting with just one central purpose, and that was to "Work 'em up, work 'em up, and keep right on working 'em up," until he got them to "climbing over each other to get to the mourners' bench."

With much enjoyable enthusiasm he recounted an instance wherein he succeeded in rousing his hearers to such a pitch of emotional enthusiasm that as many as twenty or more fell in convulsions during a single service and had to be removed from the room. With the light of a splendid enthusiasm burning in his eyes, as he recalled the incident, and his face aglow with the memory of it, he washed his hands in imaginary water and repeated over and over: "My, but it was fun!"

Upon being asked what was the most difficult problem with which he had to deal in his religious work, he replied, with a twinkle of humor, "To make 'em stick." He afterward explained the meaning of this quaint phrase by stating that soon after the close of each revival season even the most ardent religious enthusiasts began to grow cold and indifferent, and within a few weeks were in the same lethargic state of religious coma as before. When the revival season came on again and he returned to them, he found it necessary to begin all over again and "work 'em up" from the beginning.

It seemed a marvelous and inexplicable thing to him that he could not "make 'em stick." Many of them had even complained to him that they had never been able to feel the "power" except in the midst of the revival services. From the hour the meeting closed they could no longer feel the wonderful "thrill" of the "Divine Presence." It was to them just as if God had left when the minister departed.

To one who is able at will to view a revival service from the spiritual plane as well as from the physical, these perplexing questions are all fully and rationally answered.

There are within the first spiritual sphere vast multitudes of spiritual intelligences who actively participate from the spiritual plane in these revival services. Many of these are religious fanatics who have carried their religious enthusiasm with them into the spiritual life. After the natural period of adjustment to the new condition of things they take up the lines of religious work there with the same enthusiasm as here. They find a character of sensuous satisfaction in the magnetic conditions which result from these revival services. From the spiritual plane they supplement the work of the minister as far as possible. Whenever and wherever they find it possible to do so they bring to those who are upon the earth plane definite psychical experiences. It is these and such as these who furnish the "power" which is so distinctly felt by many of the most emotional workers from the physical plane.

Then again, in addition to these religious devotees upon the spiritual plane there are also vast multitudes of "earth-bound" spirits who find a wholly different and much less worthy character of satisfaction in these revival meetings. Through the negative condition of intense emotionalism these often find it possible to ride into the consciousness of the sinner "under conviction," as it were, and take complete control of all his intelligent faculties, capacities and powers. In such instances the unfortunate individual is generally pronounced insane and sent to an insane asylum, from which statistics show that comparatively few escape.

When the meeting closes and the revivalist goes to another field of labor his spiritual helpers accompany him. And thus it is that their influence is no longer felt by those who are left behind. This is why it is that to many an earnest soul it appears that God leaves when the revivalist goes away. This is why it is that the revivalist finds it impossible to "make 'em stick." This is the solution of the mystery of "backsliding." This is the reason it becomes necessary to "work 'em up" each time from the beginning. This also explains why it is that many a troubled soul is unable to feel the "thrill" of the "Divine Presence" except when the revival is on. To feel good is one thing. To be good or do good is quite another.

It not infrequently occurs that those upon the earth plane who have been most successful in reaching a state of emotional subjectivity are left unprotected upon the spiritual plane when the revivalist and his helpers pass to other fields of labor. In such instances it almost invariably follows that evil spirits take the place of the helpers and gradually obtain complete control of the individual. The result is some form of insanity or religious mania, often ending in murder, suicide, or a formal commitment to an insane asylum.

The magnetic conditions which accompany the religious revival closely resemble those of the spiritualistic seance. They are such as to enable the spiritual workers to approach very closely the plane of physical nature and exert their influence with more or less directness upon those in the physical body. There is, however, one essential difference. In the spiritual seance those upon the physical plane understand with some degree of accuracy the specific purpose of the meeting. They therefore more or less intelligently supplement the spiritual intelligences in their efforts to develop mediumistic control.

In the religious revival this is not true to the same extent. Few, if any, of the members of the church know that the "power" they feel and recognize is the result of spiritual intelligences working upon them by and through the magnetic conditions which surround them. Most, if not all of them, attribute the "power" to nothing else than God himself. Few, if any of them, understand that intense emotionalism produces paralysis of the will and thereby a psychically negative condition. They work upon each other's emotional natures without definite purpose. They only know that this, in course of time and persistent effort, will produce a condition of emotional ecstasy which, during the period of its transcendency, puts them in touch with the spiritual world. To them this spiritual touch is the "Divine Presence." This is the religion of feeling.

A few years ago the writer attended a series of revival services under the direction of the Rev. Dr. D., at that time a prominent and successful revivalist. One evening in the midst of the service the writer very unexpectedly found himself the central object of a most earnest exhortation by the minister ably supplemented by a number of his leading co-workers. After an hour of most interesting and pleasant discussion the Rev. Dr. closed the incident with an invitation to call upon him the following afternoon at his study to listen to the narration of what he evidently regarded as a most unusual and wonderful personal experience. The invitation was cordially accepted and at the appointed hour the writer found himself closeted with the good man alone in his study.

In the course of the talk which followed the minister narrated the following experience which he evidently hoped and expected would carry conviction with it and win for him a new convert to the Faith.

It was his custom before each regular service to spend half an hour alone in his study in silent prayer. It had recently come to be that whenever he thus knelt in prayer the room would soon be filled with "angels" who gathered about him in solemn service and gave him their benediction. Following this, when he entered the pulpit and began to preach, he had come to be fully conscious of the personal presence of Christ, who always stood just back of him and slightly to his right.

In reply to questions concerning these experiences he stated that on one or two occasions he had been able to see the "angels" very distinctly as they gathered about him and at times could even hear their words. But he had never looked into their faces for the reason that the experience was to him too sacred to admit of any exhibition of curiosity on his part. He had been able to note the fact, however, that, so far as he had observed, they appeared to be much like men and women upon the physical plane, except that they were always in white robes and seemed to bring with them a luminous atmosphere.

During his sermons and exhortations, while fully conscious of the presence of Christ, he had never seen him distinctly for the reason that the "Master" always stood somewhat back of him. He had, however, on a number of occasions seen the folds of his flowing white robe and had distinctly felt the touch of his hand upon his shoulder. On a number of occasions he had also found himself preaching upon a topic wholly foreign to his intentions and repeating words which were impressed upon him by the "Master," as if they were his own.

When the subject had been carried to a point where it seemed possible and expedient to do so, the writer confessed that he too had seen the "angels" even during the course of their then conversation, and that during the services of the preceding evening he had distinctly seen the spiritual individual who stood back of him in the pulpit, and that from his own personal observation he was fully convinced that the white-robed individuals who came to him in prayer were only ex-human beings, some of whom the minister had known upon the earth plane in other days as relatives and friends.

The writer further stated that the individual whom the Rev. Dr. had supposed to be Christ was none other than an ex-human minister of the Gospel whom the Dr. had at one time known upon the physical plane. It was then suggested that he might be able to verify these statements by a personal inspection, if he cared to do so, and deemed it a matter of sufficient importance to command his attention.

It would seem that this suggestion had left its impression, for the following afternoon when the writer again called upon him by appointment he found the good Dr. deeply troubled. He had looked into the faces of his "angel" friends and had found that one of them was his own father, another his brother, and that among the number were other relatives and former friends whom he had known during their sojourn upon earth. He had also turned from his pulpit and suddenly looked into the face of the "Master" and had found to his amazement that he too was only an ex-human friend of other years.

This particular incident has its value in that it illustrates, among other things, the following specific points of interest:

1. Every religious devotee who has come into conscious touch with the world of spiritual nature, regardless of sect, creed or denomination, naturally endeavors to fit his psychic experiences to his then existing religious beliefs and convictions.

2. His preconceived religious ideas, therefore, unwittingly color all his psychic experiences with the peculiar tinge of his particular religious faith.

3. To the extent that this is true he is not in position to accurately understand or interpret the meaning of his religious experiences.

4. It is a fact well known to Natural Science that there are psychics in various degrees of development among all the different religious organizations.

5. The earnest and enthusiastic revivalist, through the process of emotional subjectivity, not infrequently comes into conscious touch with the spiritual plane.

6. Unless his spiritual experiences are of an unusually vivid and definite character he is able without difficulty to so interpret them as to conform with his preconceived ideas and religious beliefs.

An interesting and fruitful study of emotionalism is also to be found in the negro race. It is a fact known to science and fully recognized by the world in general, that among all the different races the negro represents the most emotional type of human nature. His life, habits, customs and character all combine to express emotional feeling. He lives almost entirely upon the plane of the senses. Naturally, therefore, the negro in his native element is the intellectual infant of humanity.

Nothing, perhaps, more peculiarly illustrates these predominating characteristics of the race than the old fashioned negro revival. They throw themselves into these services with an emotional abandon which carries everything before it. They appear to fairly revel in the sensuous pleasure it affords them. Their religion is to them very largely a matter of feeling. Even the music which best expresses their character and state of being is a sort of religious "rag-time," having a rhythm and a swing which act as a powerful emotional excitant.

It is a matter of interest in this connection to note the characteristic difference between the negro and the American Indian. The ruling characteristic of the negro is emotionalism. He has never tried to control it. It is everywhere and at all times at the very surface of his nature and ready to demand expression. For this reason the negro finds it not only easy but perfectly natural to fall into a state of emotional subjectivity. An hour of religious emotionalism is sufficient to carry an entire negro camp meeting to the verge of hysteria, if not to a state of complete trance.

The ruling characteristic of the American Indian, on the other hand, is his indomitable will. He has cultivated this with even greater care and persistence than the negro has cultivated emotionalism. His own emotional nature is under the absolute control of his will. As might be expected, he finds it much more difficult to produce in himself the condition of subjectivity necessary to reach the plane of psychic experiences. His religious dance is a complete verification of this fact. He usually prepares for it with fasting and solitude. He proceeds to the task deliberately and methodically. He begins with slow and measured tread and for hours, often days, without ceasing goes on and on with an ever ascending scale of enthusiasm until at last physical nature is completely exhausted and he finds himself in touch with the spiritual plane, whereupon he falls into a state of trance. Then it is that he communes with the spirit braves of his tribe.

In perfect harmony with their characteristic natures it is found that the negro race is the most susceptible to the hypnotic process while the Indian is among the least so.

With perfect consistency it is also found that the animal which has not yet risen to the plane of intellectuality is nevertheless an intensely emotional being. He lives entirely upon the plane of the senses. In his emotional nature he approaches very closely the level of human nature. He experiences with intensity the emotions of jealousy, affection, anger, fear, joy, and sorrow, and he gives instant and unrestrained expression to his emotional nature only because he does not possess the power of reason.

There is never a time when men and women so much resemble the animal as when they give unrestrained expression to ultra emotionalism. Why? Because then it is that they manifest the least reason and the most feeling. In proportion as an individual lives upon the plane of his sensuous nature he gives expression to his animal nature. In proportion as he lives upon the plane of his intelligence he manifests his distinctively human nature.

It is therefore a fact of Nature that unrestrained emotionalism, like mediumship and hypnotism—and for the same reason—tends toward animalism. This is a scientific fact from which there is no escape.

Nota bene.

CHAPTER XIV.

MEDIUMS AND THEIR MOTIVES.

From the standpoint of the actor the moral quality of every act of an intelligent individual must be measured by the motive which prompts it.

Measuring the subject of mediumship from the standpoint of the medium, therefore, it is only fair that each individual medium should be given credit for whatever worthy motives inspire him in his mediumship and charged with only those which are manifestly unworthy.

Measured by their motives and intentions alone mediums naturally divide themselves into three distinct and separate classes, as follows:

1. Those whose motives and intentions are good.
2. Those whose motives and intentions are indifferent.
3. Those whose motives and intentions are bad.

Let it be remembered that the actual results accomplished do not necessarily correspond with the motives and intentions of the medium in any case. Results, therefore, cannot be taken as an index of the motives which inspire them. It is especially necessary to bear this in mind so that the ethics of the subject may not be lost sight of.

Among those mediums whose motives and intentions are admittedly good, are:

1. The religious medium.
2. The melancholy medium.
3. The student medium.
4. The healing medium.

The religious medium, like the religious minister, verily believes that he is divinely called to do an important work among men. His mission is to preach and teach the gospel of truth as he sees it and understands it. His confidence in the integrity and the wisdom of his spiritual guides and controls is as implicit as that of the minister in his God, and, as a general rule, far more definite and intelligent.

If he receives money for his ministrations he does no more

than the teachers of other religions. Even the most humble and devout minister of Christ, the Master whose personal example would condemn such a practice, preaches and teaches for money. He does this upon the theory that "The laborer is worthy of his hire." He must live. He cannot devote his life to preaching the gospel, even the gospel of Christ, if he must in other ways earn the money necessary to provide for his physical necessities.

The same is literally true with the medium, but with added emphasis. His mediumship absorbs his time. It saps his physical and mental vitality. It unfits him in every way for earning by other methods the means which his physical necessities demand. The fact, therefore, that he receives a money consideration for the labor he bestows upon the world must not be counted against him any more than it is counted against the Christian minister. The two stand upon precisely the same ethical platform in this regard. If it is admissible under any conditions or circumstances whatever to receive material dollars in return for spiritual dogmas and doctrines, then it is as proper for the medium to do so, as it is for the minister.

The melancholy medium has but one motive. He desires to be reunited with the loved ones who have descended ahead of him into the valley of the shadow and have passed from his physical vision. The impelling motive is love, the highest and noblest activity of the soul. It is the one motive of all motives which commends itself to every intelligent man and woman. Inspired by the hope of bridging the dark gulf which separates the average mortal from the absent loved ones, many an honest man and woman have submitted to the mediumistic process with no thought of its possible danger or harmfulness or immorality.

The student medium is in search of knowledge. He devotes himself to the practice of mediumship in order that he may acquire it. There is not so much of the altruistic in his motives and intentions as there is in those of the religious medium. But we all recognize the value of knowledge, even though the purpose which inspires the search for it may be more or less tinged with selfishness.

The student medium honestly believes that he is pursuing a legitimate and proper method of acquiring the knowledge he most desires. He believes that he is justly entitled to whatever he can thus obtain. He therefore stands upon the ethical platform with the physical scientist who delves into the mysteries of nature solely for the satisfaction it affords him individually. His position, however, is perhaps more nearly identical with that of the metaphysical student. Both of these are in search of spiritual truth. Each pursues his own particular method of obtaining it, but the object sought is the same, knowledge. No one thinks of condemning the metaphysical student, because it is known that he is in search of knowledge. But so is the student medium. If we are to judge men solely by their motives and intentions why should we condemn the one and not the other? This is a question for the metaphysician.

The healing medium occupies a somewhat different position. He is led by his controls to believe that he possesses great healing powers which he is under obligation to devote to the interests of humanity. By a sort of compact between him and his controls he surrenders himself as an instrument in their hands for healing purposes in return for the services they render him in a financial way. It is a species of bargain and sale which is recognized by most men and women as entirely legitimate. From the standpoint of motive alone, quite aside from the question of the principle and the process involved, we are therefore not in position to condemn the healing medium any more than we are the Christian Scientist or the metaphysical healer.

It must not be forgotten, however, that in all these instances we are always compelled to consider the results to both the individual and society. Therefore, in the final analysis of mediumship and the mediumistic process we cannot stop with the motives and intentions of the medium any more than we can with those of the anarchist who assassinates the president of a great nation under the mistaken conviction that he is thereby rendering a great and valuable service to society. The final tribunal to which all these questions must be submitted for ethical judgment must take into account not only the motives and intentions of the individual, but his rights, duties and obligations as well, both to himself and to society of which he is an integral part.

Among those mediums whose motives and intentions are neither good nor bad, but more properly designated as indifferent, the following classes are most conspicuous:

1. The curiosity seeker.
2. The entertainer.

There are a good many mediums who become such solely because of their desire to satisfy their sense of curiosity concerning mediumistic phenomena. After this has been satisfied their interest in the subject ceases. They have in their minds neither good nor evil, and think little or nothing of the results to either themselves or others.

There are many others who submit themselves to the mediumistic process solely for the pleasure it affords their friends. By this method they become successful entertainers and thereby gratify a certain sense of vanity which is not at all uncommon among both men and women. The motive, therefore, is more or less complex in its essential nature, but when analyzed carefully, defines itself as neither essentially good nor essentially bad.

Since there is little, if anything, to condemn and practically nothing to commend in the motives of these two classes of mediums, it seems both consistent and proper to classify them among those whose motives and intentions are indifferent.

Those mediums whose motives and intentions are unquestionably bad naturally group themselves as follows:

1. The business medium.
2. The ambitious medium.
3. The vicious medium.
4. The fakir medium.

In the first and fourth classes here mentioned the impelling motive is money, in the second power and popularity, and in the third self-gratification and conquest. The first and fourth, therefore, stand for the gratification of greed, the second for the gratification of vanity, and the third for the gratification of all the baser appetites, evil passions and criminal desires of degenerate human nature.

Those who are at all familiar with the subject will be able to identify among their mediumistic acquaintances one or more representatives of these various classes.

The business medium flourishes in great abundance in all the large cities of the country. His advertisements are found in all the leading metropolitan journals. They are,. for the most part, as false as it is possible to frame falsehoods in human language. The following extracts taken at random from one of the leading Chicago journals will give some slight impression of the depths of moral turpitude to which the average professional business medium is ready to descend in his greed for money.

"Hundreds turned away! Doubters awe-stricken! Your life an open book! Wonderful gifts! Extraordinary clairvoyant powers combined with superior knowledge of occult forces. Tells you names of your friends and enemies, who is true and who is false. Who you are, your name, age, occupation, where you live, the number of your house, and street you live on. Settles lovers' quarrels, reunites the separated. Causes a speedy and happy marriage with the one of your choice. The earth reveals to him her hidden treasures. He locates mines, removes evil influences, locates buried treasures, settles old estates that time has placed beyond the lawyers' shrewdness, makes you successful in business, restores lost affections, locates lost friends. Pretenders copy his advertisements! Beware of FRAUDS! Consult ONLY THE BEST! $5 READINGS FOR $1!!"

The great marvel of it all lies in the fact that such unmasked and manifest perfidy should be able to find sufficient credulity among the average human intelligence to pay the advertiser for his time, trouble and advertising.

Every man and woman with sufficient intelligence to seek shelter when it rains knows that if any one of these wonder-workers were able to discover "the hidden treasures of earth," or could successfully "locate mines," he would be selling $1 shares of mining stock at $5 each, instead of $5 readings at $1 each. It would require the location of but just one good gold, silver, copper, iron, or even coal mine to make a multi-millionaire of any one of these exalted seers and seeresses to whom God has turned over the keys which unlock the doors to the most profound secrets of Nature.

The falsehood is so glaringly patent it would seem utterly impossible that anyone should fail to see it and note it and profit by it. And yet, there are supposedly intelligent men and women in all the varied walks and stations of life whose patronage makes it possible for such charlatans to thrive.

Many of these advertisers are mediums in fact. That is to say, they have been regularly "developed" as such, and might be able to demonstrate some degree of reliability within certain fixed limitations. But they are not satisfied with their limitations. The great speculative world that gambles in spiritualistic stocks demands something more occult and more wonderful than they are able to furnish. In other words, there is not sufficient merit in their mediumship to command the money they so much covet. They, therefore, supply the deficiency by falsehood and fraudulent promises in their advertisements, never intending to fulfill them.

It is safe to say that there is not a professional business medium before the public today who advertises himself strictly within the lines of truth when stating his claims to the world.

The fakir medium differs from the ordinary business medium only in the fact that he does not stop at simply advertising more than he can perform. He resorts to deliberate legerdemain. What he is unable to accomplish honestly and legitimately he attempts to cover by sleight-of-hand. By a species of artifice, jugglery and fraudulent pretense he attempts, at the risk of exposure, to satisfy his patrons with deception and purchase their confidence with trickery. It is astonishing how many of these succeed and how well they manage to avoid detection.

This phase of the subject, it would appear, now and then makes its impress upon the minds of spiritualists themselves, as shown by the following quotation from the current issue of a leading spiritualistic journal. The author says:

"Is it the law of the survival of the fittest, or is it merely the fault of spiritualism that only the most impudent quacks and impostors of all kinds should flourish and fatten under its banner?

"Having for many years traveled in England, France, Germany,

Australia, New Zealand, and America, and throughout the best part of twenty years taken an intelligent interest in spiritualism and its adherents, the above query is the result."

There are many other honest spiritualists who have made the same inquiry.

The ambitious medium is the "politician" of his cult. He is forever "playing for place." It is not so much money as popularity, or even notoriety he seeks. He employs his mediumistic arts, "gifts" and "powers" to attract the attention and command the homage of the world to him as a sort of "superior being" or "special creation." This flatters him and satisfies his vanity. The motive is almost as base as that which inspires the business medium and the fakir.

The vicious medium belongs to a class by himself. His central purpose is to gratify as far as possible the baser appetites, evil passions and criminal desires of a perverse and degenerate nature. He lives entirely upon the plane of the senses. His mediumship represents a voluntary alliance between degenerate spiritual intelligences on the one side and a depraved human intelligence on the other. The purpose is mutual sensuous gratification.

It is a well known fact of Natural Science that between the licentious of earth and the licentious of the spiritual world the sex appetites, passions and desires constitute a powerful magnetic bond. It is known that through the mediumistic process these libidinous appetites, passions and desires may be gratified, to a considerable extent. It is also known that in many instances this abnormal and illegitimate relation between medium and control is substituted for the normal relation upon the plane of physical nature.

The fact that prostitution of this lascivious character is a possibility will come to many an honest soul with a shock of horror and profound disgust. The extent to which it is actually practiced would seem to those who are not acquainted with the facts to be an utter impossibility.

For instance: One of the best known and most prominent mediums of the United States, whose mediumistic work has favorably impressed many of those who have known her, has confessed to her friends that she sustains such a relation to a spiritual lover who is her chief control, and that she has done so for many years.

This subject is one upon which the world in general needs exact and definite information. The time is coming when this will be demanded. At the present time, however, it would seem impossible to so state the simplest facts without offending those who most need to understand the principle and the process upon which such a relation depends.

This is the legitimate field of the medical profession. Thus far it has been ignored by that profession. It cannot be longer. In the name of humanity the demand is made. To humanity the answer must be given.

CHAPTER XV.

MEDIUMSHIP AND INSANITY.

In one of the largest western institutions for the insane in the United States, six hundred diagnoses have been made showing with absolute certainty that in fifty-eight per cent of the cases thus examined the sole immediate cause of insanity was mediumistic subjection. That is to say, these diagnoses showed that fifty-eight per cent of those examined were at the time under the domination and control of outside, spiritual intelligences.

It is a well known fact that climatic conditions have something to do in determining the percentage of insanity to population. Local conditions, therefore, must be taken into account in arriving at the exact figures for any larger or different territory than that covered by the institution in which these examinations were made.

Making ample allowance for local variations, however, it is reasonably certain that more than fifty per cent of all the insanity of the United States is the direct result of the mediumistic process. There is every reason to believe that the same percentage will hold good for all European countries.

It is due to spiritualists and the friends of spiritualism in general, however, to carefully explain that by no means all of this insanity is due to the specific work of those who are known to the world as "mediums." In fact, a very considerable percentage of it is found to exist among men and women who have never sat for mediumistic development and who know practically nothing of the mediumistic process or of the philosophy of modern spiritualism.

Many of these have unwittingly fallen into a negative condition of both mind and body as a result of a wide variety of causes which are in no wise due to what is popularly known as "mediumship."

The point of specific importance, however, to be noted in this connection is the fact that whether the world or the individual himself knows it or not, his insanity is the result of the same process by and through which mediumship is developed, namely, the subjective, psychic process which forms the subject matter of this volume.

There are many different methods of developing the negative state or condition necessary to place a man or woman subjectively in touch with the world of spiritual intelligence, without regularly sitting for mediumistic development. When this state or condition is once developed, by any of the different methods known to science, it exposes the individual to mediumistic control just the same as if he had acquired it through the regular methods known and practiced by mediums and spiritualists. The only difference lies in the simple fact that the acknowledged medium goes about it intelligently and purposefully, while those who are ignorant of spiritualistic methods stumble into the condition without knowing it or intending to do so. These latter are pronounced "insane" and promptly locked up in the various insane asylums throughout the country while the regular medium is permitted to run at large merely because he calls himself a "medium." This "distinction without a difference" has lodged many a man and woman in the insane asylum, who is no more "insane" than the average medium.

There are various different and specific causes which lead men and women into the negative state or condition which opens the door to mediumistic control. Among the most important are the following:

1. Heredity and prenatal conditions.
2. Diet.
3. Solitude.
4. Darkness.
5. Introspection.
6. Emotionalism.
7. Self-indulgence.
8. Fasting.

Cases almost without number might be cited showing the effects of heredity and prenatal conditions upon children. The following, for which the writer can personally vouch, will be sufficient to illustrate the principle involved:

Mrs. W. was, in her essential nature, of the negative type of physical organism and intelligence. In addition to this natural condition, however, she became interested in the subject of spiritualism and was ultimately developed as a medium. After this, for some time, she devoted the larger part of her time and energies to her mediumistic work. During the entire year immediately preceding the birth of her daughter she was the principal medium for a group of scientific investigators of psychic phenomena. The daughter was born under these conditions.

From the time she was old enough to express herself this child was what is often termed a "natural psychic." She saw clairvoyantly and heard clairaudiently without the necessity for any effort on her part. Until she was six years old she spent the greater portion of her waking hours playing with her "invisible" playmates from the spiritual world. At the age of seven she was regularly developed as a trance medium, and so far as the writer knows has never recovered from that condition.

This instance clearly shows the effects of heredity as well as those of prenatal conditions upon the development of children.

Those who reach the negative condition of mediumship through the process of dietetics alone represent a very considerable number of those who afterwards become known either as mediums or as insane. Diet has its most direct and positive effects upon the purely physical organism of the individual. It is a fact of science, well known to most physicians, and especially to those who are known to the world as dietetists, that foods as well as medicines naturally divide themselves into two great general classes which are known and designated as "positive" and "negative."

Positive foods and medicines have the general effect of producing positive magnetic conditions within the physical organism. Negative foods, on the other hand, as well as negative medicines, produce the opposite or negative condition of the physical organism.

Generally speaking, a strictly vegetable diet of any kind

is, comparatively, a magnetically negative diet. While this is a scientific fact, it is also true that vegetables differ very widely in the degree of their positive and negative properties, qualities and effects.

For instance: As a general proposition, all vegetables which develop under the soil (such as the potato, the turnip, the radish, the carrot and the beet) are the most positive (or least negative) vegetable foods known. Those which grow upon endogenous plants, generally speaking, are second in order. Those which grow upon exogenous trees, with some exceptions, are third in order, while those which grow on vines take rank among the most negative foods. There are exceptions among all these various classes.

A strictly meat diet is the most positive magnetic diet known. While the meats of different animals possess radically different degrees of positive force and magnetic energy, it is nevertheless true that, generaly speaking, meats of all kinds are more positive than vegetables. The meats of wild animals are, for the most part, more positive than those of domestic animals. Meats of carnivorous animals are more positive than the meats of herbivorous animals. The meats of animals that live under ground are more positive than the meats of animals that live above ground. Meats of all animals that live upon the surface of the earth are more positive than those of birds that fly above the earth.

With the simple principle of food values in mind it will not be difficult to understand that diet is a most important factor in the development of the positive or negative magnetic condition of the physical organism. In like measure it has its effects upon the relation of the individual to his spiritual environment.

It often occurs that a man or woman is physically positive and mentally negative at the same time. In all such instances a negative diet alone would be sufficient to open wide the door to mediumistic control. It is not necessary for such an individual to sit in a circle for mediumistic development. All he needs is to live for a time on a negative vegetable diet. Spiritual intelligences will do the rest.

Solitude has the effect of producing a mentally negative condition. This is because of the natural tendency to mental abstraction which follows from solitude. Man upon the physical plane is eminently a social being. If deprived of the society of his kind his mind involuntarily seeks companionship in the realms of thought. This habit of contemplation without definite purpose produces a psychically negative condition. The developed medium is able to demonstrate the truth of this proposition at any time. The presence of his friends occupies his mind upon the plane of his physical environment and he accordingly finds it difficult to surrender himself to the mediumistic process in their presence. But a few moments of solitude produces the negative condition necessary and he falls into subjection without effort.

Darkness is a negative physical condition. It has upon man, however, a double negative effect. It produces natural relaxation of the physical organism and at the same time an introspective condition of the mind. Both of these are negative in effect. Darkness, therefore, is most favorable to mediumistic control. This has been fully demonstrated by mediums themselves very often. This is the secret of the dark circle. It is the principle at the foundation of the dark cabinet and the dark materializing seance.

Introspection means "looking within," or, "inspection of the within." As a metaphysical proposition it is a condition of consciousness in which the objective faculties of the mind are inactive. The mind takes no note or account of the things that are at the time occurring upon the physical plane. It is concerned with those things only which lie within the conscious soul of the individual himself. It is occupied with the internal plane of conscious intelligence. In this condition the physical body is always in a negative or passive state. In this condition the active, dominating intelligence from without may ride into the very center of individual consciousness and, unless opposed, may assume control of all the faculties, capacities and powers of the soul.

Introspection is therefore conducive to mediumistic subjection.

Emotionalism and Self-Indulgence have been sufficiently considered in previous chapters and therefore do not require further exposition in this connection.

.Fasting is, primarily, a purely physical process, although it has a strong reflex action upon the mind also. When the stomach is supplied with food all the organs of the physical body related to the processes of digestion, distribution, assimilation and secretion are in a state of involuntary activity. The physical organism is then busy with the renovating and renewing processes. When, through the process of fasting, all the nutriment supplied to the system has been disposed of, the physical organism has nothing more to do in its own behalf but wait for more food. During this period of waiting the internal organism of the physical body is in a negative or passive condition. It then becomes a magnet which strongly attracts those upon the spiritual plane, and (unless the mind is properly schooled and on guard) opens the door to mediumistic control.

No more powerful sermon could be preached to the great world of intelligent humanity than that which is contained in the simple but vital suggestion that something like 58 per cent of all the insanity of the country is the result of the mediumistic process. This fact alone is a commentary in itself which should convey to the mind of every intelligent man and woman throughout the land and throughout all the nations of earth, the fundamental fact that there is something radically wrong and fatally destructive in the subjective process of mediumship.

It is not the intention of this work to offer to the world a scientific classification of insanity upon the principle of primary causation. Such an effort could not be deemed other than grossly presumptuous. Medical science has been, for many years, actively engaged in this great work in the cause of humanity. The progress made would seem to justify the hope that its ultimate and successful completion will be accomplished within the comparatively near future. Up to the present time, however, there is a wide and prolific field of insanity which the medical fraternity find it necessary to classify under the general heading of "Causes Unknown."

In this great class, generally speaking, will be found at the present time, for the most part, the various forms of Hysterical Insanity, Religious Insanity, Religious Mania, Emotional Insanity, and so-called "Delusional Insanity" of all kinds and degrees. These, however, might all be included in one general class and properly designated as "Mediumistic Insanity" or "Subjective Insanity."

There is material here for an entire volume upon this subject alone. The importance of the theme will be suggested when it is known that, with very few exceptions, all these various forms of insanity last above mentioned are due to the interposition of outside, spiritual intelligences. They, therefore, only represent certain specific and definite degrees of mediumistic subjection.

With these simple and easily demonstrable facts of nature admitted and intelligently understood, the medical profession has the key in its own possession by which it may open the door to this seeming mystery and lay bare to medical science and to the world *The Destructive Principle of Nature in Individual Life*, which is at the foundation of *THE GREAT PSYCHOLOGICAL CRIME*.

Part III

Retributive Justice

CHAPTER I.

THE GENESIS OF "HELL."

("*The Wages of Sin Is Death.*")

As far as we are able to trace the authentic history of mankind human intelligence has intuitively sensed a great fundamental law of Equity, Justice and Right which runs throughout all the manifestations of Nature.

The application of this great law to the ethics of human life constitutes the basis of all religious and philosophic systems of the past and likewise of the present.

The limitations of human intelligence in its efforts to grasp and comprehend this law in its entirety and apply it as a rule and guide of conduct in the daily lives of men, are responsible for all the sectarianism of both religion and philosophy, as well as of all the variations in governmental systems and policies throughout all the nations of earth.

Although the law itself is a unit in essence, it manifests itself to human intelligence in its twofold aspect as one of the most stupendous and comprehensive dualities of all Nature, the duality of Construction and Destruction.

In its constructive aspect we recognize it as the Law of

Compensation, or Compensatory Justice, in acordance with the Harmonics of Evolution.

In its destructive aspect we recognize it as the Law of Retribution, or Retributive Justice, in accordance with the Discords of Devolution.

To the constructive side of this great Law of Justice is referable all that there is of individual growth, development, progress, strength, health, energy, life, love and happiness, both here and hereafter. This is the domain of Nature's compensatory rewards to individual intelligence for obedience to Nature's Evolutionary Principle.

The ultimate goal of individual achievement under and in accordance with the operation of Nature's Constructive Principle is, so far as science knows, Individual Immortality and perfect Happiness, in "the fulfilling of the law." This is the achievement which opens to the soul the "Gates of Paradise." And this is THE WAY OF LIFE.

To the destructive side of this same great Law of Justice is referable all that there is of individual atrophy, weakness, enervation, sickness, suffering, sorrow, hate, fear, disease, dissolution, disintegration, decay, unhappiness and death.

This, indeed, is the domain of Nature's Retributive Punishments to individual intelligence for disobedience of Nature's Evolutionary Principle.

The ultimate destiny of individual intelligence under and in accordance with Nature's Destructive Principle is, so far as science knows, Spiritual Death, "The Second Death," Total Individual Extinction, and a resolution of the individual Entity back into Nature's Elements from which it came.

And this is THE WAY OF DEATH and THE GENESIS OF "HELL."

CHAPTER II.

The Way of Death.

Duality is expressed in every department of Nature. Human intelligence recognizes the principle everywhere. In the following expressions we endeavor to clothe it in human language:

Finite and infinite.
Time and eternity.
Beginning and ending.
Light and darkness.
Day and night.
Transparent and opaque.
White and black.
Heat and cold.
Summer and winter.
Wet and dry.
Hard and soft.
Heavy and light.
Large and small.
Fine and coarse.
Much and little.
Many and few.
Length and breadth.
Height and depth.
Up and down.
In and out.
Back and forth.
Tall and short.
Straight and crooked.
Motion and inertia.
Expansion and contraction.
Mind and matter.
Sound and silence.
Harmony and discord.
Labor and rest.
Wealth and poverty.

Health and sickness.
Strength and weakness.
Male and female.
Man and woman.
Waking and sleeping.
Active and passive.
Positive and negative.
Sweet and bitter.
Joy and sorrow.
Pleasure and pain.
Hope and despair.
Faith and distrust.
Belief and skepticism.
Good and evil.
Right and wrong.
Truth and falsehood.
Sincerity and deceit.
Knowledge and ignorance.
Wisdom and folly.
Humility and pride.
Generosity and selfishness.
Kindness and cruelty.
Love and hate.
Receiving and giving.
Consciousness and unconsciousness.
Voluntary and involuntary.
Self-control and subjection.
Independence and dependence.
Freedom and slavery.

Responsibility and irresponsibility.

Sanity and insanity.

Evolution and involution.

Integration and disintegration.

Growth and decay.

Progress and retrogression.

Construction and destruction.

Immortality and mortality.

Life and death.

Heaven and Hell.

A study of the foregoing will disclose to the careful analyst that in whatever sphere or department of Nature the principle of duality manifests itself, it is an expression of either simple contrast or extreme opposites.

As an example, heat and cold constitute a duality which expresses a mere contrast in degrees of temperature with that of the individual. Heat merely expresses a higher degree of temperature than cold. Both, however, express temperature.

So also, the terms large and small, fine and coarse, heavy and light, express qualities of contrast only. They represent merely a difference in the degree of a single quality or property of physical Nature.

On the other hand, the terms truth and falsehood constitute a duality which represents two distinct and separate principles diametrically opposite in their essential natures. In like manner love and hate, integration and disintegration, life and death, are dual terms which express extreme opposites in Nature.

There is a principle in Nature which, in all its operations and manifestations, is creative, formative, integrating, developing, organizing and evolutionary in its nature and tendencies. It is known to science as "Nature's Constructive Principle." As such it constitutes an equal part of a most stupendous duality in Nature, the other half of which is known as "Nature's Destructive Principle."

"Construction" and "Destruction." These terms give expression to a duality of extreme opposites. They define two of the most important, extensive, conflicting and antagonistic processes of all Nature. They represent the two great fundamental and essential opposites in Nature which are known and recognized by scientific thinkers and investigators everywhere.

Nature's Destructive Principle is that half of the great

duality which is under consideration in this chapter, and may be deemed the basic principle which furnishes the text of this particular volume.

It is hoped and believed that a fair and unbiased consideration of this principle alone will establish in the mind of every honest and earnest student a clear and unmistakable line of differentiation which runs throughout all the objective manifestations of Nature. It is also believed that this principle once clearly defined and understood, will indicate more clearly and forcibly than all things else the subtle fallacies which are involved in what is known as "development" through hypnotic and mediumistic processes.

When the gigantic boulder which has been formed by and through the operation of Nature's Constructive Principle is lifted from its native bed and exposed to the summer's heat, the winter's cold, the dry winds and the beating rain, its outer surface soon begins to disintegrate and crumble away. In this we observe the first effects of Nature's Destructive Principle in operation.

The Electro-Magnetic Life Element of the great giant is being withdrawn and death is setting his seal where life has once reigned supreme.

The summers and the winters come and go. The summer sun continues to burn and the winter cold to bite. The wind's dry breath continues to blow and the rains to beat. Slowly but surely the work of desolation and destruction goes on. The giant boulder shrinks and shrivels away beneath the continued play of Nature's hostile forces until at last nothing remains of its once gigantic form. Where it once rested nothing but common earth remains. The life element which once sustained it has been dissipated and its existence as an individual entity is destroyed. Its original particles, both physical and spiritual, are scattered to the ends of the earth. Its vital principle being withdrawn, under the operation of Nature's Destructive Principle the once great boulder as an individual entity has been disorganized, disintegrated, scattered and resolved back into Nature's elements from which it came, and the work of destruction is completed.

Ascending one round higher in the scale of Nature into the realm of the vegetable kingdom we find the same principle in operation.

The splendid oak which, under the power of Nature's Constructive Principle, operating through the Electro-Magnetic Life Element of mineral Nature and the Vito-Chemical Life Element of vegetable Nature, has grown from the tiny acorn to its full and majestic maturity, stands a veritable "Monarch of the Forest." But the storm comes. The lightning flashes. The great monarch is torn from the earth. Its huge body lies prostrate upon the ground.

Soon the green leaves begin to fade. Then they wither and fall from the branches. The corpse of the dead monarch lies bare upon the earth. Its naked body and bare limbs glisten in the sunlight.

The waters come and cover it over. The soil of the earth is washed around and over it. At last, after many ages, it lies buried deep within its earthly grave. The centuries come and go. Other great trees have grown to maturity above it. The once mighty monarch has become a bed of coal. At last the waters recede. Man comes with his pick and shovel. The bed of coal is lifted to the earth's surface. Thence it is carried into many homes and there burned to ashes. These ashes are scattered to the four winds, and where is the once stately oak?

With the lightning's stroke began the dominant play of Nature's Destructive Forces. When the great tree lay prostrate upon the ground and its roots glistened in the sunlight the channel of Nature's Constructive Energy was broken. The Vito-Chemical Life Element of vegetable Nature, the highest Life Element upon which the oak was integrated, escaped from the body, branches and leaves and was dissipated.

When the waters came and buried its great form deep down beneath the surface of the earth the chemical action of Nature's elements transmuted it into the bed of coal. In this transition we note another step in the destruction of its individuality as a tree. When man with his pick and shovel uncovered the bed of coal, lifted it to the earth's surface and carried it into the many homes, this marked another step in the process of disintegration. Then it was consumed as fuel and converted into heat and ashes. This marked yet another step in the process of dissolution. When these ashes were scattered and lost and the heat was diffused into space the operation of Nature's Destructive Principle was completed.

The splendid oak, the monarch of the forest, typifying vitality, strength, organization and constructive energy, under the operation of Nature's Destructive Principle has been both physically and spiritually disorganized, disintegrated, scattered and resolved back into Nature's elements from which it came. Its individuality on both planes of life as an organic entity is destroyed. And thus is acomplished its complete individual extinction.

But what is the primary cause of this wonderful change? Only this. The organizing, integrating, developing and renewing processes of vegetation depend upon the active principle of the Electro-Magnetic and Vito-Chemical Life Elements of Nature. The supply of these Life Elements has been cut off and the process of growth has ceased. At the point where growth ceases decay inevitably begins. The ultimate end of this destructive principle in operation is complete individual extinction.

Let us now go one round higher in the scale of organic Nature to the plane of the animal kingdom.

Under Nature's Constructive Principle—operating through the two lower Life Elements of the mineral and vegetable kingdoms and the Spiritual Life Element of animal Nature— the single, nucleated life cell germinates, grows, multiplies and develops into aggregates which form themselves into definite organs. These organs constitute the structural basis upon which the physical and spiritual bodies of the infant lion are integrated.

The baby lion is born. It grows and develops from infancy to full maturity. It becomes another veritable "Monarch of the Forest." At the zenith of its individual strength and animal development the hunter's bullet pierces its heart. The physical lion lies prostrate in death.

The process of physical dissolution immediately begins. The flesh is torn from the bones and devoured by other animals. Its constituent physical parts enter into the texture and organic structures of many animals and plants. The bones bleach in the sun. They crumble and disintegrate. Their individual particles are scattered over the earth and enter into other chemical, vegetable and animal combinations and are lost. The work of physical dissolution and disintegration is complete.

Under the operation of Nature's Destructive Principle the physical organism of the mighty monarch is disorganized, disintegrated, scattered and resolved back into Nature's elements from which it came.

Its individuality as an organic physical entity is destroyed, and thus is accomplished its individual extinction upon the physical plane of its being.

But what of the finer spiritual organism? Is this also disintegrated and dissolved? No, not yet.

When the hunter's bullet pierced the lion's heart the chain of vital relationship, which bound the two organisms together in one individual animate entity, was broken. The two bodies immediately separated. Had he possessed the independent power of spiritual vision, the hunter might have witnessed with perfect distinctness and absolute certainty the separation of the two bodies at the moment of physical death.

With his physical eyes he would have seen the dead physical form and with his spiritual vison he would have seen the live and active spiritual body—a perfect duplicate of the physical, except that the one is dead and the other is alive.

These observations would have put him in possession of the facts of Nature stated in a previous chapter, viz.:

1. That the physical death of an animal does not immediately result in the total and complete individual extinction of the entire animal entity.

2. That the animating principle accompanies (or is accompanied by) the spiritual body at the point of physical death.

3. That the spiritual animal appears to possess all the

natural faculties and intelligent capacities and powers which were manifest in the physical animal.

If the intelligent student should, perchance, be interested in pursuing the subject further, he would most naturally desire to know something concerning the destiny of the spiritual animal; whether it persists upon the spiritual plane of animal life forever; if not, how long it so continues to persist; whether it retains the same form indefinitely, or undergoes a metamorphosis after a time and takes on a different form; whether it develops and improves as an animal entity until it passes to higher spiritual planes; or, whether it disappears entirely from the spiritual plane of animal life and reappears upon the physical; if so, whether it appears as an animal of the same species, or transmigrates to a different species; if not, then, whether its disappearance is in reality its second death and means individual extinction.

All these suggestions and many more would naturally be of interest to the student of science. In other words, he would find himself in the midst of a problem of Nature which has defied the best intelligence of the ages, and still occupies a position of absorbing interest in the field of Natural Science.

Many of these questions, however, have been settled with definite, scientific certainty.

For instance: It is found that the animal does not persist upon the spiritual plane of animal life forever. It does not take on a different form during the period of its persistence on the spiritual plane. The period of its persistence upon the spiritual plane varies in time somewhat as it does upon the physical plane. It does not pass upward to higher planes of spiritual life, etc.

It is found that in the course of the years the animal upon the spiritual plane of animal life undergoes what appears to be a second death. The animating principle is withdrawn from the spiritual organism—or is dissipated with it—and the spiritual body is dissolved, disintegrated, and resolved back into Nature's elements in a manner somewhat analogous to the dissolution and disappearance of the physical body at physical death.

The lion, therefore, in the course of the years, reaches this second climax which we may, without confusion or misunderstanding, designate as "spiritual death," or the "Second Death."

But what is the exact scientific meaning of this spiritual or second death?

Leaving this great problem unsolved for the present, let us now proceed to the next higher round of individual life and in the kingdom of man see how far we may be able to trace the same principle of Nature in operation.

Under Nature's Constructive Principle, operating through the three lower Life Elements of Nature and the Soul Element of human life, the human infant is born upon the physical plane of its being. As a physical organism it grows and develops from infancy through childhood and youth to full maturity.

Up to this time the constructive forces of its physical being have been in the ascendency. But there comes a time when physical maturity is fully reached. At this point the constructive forces of the physical body begin to wane and the destructive forces begin to augment. This transition continues until the meridian line of physical life is reached. From this point we mark the declining years of old age. When Nature's Destructive Principle reaches its climax upon the physical plane man's physical death ensues.

At this point, as in the case of the animal, the physical body and the spiritual body separate. One who possesses the power of independent, spiritual vision is able to observe this transition with perfect distinctness and absolute scientific certainty.

In this observation he is able to demonstrate those additional facts of Natural Science previously stated, viz.:

1. That this separation of the two material bodies of man at the point of physical death corresponds, to all appearances, with the same process in the animal.

2. That the vital or animating principle of the double organic entity either follows (or is followed by) the spirit-

ual body only, and that in this respect it corresponds, to all appearances, with the same process in the animal.

3. That the spiritual man appears to possess all the natural faculties and intelligent capacities and powers with which he was invested at, or prior to, the time of physical death.

The establishment of these facts brings us at once to the most difficult and at the same time the most absorbing problem of Natural Science, the stupendous problem of man's ultimate individual destiny, the destiny of the soul.

Once in its presence we are no longer so deeply absorbed with the lesser problems of physical evolution, except in so far as they may throw light upon the greater question. Whether man upon the physical plane is but an ape evolved, or is a distinct creation without a physical progenitor, is a question which loses much of its interest in the presence of the greater problem of his ultimate individual destiny.

Man, to sustain himself upon the higher rounds of spiritual life, must find occupation in more beneficent pursuits than that of reveling in the memories of the past. To him the past becomes but a storehouse of experiences to which he returns only when in need of the materials it can furnish him for the solution of the more vital problems of the present and the future.

It is true that the most advanced student of Natural Science seeks knowledge upon all the planes of individual life and being. He finds it all along the way, from the lowest round of physical Nature to the highest plane of spiritual life to which he has attained. But his desire for the accumulation of knowledge is inspired by his appreciation of the possibilities which lie above and yet beyond.

If he delves into the problems of physical life and physical evolution it is only in order that he may, perchance, find there a key with which to unlock the door to a more exalted knowledge of spiritual life and spiritual unfoldment. With this key at his command he may then be permitted to open the door of the higher life to others who are seeking for the light of truth.

It is in this spirit that Natural Science has delved into the mysteries of Nature in search of the magical key of knowledge and power with which to unlock the secrets of ultimate individual being.

From this scientific point of view the course of individual life upon the spiritual planes has been observed, its various phases noted and a considerable amount of scientific data accumulated and classified. A few of the most conspicuous and significant "facts demonstrated" have been carefully stated in a previous chapter.

The present purpose is to amplify to some extent such of those facts as will serve to bring out more clearly man's relative position as an individualized intelligence upon the spiritual planes of life. With this in view it is especially important to note what appears to be a well defined principle of differentiation which gives to man upon the spiritual planes, as well as upon the physical, a status which is unique and at the same time deeply interesting and seemingly of scientific significance and value.

First.

It is observed that the dissolution of a physical mineral carries with it almost instantly the dissolution of its ethereal or spiritual duplicate. This almost simultaneous or synchronal dissolution of the two bodies appears to be significant from a scientific point of view, in that it would appear to establish with a reasonable degree of scientific certainty the following deductions:

1. That the constructive process or growth of the spiritual duplicate of a mineral ceases when its physical growth or integrating process is arrested, and *vice versa*.

2. That the relation between the physical and spiritual bodies of the mineral is of such a character as to establish what appears to be their absolute interdependence.

3. The integrating process in this case, therefore, appears to be but a single process manifesting upon duplicate planes of mineral existence.

SECOND.

In the vegetable kingdom just one important variation from the mineral process appears, namely: The dissolution of the two bodies of a plant is by no means so nearly simultaneous or synchronal as in the case of the mineral. The length of time intervening is very much increased. In other words, the spiritual organism of a plant appears to possess the power of individual persistence after physical dissolution to such an extent as to plainly suggest a possible design of Nature, which design would seem to become more clearly defined as we ascend to higher planes of organic life.

But a study of vegetation on both its planes of life appears to establish with a reasonable degree of certainty the following deductions, viz.:

1. That the spiritual organism of a tree or plant ceases to grow or develop whenever physical development is arrested. That is to say, its spiritual dissolution actually begins at the point of physical death just as appears to be the case with the mineral.

2. In so far as the principle of growth or accretion is concerned there seems to be the same general interdependence of the two bodies in the vegetable kingdom as in the mineral.

3. Here also integration appears to be but a single process manifesting upon two planes of material existence.

THIRD.

In the animal kingdom some important variations or modifications appear, among which the following are most important:

1. The length of time a spiritual animal persists as an individualized entity, after its physical dissolution, is many times greater than that during which the spiritual vegetable persists after its forced physical dissolution.

2. The spiritual growth and development of an animal does not necessarily stop at the point of physical death. At the death of infant animals, spiritual growth, in most instances, appears to cease immediately and spiritual death follows within a comparatively short time.

On the other hand, if the period of animal infancy is past before physical death occurs and the process of physical development and growth is well under way, the spiritual organism continues to develop until it reaches what appears to be full maturity upon the spiritual plane.

3. In this latter case spiritual disintegration does not begin at the point of physical death, nor until long thereafter. In this respect the animal differs very radically and essentially from the mineral and the vegetable.

4. Here also the principle of growth does not appear to bind the two organisms together in an indissoluble bond of interdependence. Indeed, the dependence appears to be almost entirely on the part of the physical.

5. Another important distinction or variation is here noted, in that the integrating process appears to be a double process instead of a single one, as in the two lower kingdoms of Nature. Or, if it be not a double process, then at the point of physical death that which produces growth is detached from the physical and unites with the spiritual.

FOURTH.

In the kingdom of man these variations or modifications appear with even greater distinctness. They stand out in such vivid contrast with the conditions which obtain in the lower kingdoms of Nature that the mind almost involuntarily forecasts a possible design which the great Universal Intelligence appears to be working out.

The variations and modifications here to be specially noted are:

1. However young the human infant may be when its physical death occurs, if it has once co-ordinated with the Soul Element of Nature and "breathed the breath of life," its status as an individualized intelligence is determined.

In this case its physical death does not appear in the least degree to suspend, retard or check the growth and development of the spiritual organism. The human infant upon the spiritual planes passes through all the phases and stages of spiritual growth and organic development to its full spiritual maturity, in a manner closely analogous to its growth and development upon the physical plane.

2. Man appears to be inherently invested with the power and ability to perpetuate his own organic individual existence upon the spiritual planes of life indefinitely. This is accomplished by his personal knowledge and right application of the laws, principles, forces, activities and processes of Nature which govern the conservation of his spiritual life and energies.

3. By the right application of his knowledge and the right use of all his acquired powers he comes into full co-operation with Nature's Constructive Principle. He thus adds to the great upward evolutionary impulse of Universal Intelligence the impetus of his own individual powers. He becomes an active, independent, self-conscious, rational and voluntary factor and power in his own individual evolution. By and through this voluntary and rational co-operation with the great Universal Intelligence he severs the last destructive tie of his individual being and rides upon the current of Nature's constructive, sustaining, renewing and living forces onward and upward through the realms of spiritual light and life until he passes beyond the limit of all our present knowledge.

4. Another significant variation or modification is found in the fact that, although man is unquestionably invested with the power and ability to perpetuate his individual existence upon the spiritual planes of life indefinitely, yet he does not always elect to do so.

This suggestion brings us to what appears to be another interesting fact of spiritual Nature, namely, that man is invested with the power of individual choice in the spiritual life as well as in the physical. This, in fact, appears to be one of the inalienable rights of every responsible individual intelligence.

It is a well-known fact that in this physical life man may defy every principle of Nature which makes for his own up-building. In other words, he may defy Nature's Constructive Principle. This is true as to every phase of his being. He may destroy his own physical life by any one of the numerous methods employed by the suicide. Or, he may wreck his physical health and strength by overindulgence of any or all of his physical appetites, passions, emotions or desires, and thus reach the same physical end through a slower and more gradual process.

He may defy every moral principle of equity, justice and right, and in a similar manner accomplish his moral suicide or death.

In the same absolute and definite manner the power of individual choice obtains upon the spiritual planes of life. By the wrong application of his knowledge and the abuse of his acquired powers man in that life, as in this, can, if he so elect, come into full co-operation with Nature's Destructive Principle. In this event he becomes an active, independent, self-conscious, rational and voluntary factor and power in his own devolution and spiritual retrogression.

By and through this voluntary and intentional violation of the constructive, sustaining, renewing and living principle of individual continuity, he may, of his own choice, ride upon the strong current of Nature's Destructive Forces backward and downward into the realm of spiritual darkness, to disintegration, dissolution, individual extinction and a final resolution back into Nature's elements to a point beyond the limits of all our present knowledge.

And THIS IS THE WAY OF DEATH.

CHAPTER III.

IN PERSPECTIVE.

A clear and comprehensive understanding of Nature's Destructive Principle is of such transcendent importance that a brief perspective view of the preceding chapter may be of value. The specific purpose of such a view is to fix indelibly in the mind an accurate conception of one fundamental deduction of Natural Science which gives to man a unique and distinctive place in Nature.

(I.) LIFE ELEMENTS.

In order that all phases of the subject may be observed in true perspective it is necessary to view it from as many different points of vision as possible. With this suggestion in mind, let us first proceed to the plane of the mineral kingdom and from that level look upward over the two intermediate kingdoms of the vegetable and the animal to the plane of human life. From this point of vision let us study the evolutionary ascent from the lowest and simplest form of life to the highest and most complex, as it is indicated in the Life Elements of Nature themselves. Viewed from this point we are able to note the following significant facts of Natural Science:

1. In the mineral kingdom the constructive or integrating principle of Nature operates through the Electro-Magnetic Life Element alone. Upon this single Life Element, therefore, the integration and growth of minerals depend.

2. In the vegetable kingdom the constructive, integrating and organic principle operates through two Life Elements instead of one. That is to say, it operates through the Electro-Magnetic and the Vito-Chemical Life Elements.

Of these two Life Elements the Vito-Chemical is the dominant one in the vegetable organic process. It controls that higher function of Nature known to science as the organic principle or process in vegetation, as this process is distinguished from that of mineral integration.

3. In the animal kingdom there is yet a higher, third Life Element through which the constructive principle operates. This third Life Element is the spiritual Life Element of Nature. It is the dominant factor in the organic process of animal Nature. It is that element which lifts the animal to a plane above the vegetable and gives to it those added characteristics which so clearly manifest themselves in the faculty or capacity of consciousness and the power of voluntary action.

4. In the kingdom of man the fourth Life Element of Nature—the Soul Element—is the principal factor in the constructive process. Here we have the constructive principle of Nature operating through four Life Elements in harmony instead of through one alone. Of these four the Soul Element is the dominant one in the human organism and gives to man those added characteristics of self-consciousness, independent choice, reason and the power of independent, self-conscious and rational will or volition.

From the foregoing it will be observed that in the mineral kingdom Nature's Destructive Principle, in order to prevail, must overcome the integrating power of but a single Life Element. In the vegetable kingdom it has to contend against the combined integrating and organizing forces of two Life Elements of Nature. In the animal kingdom it must oppose the combined integrating, organizing and sustaining forces of three, and in the human it is pitted against the combined forces and energies of all four of Nature's Life Elements working in harmony.

In this view of the subject it is not difficult for the mind to anticipate what would appear to be a perfectly natural result, namely, that the higher we proceed in the evolutionary process and the further we get away from the plane of the mineral kingdom the more powerful become the forces of Nature which we recognize as constructive, and the more difficult becomes the task set for Nature's Destructive Principle.

From this point of vision, therefore, the mind is able to note what appears to be a far-reaching design of Universal

Intelligence, namely, to ultimately evolve an order of being which shall possess within itself the power and ability to transcend the operation ,i Nature's Destructive Principle.

(II.) GROWTH.

In order to obtain a more perfect view of the subject, let us now return to the plane of the mineral kingdom, and, looking upward from another point of vision, study the evolutionary ascent of Nature as it is indicated in the principle of growth or accretion. And in this examination let us view the subject from both the spiritual and the physical planes of life at the same time.

1. It will be remembered that in the mineral kingdom growth of the spiritual body ceases when the growth of the physical is arrested.

2. In the vegetable kingdom this appears to be the case also, but there are some well defined indications which suggest that this may be only an appearance and not a fact.

3. In the animal kingdom all uncertainty is dispelled. Here it is determined with absolute certainty that, in the case of infant animals, growth of the spiritual body appears to cease soon after physical death. This, however, is not true of those animals which pass the stage of infancy before physical death occurs. In this latter case the spiritual body continues to grow after physical death, and in most instances— more especially among what we term the higher animals— spiritual growth continues until the spiritual organism reaches what appears to be spiritual maturity.

4. In the kingdom of man, again, this evolutionary phase of life reaches its climax. Here it is observed that however young the infant man may be, if it has reached co-ordination with the Soul Element of Nature and breathed the breath of its higher life, the death of the physical body appears to have no effect whatever upon the continued growth of the spiritual. It proceeds to grow and develop without interruption or lapse of any kind until it reaches what appears to be full spiritual maturity.

Indeed, in this field of observation growth appears to be

much more exclusively a spiritual process, with an incidental manifestation upon the physical plane. It is moved
primarily by a spiritual impulse rather than by a physical, as
indicated in the fact that physical death does not affect the
process of growth in the spiritual organism in any way.

From this second view point the mind seems to see with
added clearness the possible design of Universal Intelligence
as it appears to manifest itself in the wonderful scheme of
evolution. We are able to clearly note the unfaltering march
of development toward the consummation of what appears
to be a fixed and steady purpose, the evolvement of an indi-
dividual organism which shall be able to transcend the limited possibilities of Nature's Destructive Principle.

(III.) Psychical.

Once more let us stand upon the level of the mineral kingdom and from yet another point of vision view the subject.
In this observation let us study the evolutionary rise of the
individual entity in its purely psychical aspect.

1. It is clear to the scientific observer that in the mineral
world the constructive or integrating process is one in which
the mineral entity itself, as such, has no intelligent or conscious part. The integrating power of the mineral world, to
every appearance, is automatic and involuntary so far as the
mineral itself is concerned. The mineral, in fact, appears to
grow and decay, integrate and dissolve, in neither a conscious
nor voluntary manner, but rather in obedience to the operation of the great law of Universal Intelligence.

In the mineral, therefore, we are unable to discover anything which suggests to our minds an individualized intelligence. Whatever manifestations we are able to observe which
might suggest consciousness, volition or intelligence, appear
to reside in the individual, chemical particles of which chemical aggregates are composed, and not in the aggregate as a
distinct and separate entity or individuality.

For illustration: The energy or impulse which unites the
particles of gold or silver into one common mass manifests
itself in the individual particles of which the mass is com-

posed, and not in the mass as a whole. For this reason we are able to assert with seeming scientific certainty that the stone, or the crystal, or the boulder, or the nugget, or any other mineral aggregate, as an individual entity, has neither consciousness, volition, intuition nor intellectuality in any of its individual manifestations.

2. In the vegetable world we seem to cross a distinct line of differentiation which suggests at least a different character or grade of intelligence. Here the manifestations of intelligence do not appear so exclusively in the individual particles of which the various aggregates are composed.

For illustration: The sunflower turns its face to the sun. In the morning it looks to the east. During the day it follows the course of the sun in its flight across the heavens from east to west and at night bows its head to the west.

The sensitive plant shrinks at the touch of the human hand as if it were conscious of possible danger.

The little "Fly-Trap" opens its cup-like flower as if to await the coming of the unsuspecting insect. When the busy bee comes and enters in search of honey, or the fly in search of food or drink, the little flower quickly closes its door-like lid or mouth, and the insect is a hopeless and helpless prisoner. Here it is securely held until death comes to its relief. Then its decaying body is absorbed and assimilated by the plant as food.

The wild morning-glory vine of rapid growth reaches the limit of its support and gropes about in search of something new upon which to support itself. Place another support within a few inches of the end of the vine, but slightly to one side, and then watch the result. Within a few hours you will observe that the vine is reaching out to the new support. Then shift the object to the other side and in a short time you will see that the vine has turned about and is reaching for it in the opposite direction.

In all these instances, and many more which might be mentioned in connection with the vegetable world, there appears to be a very low grade of instinct or semi-consciousness as well as volition, which resides in the plant itself as an individual entity, and not alone in the particles of which it is composed.

It is true that science is not able to assert with certainty that any plant actually possesses individual consciousness, instinct or volition, but it is compelled to note the fact that in the evolution of vegetable life Universal Intelligence has taken a long step in the direction of an individualized intelligence and seems to be anticipating that ultimate result.

3. In the animal kingdom we cross another distinct line of differentiation in psychic conditions and development. Consciousness is here well defined as a faculty or capacity of the individual animal. Volition is also a well defined power of the individual entity, and not wholly an automatic result of general laws operating through the individual particles of which the individual animal is composed.

Here we also note for the first time that the individual entity possesses the power of independent locomotion. It is also invested with appetites, passions, emotions and desires, and, excepting in so far as the vital processes are concerned, the individual animal has full control of its muscular organism.

Here also we observe for the first time in the upward march of evolution what we have defined as animal instinct. So closely does it seem to approach the limit of the purely intellectual that wise men of all the ages have differed in their judgments concerning the ability of the animal to reason from cause to effect. Certain it is that if the animal does not rise to the level of the purely intellectual, its individuality most clearly and unmistakably foreshadows such a possible development in the yet higher kingdom of man.

4. In the human kingdom we find the full realization of all that is foreshadowed in the lower kingdoms of Nature. Man possesses all that the animal does and something more. Added to the consciousness of the animal is the self-consciousness which is distinctively a human faculty or capacity. Animal instinct assumes the higher form of intuition in man. The volition which in the animal is apparently but a reflex of

animal appetites, passions, emotions and desires, in man becomes an independent, self-conscious and rational power.

In other words, in his intellectual activities, processes, capacities and powers man rises to a plane of life and being unknown to and untouched by all the rounds of individual life which lie below the level of the Soul Element of Nature.

(IV.) PERSISTENCE.

One more view of the subject from the plane of the mineral will enable us to complete the picture. This time our task is to note the upward movement of evolution as it is indicated in the persistence of the spiritual body beyond the point of physical death.

1. It will be remembered that in the mineral kingdom the dissolution of the two bodies is almost simultaneous or synchronal. The spiritual body persists but a comparatively brief period of time after physical dissolution, even where the process of physical dissolution is forced and instantaneous.

2. In the vegetable kingdom the length of time the spiritual body persists after physical death or dissolution is many times longer than in the case of minerals.

3. In the animal kingdom this progression goes on.

4. And in the kingdom of man we again reach a natural and sequential climax. Here we find that Nature, or the great Universal Intelligence, appears to have shifted the burden of responsibility to man himself. As a result man possesses the power within himself to determine or to extend the period of persistence of the spiritual body beyond the point of physical death indefinitely. In a much more exact and literal sense, therefore, than is generally understood, man appears to be "the arbiter of his own destiny."

As clearly and as explicitly as may be expressed in the language of Nature's evolutionary processes, man appears to hold the key of individual immortality in his own hands. He may, if he so choose, ally himself with Nature's Constructive Principle in all its majesty, power and glory, and in so doing seemingly defy the powers of darkness, death and destruction forever.

In this he chooses THE WAY OF LIFE.

On the other hand, he may elect to co-operate with Nature's Destructive Principle, if he so desires. If so, and he persist in this election, his inevitable destiny, so far as known to science, is what we have designated as "Spiritual Death," or "The Second Death."

The exact scientific significance or meaning of this spiritual or second death is not yet known with absolute certainty. But it is known that whosoever chooses this road travels THE WAY OF DEATH.

A brief summary which presents the subject in its full and complete perspective is as follows:

MINERAL.

1. One Life Element.
2. Spiritual growth ceases at physical death.
3. Spiritual and physical death practically synchronal.
4. Without individual consciousness, instinct or volition.
5. Death of both bodies ultimately inevitable to all appearances.

VEGETABLE.

1. Two Life Elements.
2. Spiritual growth appears to cease at physical death, but there are some indications to the contrary.
3. Spiritual and physical death clearly not synchronal.
4. Some indications or shadowings of individual consciousness, instinct and volition.
5. Death, both physical and spiritual, ultimately inevitable to all appearances.

ANIMAL.

1. Three Life Elements.
2. Spiritual growth continues after physical death.
3. Spiritual life continues long after physical dissolution.
4. Individual consciousness, instinct, volition, appetites, passions, emotions and desires, with strong suggestions or shadowings of developing intellectual activities, faculties, capacities and powers.

5. Death, both physical and spiritual, ultimately inevitable to all appearances.

MAN.

1. Four Life Elements.

2. Spiritual growth not interrupted nor in any manner retarded or interfered with by physical death.

3. Persistence of spiritual life after physical death under the control and within the power of the individual and dependent on his individual choice.

4. Individual self-consciousness, intuition, appetites, passions, emotions and desires; independent, self-conscious and rational volition, and all intellectual faculties, capacities and powers fully defined.

5. Spiritual death not necessarily inevitable, but under control of the individual. Individual Immortality a possibility to all appearances.

CHAPTER IV.

INDIVIDUAL IMMORTALITY.

What is Immortality?

The answer to this important question must depend entirely upon the view point from which we examine the subject.

For illustration, the lexicographer tells us with every evidence of assurance that immortality is:

1. "Exemption from death and annihilation."
2. "Unending existence."
3. "Life eternal."

The metaphysician and the theologian generally accept these as consistent and satisfactory definitions of the word, and we are not disposed to find fault with them for the reason that they are looking at the subject from a particular standpoint.

But the scientist who is compelled to view the subject from the standpoint of knowledge alone, says that so far as we know there is no such thing as "Unending existence" or "Life eternal." Our actual knowledge is limited to matters which lie within the range of our own personal experiences. These matters, it will no doubt be admitted, all lie a long way this side of eternity, or never-ending time, if, indeed, there be such a time, place, condition or state of being.

Therefore, from the standpoint of science there may or may not be immortality in the sense expressed by the lexicographer and the theologian. No one, so far as men of science know, has, up to this time, lived out an "eternity" or an "unending existence," and therefore, so far as we know, the question of eternity is yet one of the unsolved problems.

From the standpoint of this work, therefore, the meaning of immortality is quite a different thing from that expressed by any of the definitions above quoted.

Viewed from this standpoint, Individual Immortality means nothing more and nothing less than a condition or state of being wherein the individual possesses the knowledge and the power to come into full co-operation with Nature's Constructive Principle.

From the standpoint of this work, therefore, we are not concerned with the question as to whether this may or may not mean "Life eternal" or "Unending existence," any more than the astronomer who first accurately determined the precession of the equinoxes was, at the time, concerned with the question as to how many such cycles of time it would require to constitute an "eternity."

The coming into possession of such knowledge and such power may mean "Life eternal." It may mean an "Unending existence." If so, then science and theology quite agree. If not, then science occupies the stronger ground by withholding its judgment upon a question of the ultimate, which, of necessity, lies far beyond the limitations of its power of judgment.

To make this distinction entirely clear, our astronomers are to-day able to calculate the distances, relative locations, lines of motion and velocity of the planets with such mathematical exactness as to determine within a very few seconds the time of an eclipse of the sun, or of the transit of Venus. All of their calculations, however, are based upon a very broad hypothesis, namely, that the planets will continue to move in the future just as they have done in the past.

But no astronomer would be rash enough to guarantee that the sun will even be in existence at the time fixed for the next eclipse, or that Venus will not have exploded long before the time set for its next transit of the sun. These are questions he at once recognizes as beyond the limits of his jurisdiction.

The most he can truthfully say is that, inasmuch as history informs us that these planets have been in existence many hundreds of years, during which time their movements have been observed and calculated with comparative certainty, we have the scientific right to assume, for the purposes of these calculations, that they will go on in the same way for some time to come. But we have no scientific license to declare that they are absolutely unchangeable, or that in their individual capacity they are necessarily "eternal."

And so, when Natural Science comes to know that man upon the spiritual planes of life is invested with the power to come into full co-operation with what we have designated as Nature's Constructive Principle, it can only declare that fact and nothing more. But it can without impropriety suggest that man thus appears to possess the power of indefinite individual persistence. It can also point out that to all appearances this would seem to indicate "Eternal life" or "Unending existence." But it dares not dogmatize concerning ultimates.

And therefore wherever the term "immortality" is employed in this work or in subsequent volumes of this Series, it must be understood in the limited and scientific sense above suggested.

•

CHAPTER V.

ON WHAT IT DEPENDS.

By reference back to Part II, Chapter IV, Paragraph 23, it will be observed that in the spiritual life man's ability to persist and to advance from lower to higher spheres of spiritual existence is commensurate with his independent control of all his individual faculties, capacities and powers, and is in response to his independent, self-conscious and rational volition and desire to so persist and advance.

In this fundamental fact we strike what appears to be the keynote of Nature's harmonic principle. Here it is we find what appears to be a rational and scientific answer to the great problem of evolution.

If the student has followed the subject closely to this point he cannot fail to be impressed with what appears to be a far-reaching design of Universal Intelligence as it expresses itself in the ever onward and upward movement of evolution.

From the lowest round of physical Nature to the highest plane of spiritual life we have been able to note the steady, unfaltering, upward march of Nature toward the consummation of what appears to be a fixed and definite purpose.

Out of the seeming chaos of inorganic conditions we have noted the slow but inevitable rise of individual life. We have observed that from the time of its first appearance upon the plane of physical life each evolutionary round has invested the individual entity with higher, stronger and more enduring individual characteristics.

We have seen this individual entity at each higher round in the ascent of life develop new capacities and added powers, and each step has been in the direction of individual independence, emancipation and supremacy.

From the individual crystal to the individual man there has been and is a steady and seemingly intelligent and purposeful graduation from lower to higher rounds of individualized existence.

And what, in all this, is the one most conspicuous, significant and salient fact which impresses the mind as of paramount value and importance?

It is this, that out of all the struggles of Nature, out of all the seemingly uncertain conditions of individual existence, out of all the play of Nature's laws, principles, forces, activities and processes, out of all the mystery which surrounds the ultimate destiny of individual life, there has at last emerged an individualized, intelligent entity which possesses the inherent power of indefinite persistence, as an individualized intelligence upon the spiritual planes of existence, by and through co-operation with Nature's Constructive Principle.

In other words, out of all the complex operations of the seemingly automatic and mechanical processes of lower Nature has at last been evolved an individualized, intelligent entity, possessing the one transcendent power of Individual Immortality.

Man is that individualized, intelligent entity. He stands solitary and alone upon the summit of that splendid ascent of individual life, a fitting expression of the consummation of Nature's stupendous scheme of evolution.

As he stands thus majestically upon the pinnacle of the ascent of individualized life and intelligence, he presents to the mind a splendid picture in evidence of Nature's evolutionary triumph.

As we study the picture in all its outlines, the mind turns with an irresistible impulse to a search for the hidden springs of that subtle, sustaining power by and through which man is able to rise superior to the operation of Nature's Destructive Principle and achieve that final triumph which Nature has placed within his possibilities, the triumph of Individual Immortality.

Here in this fertile field of spiritual life, which physical science dogmatically placards "The Unknowable," and which speculative philosophy generously concedes to be "The Unknown," Natural Science and true religion find a common ground of sympathy in their search for truth.

Here in this apparently unlimited field of research and experiment is again illustrated the process by which science has so often worked out its verifications of the soul's intuitions and its unanswerable demonstrations of the fallacies of unenlightened dogmatism.

With seemingly unanswerable logic Natural Science proceeds to the solution of the great problem of Individual Immortality, and in that scientific solution the following facts have a special value:

1. It has been demonstrated that death, both physical and spiritual, is the inevitable heritage of all forms of individual life below the level of man.

2. It is found that man possesses the power, if he will but use it, to rise superior to the operation of Nature's Destructive Principle. By the exercise of this power he may perpetuate his individual life upon the spiritual planes indefinitely. He may advance from lower to higher planes of spiritual life by an ever increasing acquisition of individual power, until he passes to realms above and beyond the range of all our present knowledge.

In other words, he possesses that wonderful and mysterious acquisition which we may designate as the power of individual persistence upon the spiritual planes of life. He is likewise the only individualized, intelligent entity of which we have personal and definite knowledge, who is capable of rising to this transcendent state of Individual Immortality.

3. It is found that man possesses certain well defined capacities, faculties and powers not found to exist in any of the rounds of individual life which lie below him in the scale of evolution.

That is to say, he possesses all that is found in the world of individual life below him, with something added. He therefore possesses something which is distinctively and exclusively his own, something not possessed by animal Nature. And it is this distinctive and exclusive possession which, in fact, makes him man.

To these superior endowments of Nature, which are exclusively his own and distinguish him as an individualized intelligence from all that lies below him, Natural Science turns in its search for that which lifts him to his higher round of individualized existence. To these it looks for the secret which gives to him his distinctive place in Nature. To these and these alone it turns for the key which unlocks to him the door of Individual Immortality.

WHAT ARE THEY?

It is found that among those specific and individual capacities, faculties and powers which are distinctively and exclusively human are:

1.   SELF-CONSCIOUSNESS, as distinguished from mere Consciousness.

2.   REASON, as distinguished from mere Intelligence.

3.   INDEPENDENT CHOICE, as distinguished from automatic or involuntary Selection.

4.   INDEPENDENT, SELF-CONSCIOUS and RATIONAL WILL, OR VOLITION.

These are the inherent, essential and distinctive elements which are exclusively related to and constitute the background of human character. To these, therefore, and to these alone must of necessity be related whatever distinctive and exclusive powers man may possess over and above the animal.

But the one exclusive power of this character man possesses which transcends all others in value and importance to himself is that which enables him to intelligently co-operate with Nature's Constructive Principle, rise above the operation of Nature's Destructive Principle, persist indefinitely upon the spiritual planes of life, and thereby achieve Individual Immortality.

Therefore, in the above named distinctive and exclusive elements of human character, namely, Self-Consciousness, Reason, Independent Choice and an Independent, Self-Conscious and Rational Volition, we have laid out before us the subject matter for an intelligent and scientific study of the great problem of Individual Immortality.

With this thought clearly in mind, it is hoped that the following pages may contain something of special interest and possible value to every student of the higher lines of thought and inquiry. It is therefore assumed that any apology for the time and space consumed in an effort to simplify the subject and bring it within the easy understanding of the student would be out of place.

Without further explanation, therefore, let us turn our attention to a study of the great problem before us.

SELF-CONSCIOUSNESS.

In all the varied forms of animal life we are forced to recognize evidences of a certain character, degree or quality of consciousness. However low down the scale of animal life we may choose to go, we fail to reach a point where this faculty or capacity appears to be wholly wanting. This would appear to establish with reasonable certainty the fact that consciousness is a primary faculty or capacity of the individual, animal entity.

Consciousness is, indeed, that faculty or capacity of the individual intelligence, ego, soul or entity, by and through which it becomes aware of the existence of a world outside itself as well as a world of demands within. Through this faculty or capacity the appetites, passions, desires, impulses, affections, emotions, instincts and intuitions make their impression upon the individual entity and command recognition. Through this faculty or capacity alone are the five physical senses able to convey their messages to the entity itself and have them recorded.

But in all the realm of animal life there appear to be such fixed limitations upon this faculty or capacity as to mark a distinct line of differentiation between the animal consciousness and the consciousness of man. This fact would seem to indicate that the Soul Element of Nature, which is individualized in man alone, has undoubtedly added to animal consciousness something which is distinctively and exclusively human in its character, degree or quality.

To distinguish between the character, degree or quality of consciousness in animals and men we designate animal consciousness as simple "consciousness" and human consciousness as "Self-Consciousness."

Self-Consciousness is that character, degree or quality of consciousness which enables us to know and understand ourselves. It is that which enables us to perform our acts knowingly and intentionally. It involves the consciousness of the relations which exist between this self and those other selves. It is that consciousness which is able to recognize the self as a responsible, individual intelligence. It is, indeed, one of the primary, fundamental and essential elements of human character upon which individual responsibility is based and upon which it depends.

REASON.

As with consciousness, so with reason. Whatever may be said concerning the intelligence of animals, however closely they border the realm of the human, there is a subtle dividing line, which is not easily mistaken, running between the two kingdoms of Nature.

We recognize our intimate relationship to the animal kingdom in the appetites, passions, emotions, desires, instincts and impulses which we experience in common with the animal. Even our motives, when judged by our actions, are often such as to suggest the animal rather than the man.

But when we enter the realm of the purely psychical and ethical we at once become aware that we are in a field unoccupied by the animal, a field which appears to be reserved to man alone. In other words, it is in the realm of the soul that man rises to a distinct and exclusive level above and beyond the limitations of the animal.

This is not intended to deny nor in the least degree minimize the intelligence of animals. On the other hand, it will be conceded by every intelligent student of natural history that the animal displays many unmistakable evidences of a nascent or dawning intelligence. A careful investigation and study of these evidences, however, would seem to establish certain fixed and definite limitations within which the operations of animal intelligence are circumscribed.

To a considerable extent, indeed, the animal intelligence

appears to operate as a natural reflex of the purely physical motives of animal Nature. It is, to all appearances, concerned with an exclusive interest in its physical life and environment. The struggle for nutrition, for individual life, for self-protection, for the gratification of the purely physical appetites, passions, affections, emotions and desires, the instinct of reproduction, the mother's care of her young, all combine to make up the little world within which animal intelligence finds the limits of its achievements.

But not so in the larger domain of human intelligence. Here we have most clearly defined those higher, sustained activities of the analytic and synthetic mind which we designate as "Reason."

This power of inductive and deductive reasoning which appears to be almost, if not entirely, wanting in the animal, rises in man to a development apparently without fixed limitations. Man reasons analytically, synthetically, inductively and deductively on all the affairs of his own life as well as on the lives of his fellow-men. He reasons upon his physical body, his appetites, passions, impulses, desires and functions. He reasons upon this life and the life to come. He reasons upon the spirit and likewise upon the soul. He reasons upon what he is, what he has been, and what he may yet become. He reasons upon himself as an individual intelligence and as a part of the great aggregate of Universal Intelligence. He reasons upon things finite and things which appear to him to be infinite. He reasons upon God and Nature, finite intelligence and infinite intelligence. He reasons upon reason itself, and in all his reasoning he is seldom content to stop short of the ultimate.

It is upon this power of reason that he depends to guard himself from the errors, mistakes and accidents of life. This is the power which enables him to anticipate the natural and logical results of his own actions.

Reason, in truth, is another of the primary, fundamental and essential elements of human character at the basis of individual responsibility.

INDEPENDENT CHOICE.

A further study and comparison of animals and men discovers another marked distinction between them, namely, in the power of independent choice. The distinction here, as in the case of consciousness and reason, is undoubtedly of a psychic nature and referable to the Soul Element of Nature, which is individualized in man alone.

The power of individual choice in the animal is so nearly a reflex of the physical appetites, passions, affections, emotions, desires and instincts that it apparently loses the element of independence to a very large extent. In the elections and selections of the animal we seldom discover anything to indicate a clear and unqualified act of reason overthrowing the appetites, passions, affections, desires, emotions and instincts. But a careful analysis of the act and its motive seems to establish a natural concurrence of whatever reason is manifested, with the physical and spiritual demands above enumerated. In other words, the moral element appears to be wanting in the motives which govern animal life and action.

But in man this power of independent choice rises to the highest level of his ethical nature. To the extent only that man may, in truth, be said to be a creature of environment would his power of individual choice appear to lack the element of independence.

However much we may endeavor to excuse ourselves from the natural penalties of our own mistakes, derelictions and transgressions upon the theory that we are but "creatures of circumstances," we know that our fellow men almost unanimously deal with us upon the assumption that we really do possess the power of independent choice. Nor do we even protest against such an assumption. On the contrary, we encourage it. Indeed, our pride of intelligence would be most deeply offended if our friends and fellows should presume to doubt or question our perfect independence. We therefore accept the common judgment of our fellow men and in return we hold them to the same standard of accountability.

In this power of independent and rational election, selection and choice we recognize another of the primary, fundamental and essential elements of human character at the foundation of individual responsibility.

INDEPENDENT, SELF-CONSCIOUS AND RATIONAL VOLITION.

Those who have given the subject any considerable amount of thought and consideration have already discovered that an independent, self-conscious and rational act is never performed without an impulse of the will to set in motion the processes by and through which the act is to be accomplished. This impulse of the will we call "Volition."

This power of volition is possessed by animals as well as by men. But here again we find a distinct line of differentiation manifest. The animal volition responds in what appears to be a semi-automatic manner to the animal impulses. It is apparently little more than a reflex of the animal appetites, passions, affections, emotions, desires and instincts.

To a marked degree, therefore, it lacks in one or more of the elements of independence, self-consciousness and reason. To the same degree it lacks the moral elements at the foundation of individual responsibility.

A brief study of human nature is sufficient to make clear the distinction which it is important to emphasize at this point. Man in his normal physical and mental state of being possesses the power to act independently. This means that he is able to act unaided and uninfluenced by his fellow men. He also possesses the power to act self-consciously. This means that he is able to act knowingly and intentionally. And finally, he has the power to act rationally. This means that he is able to anticipate the natural and logical results of his own acts within the scope of his acquired knowledge.

For the purpose of presenting this subject more vividly to the mind of the analytical student the following brief diagram is suggested as a valuable object lesson:

$$\text{VOLITION} \begin{cases} \text{INDEPENDENT} \begin{cases} \text{U n a i d e d} \\ \text{and} \\ \text{Uninfluenced} \end{cases} \\\\ \text{SELF-CONSCIOUS} \begin{cases} \text{Knowingly} \\ \text{and} \\ \text{Intentionally} \end{cases} \\\\ \text{RATIONAL} \begin{cases} \text{Anticipating} \\ \text{the} \\ \text{R e s u l t s} \end{cases} \end{cases} \text{RESPONSIBILITY}$$

This simple diagram carries its own explanation. Whether we admit it or not, the elements therein suggested are those upon which we must and do depend in determining the question of individual responsibility.

The unqualified truth of this statement will become perfectly apparent to every intelligent thinker who will take the trouble to familiarize himself with the fundamental principles underlying the criminal jurisprudence of our country. Upon this subject the ablest minds of all the ages have been employed in an effort to work out a system or standard by which to try and determine the motives and the actions of men with perfect equity, justice and right.

Should he turn to the official record of any important criminal trial he will find abundant confirmation of the foregoing statements.

From the "indictment," which is the first legal document containing the criminal charges, through all the evidence, the testimony of witnesses, the objections of counsel, the rulings of the court, the charge to the jury, the finding of the verdict and the final judgment of the court upon the verdict, there is but one general purpose. That purpose is to determine the guilt or innocence of the accused.

The first thing to be determined is whether the act charged in the indictment was actually committed. If this be proved, the second step is to determine whether the accused is the person who committed the act so charged. If this also be proved, then the third step is to determine whether he did it of his own volition. If it can be shown that he committed the act charged, and did it voluntarily, then the inquiry is narrowed to three simple questions, viz.:

1. Even though he committed the act charged and did it of his own volition, did he act entirely independently? In other words, was he aided or influenced by any one else? If so, by whom and to what extent?

2. Did he commit the act entirely self-consciously? That is to say, did he act knowingly and intentionally?

3. Was he in the full possession of his reason at the time the act was committed? Or, differently stated, was the act his own rational act? And this means, was he at the time able to anticipate the logical and natural results of his act?

If all these conditions can be shown to have existed at the time the act was committed, then the jury has nothing to do but return a verdict of "Guilty as charged in the indictment" (unless the element of self-defense enters into the case) and the accused must suffer the full penalty of the law.

But if it can be shown that he did not act independently, then it is the business of the court and jury to ascertain to what extent he was aided or influenced by others, and by whom. In just so far as it can be determined that he was aided or influenced by others to commit the act, to that extent it is the intent of the law to condone the offense. To that extent also he is relieved of responsibility. To the same extent the responsibility for his act is fixed upon those who are found to have aided or influenced him to commit it, and it becomes the duty of the court to see that they are adequately punished, if this be possible.

Again, if it can be shown that at the time of the commission of the act complained of he was not entirely self-conscious; in other words, if in any measure the act was committed without knowledge or intent on his part, then it is necessary and proper to ascertain to what extent this was the case. When it is determined to what extent the element of self-consciousness was lacking at the time the act was committed, to that extent he must be held not responsible. In the verdict of the jury and the final judgment of the court upon the verdict and in the sentence pronounced by the court the effort will be made to give him the benefit to whatever extent he is found to be not responsible.

And finally, the question of his sanity must be determined. If it can be shown that at the time of the commission of the act he was not in full possession of his reason, it becomes the duty of the court and jury to ascertain to what extent he was unable to exercise his rational faculties, capacities and powers. To what extent was he at the time unable to rationally anticipate the logical and natural results of his act? When this question is determined it is the intent of the law to condone the offense to a degree commensurate with his lack of rational understanding.

In other words, in just so far as it can be determined that he was, at the time of the commission of the act, not in possession of all his rational faculties, capacities and powers, to that extent he is relieved from responsibility for the act so committed. To that extent he is held to be excused from the consequences of his act, and to the same extent his sentence will be mitigated.

It is equally true that if it can be shown that he was deprived of the use of any of his natural faculties, capacities or powers through the independent, self-conscious and rational volition of another party, then he is not only relieved from responsibility but the responsibility for his act is transferred to such third party, who must suffer the law's penalty therefor.

Thus it is found, and universally admitted, that the primary, fundamental and essential elements of individual responsibility are:

1. SELF-CONSCIOUSNESS.
2. INDEPENDENT CHOICE.
3. REASON.
4. INDEPENDENT, SELF-CONSCIOUS AND RATIONAL VOLITION.

Upon the basis of these elements of human character and by the standard which they establish we judge our fellow men, whether we admit it or not, and upon the same basis and by the same standard we are judged by them, whether we will it or not.

But by reference to the introductory pages of this chapter it will be observed that these elements of individual responsibility are identical with those faculties, capacities and powers of the Soul which are found to be distinctively and exclusively human. These, it will be remembered, are the faculties, capacities and powers which distinguish man from all the rounds of animal life which lie below him in the scale of evolution. Animals do not possess them. Man does, and they belong to man alone.

To these distinctive and exclusive, human possessions, therefore, science is compelled to turn for the key which unlocks to man the door of Individual Immortality.

It is found:

1. That man possesses the power of Individual Immortality.

2. That he is the only individualized intelligent entity which does possess it.

3. That he is the only entity within the range of scientific knowledge in which are present all the elements of character upon which individual responsibility depends.

4. That these elements of human character which constitute the basis of individual responsibility are identical with those distinctive and exclusive faculties, capacities and powers which distinguish him from the animal, and on which he must therefore depend in his struggle for Individual Immortality.

In other words, Universal Intelligence has invested man with certain intelligent faculties, capacities and powers which make him individually responsible under the law of his being. By the proper exercise and use of these intelligent faculties, capacities and powers he discharges his individual responsibility and at the same time achieves Nature's just reward therefor, which is Individual Immortality.

By the surrender or abuse of these intelligent faculties, capacities and powers he violates the constructive law of his being, invokes upon himself the operation of Nature's Destructive Principle, and enters upon the downward path of life, the ultimate destination of which appears to be individual extinction, dissolution and a resolution back into Nature's elements from which he came.

From the foregoing facts and analysis we are brought face to face with the following irresistible and irrefutable conclusions, viz.:

1. Whatever in Nature shall interfere with the free and independent exercise and use of those primary, fundamental and essential faculties, capacities and powers which form the basis of man's individual responsibility, must inevitably obstruct his pathway toward Individual Immortality.

2. Whatsoever, or whosoever shall divest or deprive man of the free exercise and use of those faculties, capacities and powers upon which his individual responsibility depends attacks the very essence of his being and invokes upon him the operation of Nature's Destructive Principle.

3. Whosoever attacks those distinctive and exclusive faculties, capacities and powers by and through the free and independent exercise and use of which man asserts and maintains his position as a responsible individual intelligence and upon which he must depend for the achievement of Individual Immortality, is a menace to society, an obstruction to individual progress and an enemy of mankind. For,

THIS IS THE WAY OF DEATH.

CHAPTER VI.

SELF-CONTROL, THE APPLICATION.

The following brief recapitulation will make clear the application of the principle under consideration:

1. There are two great fundamental principles of Nature which are forever contending for supremacy in the life of every intelligent soul.

2. One of these is known to science as the Constructive Principle of Nature in Individual Life.

3. The other is known and designated as The Destructive Principle of Nature in Individual Life.

4. Man possesses the power to conform his life to either of these fundamental principles at will.

5. By conforming his life to Nature's Constructive Principle he discharges his individual responsibility to himself, to his fellow man and to Nature, or Universal Intelligence.

6. By this discharge of his individual responsibility he earns Nature's reward therefor, which is Individual Immortality, Self-Completion and perfect Happiness both here and hereafter.

7. By the achievement of Individual Immortality the individual rises superior to the Destructive Principle of Nature, and triumphs over all things whatsoever that obstruct his pathway toward the ultimate evolutionary goal of individual life and intelligence.

8. By conforming his life to Nature's Destructive Principle he fails in the discharge of his individual responsibility to himself, to his fellow man and to Nature, or Universal Intelligence.

9. By such failure or refusal to discharge his individual responsibility he thereby enters upon the pathway of Death. He must inevitably suffer Nature's penalties therefor. These penalties, so far as known to science, are individual unhappiness and loss both here and hereafter, leading with unerring certainty to ultimate dissolution, disintegration, individual ex-

tinction and a resolution back into Nature's elements from which he came.

10.   Man possesses certain well defined attributes of individual nature which are distinctively and exclusively human.

11.   These are the attributes of the Soul.

12.   They are Self-Consciousness, Reason, Independent Choice, and Independent, Self-Conscious and Rational Volition.

13.   Upon his own free and independent control and exercise of these individual attributes of the soul man must depend for his ability to co-operate with Nature's Constructive Principle, discharge his individual responsibility, achieve Individual Immortality and Self-Completion, and attain Happiness both here and hereafter.

14.   Whatever deprives him of his own free, independent and voluntary control and exercise of these fundamental attributes of the soul thereby robs him of his power to co-operate with Nature's Constructive Principle, discharge his individual responsibility or achieve Individual Immortality and Self-Completion, and destroys the possibility of his happiness both here and hereafter.

THE APPLICATION.

Hypnotism is a subjective, psychic process.

In so far as it exists at any given time it paralyzes the will and voluntary powers of the subject.

To exactly this extent it deprives him of his own free and independent control and exercise of all those attributes of the soul upon which he must depend for his ability to co-operate with Nature's Constructive Principle, discharge his individual responsibility, achieve Individual Immortality and Self-Completion, as well as Happiness either here or hereafter.

Mediumship, like hypnotism, is a subjective, psychic process.

Like hypnotism, also, in just so far as it exists at any given time it paralyzes the will and voluntary powers of the medium.

To whatever extent this condition obtains at any given time

it deprives the medium of his own free and independent control and exercise of all those attributes of the soul upon which he must depend for the achievement of Individual Immortality, Self-Completion, and happiness both here and hereafter.

Hypnotism and Mediumship, therefore, are manifestations of Nature's Destructive Principle in operation in Individual Life.

In just so far as they exist, the process involved violates every constructive principle of Nature in Individual Life, trespasses upon every inalienable right, privilege and possession of the soul, and invokes the immediate operation of the Destructive Principle of Nature in Individual Life.

The individual who makes this election and consistently adheres to it thereby places himself upon the broad highway to unhappiness here and hereafter, the ultimate destination of which, so far as science knows, is ultimate dissolution, disintegration, total individual extinction and a resolution of the individual entity, physically, spiritually and psychically, back into the original elements from which it came.

This is "The Second Death."

This is "Spiritual Death."

This is Psychical Death, "The Death of the Soul."

And this is—THE GREAT PSYCHOLOGICAL CRIME.

CHAPTER VII.

THE LINE OF DESPAIR AND THE POWERS OF DARKNESS.
"Who enters here leaves Hope behind."

Hypnotism and Mediumship are not the only psychological crimes possible to individual intelligence. Indeed, they exemplify but two of the many methods or processes by and through which man may subject his fellow man or be subjected to the operation of Nature's Destructive Principle in such manner as to invoke the penalties which Nature prescribes therefor.

The scope and purpose of this volume, however, are such as to preclude the consideration of other subjects and limit us to an examination of Nature's Destructive Principle in Individual Life as it exemplifies itself in these particular processes of psychic subjectivity and psychic control.

Notwithstanding these limitations it would seem proper to call attention at this point to the important fact that while there are many different methods and processes by and through which Nature's Destructive Principle may be invoked, yet the fundamental principle itself is always the same. It involves the relationship of activity to passivity, positive to negative, energy to inertia, strength to weakness, aggression to suppression, domination to submission, Control to Subjection.

It may also be said, for it so appears from all the known facts of science, that all crime is referable to these relationships. The powerful, energetic, ambitious, positive, active, aggressive, dominating and controlling intelligence in the gratification of selfishness and vanity is guilty of the crimes and sins of commission. The weak, timid, credulous, inert, negative, passive, submissive, yielding and surrendering intelligence is responsible for the crimes and sins of omission. Acting together they accomplish all the crimes and sins known to the calendar of Nature.

In order that the subject may not be dismissed from the mind and consciousness with an imperfect conception or a defective understanding of the principle involved in Hypnotism and Mediumship, it is necessary to know something definitely of the manner in which the law exemplifies itself upon the spiritual planes of life.

To accomplish this result repetition, to some extent, is unavoidable. The importance of the subject, however, is such as to clearly justify whatever restatement of data may become necessary in this connection.

It is not the province of science to speculate nor dogmatize concerning ultimates. Natural Science does not claim nor assume to have solved the great problem of the soul's ultimate destiny. So far as it has gone, however, in its accumulation of scientific data bearing upon this subject, there appear to be three distinct psychological states of being that are suggestive of ultimate evolutionary possibilities. These may be dimly suggested by the terms, "good, indifferent and bad;" or by "improvement, uncertainty and degeneracy;" or by "progress, stagnation and retrogression."

In the first and highest of these three states the individual has reached an evolutionary altitude where truth for its own sake is more attractive to him than falsehood with all its alluring promises of selfish advantage. Light is more attractive to him than darkness. It is more agreeable and pleasant to do right for the sake of principle than to do wrong for selfish gain. It is easier to rise to higher levels of life and action than sink to lower planes of existence. In this state reason has finally triumphed over all the debasing influences of the appetites, passions, emotions, impulses and desires. Harmony and co-operation are established between the self-consciousness, reason, independent choice and volition of man, and the self-control for which he has striven is now an established fact. He is liberated from all the forces, activities and processes of Nature, both within and without, which would enslave the soul. He is emancipated from all subjective conditions and processes and all the predominating tendencies of the soul set toward light and life and the attainment of Individual Immortality.

The line which marks the level of this evolutionary development and individual triumph may well be known as "The Line of Victory." It marks the plane of the greatest victory of individual life, the final victory over self in the achievement of individual self-control.

The second or middle psychological state of being lies immediately below the first. It is the battle ground of individual life. It is here that every individual intelligence must fight the crucial battle of self. Here it is that he is subject to the active play of all the opposing and contending forces of Nature.

His intelligence, reason, intuitions and aspirations all exert their buoyant effect upon his life and tend to lift him upward into the light of a higher knowledge and a higher life. His evil appetites, passions, emotions, impulses and desires all tend to drag him downward.

His environment and associations exert the same double influence upon him. Those who are above him in point of knowledge, development and power give him courage and hope and inspiration to rise with them into the light. Those who are yet below him exert their influence with equal persistence to drag him downward to their level and into the darkness.

And so it is that here in this middle ground his intelligence, reason, conscience, intuitions and aspirations and all the powers of light are pitted against the evil tendencies of his individual nature and all the powers of darkness. This, therefore, is the realm of vacillation, and uncertainty. Today the soul sets toward the light. Tomorrow it seeks the world of darkness. Today the good triumphs. Tomorrow the evil tendencies predominate. The ultimate issue is yet undetermined. The soul is being weighed in the balance.

This is the psychological state of evolutionary development where and in which future possibilities are determined.

In this middle state the spiritual gravity of the individual is naturally downward, except for the power he possesses to lift himself by his own efforts. The following analogy will serve to make this condition more clearly understood:

For instance: The weight of an eagle's body is many times greater than that of the air in which it flies. It therefore naturally gravitates toward the earth. Under the law of its gravity, if left alone, it would fall to the ground never to rise again. But this monarch of the air has the power within itself and of its own right to overcome the force of gravity and rise at will to realms beyond the clouds and the shadows of earth into the clear sunlight of heaven.

Thus it is with man in this second psychological state or condition. When left alone to the mercy of the elements and the play of Nature's forces his spiritual gravity carries him downward toward the realms of darkness and death. But he has within himself and of his own right the power to over-come the downward tendencies of his spiritual gravity and rise at will into the realms of light and life and Individual Immortality.

It is but a question of whether he will or not. As it is with the eagle so it is with man himself. If he would rise and soar above the shadowland of earth he must do so by the self-control and exercise of those individual faculties, capacities and powers of the soul through which he is enabled to dis-charge his individual responsibility and at the same time earn Nature's reward therefor, which is Individual Immortality. From the standpoint of science it would appear that these are the wings which God or Nature has given him with which to rise in triumph above all the opposing forces of Nature.

At the lower level of this second or middle psychological state of man runs another line, a fixed and immutable line of Nature. From its portentous and appalling significance the Masters of Natural Science have aptly named it "The Line of Despair."

Below the level of this line of psychic condition lies the realm of spiritual darkness and spiritual death. Those who in their downward flight cross this line "leave hope behind." This is the bourne whence neither man nor woman ever re-turns. This line of despair marks the level at which the De-structive Principle of Nature in Individual Life becomes triumphant. It marks that point in the devolution of man-kind where all the elements of individual being, spiritual, men-tal and moral, set toward darkness and death.

Let it be remembered that so long as there remains one aspiration for good, one desire for light, one cry of conscience, one prayer for help, Nature responds and sends her messengers. But when man in his downward flight crosses this Line of Despair he passes beyond the reach of those who would or could help him to rise again. Those attributes of the soul which distinguish him from the animal no longer respond to the power of will. At the crossing of this line, therefore, he sinks to the level of animal nature. Like the animal he lives for a time in this world of progressive degeneracy and then goes down to spiritual death.

What the scientific significance of this second or spiritual death may be is, as yet, the great unsolved problem of Nature. So far as science knows, this means the death of the soul, or total individual extinction and a resolution of the individual entity in all its essential nature back into the elements from which it came. And

THIS IS "HELL."

CHAPTER VIII.

The Law of Spiritual Gravity.

The Law of Spiritual Gravity is Nature's gravimeter by which to try and determine the evolutionary status of the souls of men and women in this life as well as in the life to come.

It is therefore in essence a psychic law. Inasmuch, however, as it manifests itself upon the spiritual planes of life in terms of spiritual conditions according to the status of the spiritual body, it has come to be known as the Law of Spiritual Gravity. For the sake of simplicity and to avoid confusion it will be so designated in this work.

Under and by virtue of this Law of Spiritual Gravity each one of us at physical death either rises or sinks—as the case may be—to a level of spiritual life and evolution exactly commensurate with his life and development immediately prior thereto.

That is to say, in our essential being the transition called death does not affect us. We are neither essentially wiser nor essentially better upon our entry into that life than we are upon our exit from this, save and except in just so far as the experience of making the transit itself is concerned.

In just so far as we have been subjects of or slaves to our evil appetites, passions, desires and propensities here we remain so there until by the power of self-control we lift ourselves above them to higher levels of spiritual life. In so far as we have been subjects of hypnotism and mediumship here we remain so there until we are liberated through the development of the latent power of self-control.

Thus, under the operation of the Law of Spiritual Gravity this physical life is fraught with momentous significance and unlimited possibilities. It is, in fact, the training ground from which we pass to a higher conflict. The life we live here determines the level to which we gravitate there.

We may, if we will, so avail ourselves of the opportunities of this life as to lift the soul at physical death above the Line of Victory into the realms of light and life and Individual Immortality.   Or, we may by our indifference to the possibilities of another life develop a Spiritual Gravity which at physical death will carry us into that great middle psychological state which lies below the Line of Victory and above the Line of Despair, but still within the midst of the great battle of life.

In like manner, by complete surrender to the destructive power of our evil appetites, passions, desires, impulses, emotions and propensities, or by the deliberate and intentional abuse of the knowledge we possess and the forces we command we may destroy the powers by which it is possible for us to ascend the scale of evolutionary development.   By the intentional abuse of knowledge and the deliberate misuse of power we may establish a Spiritual Gravity which at physical death will carry us at once below the level of the Line of Despair into the realm of spiritual darkness and spiritual death.

These are not the poetic imaginings of a Dante nor a Milton.   They are not the charming mysticism of a Balzac nor a Corelli.   They are not the metaphysical misconceptions of any creed or religion.   On the other hand, they are the determined results of a definite science.

The thoughtful student will not fail to note the fact that the Catholic doctrine and dogma of Hell, Purgatory and Paradise, is not entirely without foundation in the Law of Spiritual Gravity.   It is evident to those who have followed the history of that organization that the dogmatists of that church have sensed the existence of this great law.   In its "Indulgences" and "Absolutions," however, it violates the fundamental law of Nature which underlies the development of individual life and thereby entirely nullifies the value of its near approach to this great fundamental truth.

If at this point the student should ask concerning the effect of the Law of Spiritual Gravity upon the doctrine of reincarnation, it is only necessary to state:

1.   The subject of reincarnation is not under consideration in this work.

2.   Even if it were an established fact, it could not in the least degree mitigate nor modify the law of individual life here outlined.   The Law of Spiritual Gravity has been scientifically

determined as far as it is possible for finite intelligence to determine any law, and to whatever extent the doctrine of reincarnation or any other doctrine proves to be true, it cannot conflict with an established law of Nature.

Under the Law of Spiritual Gravity in its relation to the evolution of individual intelligence, Individual Immortality is an achievement of the Soul and not an arbitrary imposition of God or Nature upon all mankind without regard to individual choice. It is a reward guaranteed by Nature to each individual man and woman for the right application of acquired knowledge and the right use of developed powers.

In its evolutionary ascent under the paternal dominion and guidance of God, or Nature, or Universal Intelligence (whichever term may best express the intelligence which manifests itself in all the forces, activities and processes of Nature) the individualized, intelligent entity reaches its "majority," so to speak, at the estate of man.

At this evolutionary point the Great Intelligence invests the individual entity with the soul attributes of Self-Consciousness, Reason, Independent Choice, and an independent, self-conscious and rational Volition necessary to its self-preservation and independent action; then severs the tie which makes it a "Child of Nature" and emancipates it from all paternal dominion and control.

The individual, by virtue of the Soul attributes with which he is thus invested, comes to his "majority" with a full and complete understanding and recognition of his emancipation from paternal authority, and voluntarily assumes the duties, obligations and responsibilities which his freedom imposes. This is why he calls himself a "free moral agent" and a "responsible individual intelligence."

The young man who reaches the period of his majority under the civil law thereby, without further act, process or formality, becomes an independent citizen of the state. He attains this status by the simple processes of Nature over which he has no control whatever. And yet, he knows that from the moment or the instant he reaches this point in the process of his individual unfoldment he occupies a wholly different position before the law.

He can no longer demand nor claim paternal protection. Neither is he bound by filial obligations and responsibilities, save and except such as he voluntarily assumes. He is now a responsible individual intelligence before the law. He is a citizen of the state, with all the rights, privileges, duties, obligations and responsibilities which are the natural concomitants of such a citizenship. He occupies a status quite different from that prior to his majority. During his minority he had neither rights, privileges, duties, obligations nor responsibilities, save such as were his by virtue of his infancy.

So it appears that under the evolutionary process the individual entity, without further act, process or formality, reaches its majority at the estate of man. From the instant he emerges from the infancy of animal nature into the estate of man he can no longer hold Nature or the Great Intelligence responsible for his own individual life or conduct. He can no longer demand or claim paternal protection as an inalienable right, save and except as he earns it. He is no longer bound by filial duties, obligations or responsibilities, save such as he voluntarily assumes.

But he is now a citizen of the great world, entitled to all the rights and privileges and bound by all the duties, obligations and responsibilities which are the natural concomitants of such a citizenship. He is therefore still within the jurisdiction of both law and order.

But like the citizen of the state, he may either obey the law or violate it at will. Neither God nor Nature assumes to compel obedience to nor prevent violations of the law. This is a matter which the individual alone must determine. Nature assumes only to reward obedience to and punish violations and infractions of her laws.

If by his own free will and independent choice he elects to acknowledge and respect the majesty of the law he thereby earns the rewards and benefits which the law guarantees. If, on the other hand, he elects to violate or disregard the duties and obligations which the law imposes he must suffer the inevitable penalties which the law prescribes therefor.

But in the realm of this higher citizenship of the Soul there is but one law, the great Law of Justice.

By obedience to this law we discharge our individual responsibility and thereby earn Nature's reward therefor, which is Individual Immortality. And this, to us, is Compensatory Justice.

By our violation of this same great law we incur the penalty which Nature prescribes therefor, which, according to the terminology of Natural Science, is Spiritual Death, the Second Death, or total Individual Extinction. And this, to us, is Retributive Justice.

Thus, in its final analysis the Law of Justice, as it is known and exemplified in the realm of the soul's citizenship, is the law of individual Life and Death. Under the operation of this law the right of individual and independent choice is an inalienable and inviolable right of every individual man and woman.

In accordance therewith man is, in the most exact and literal sense, the arbiter of his own destiny. He goes to that destiny, whether it be in the realm of light and life and Immortality, or in that of darkness, disintegration and Death, because he and he alone has so elected. And this is the scientific "Doctrine of Election."

A more comprehensive understanding of the Law of Spiritual Gravity may be obtained by noting the interesting manner in which it exemplifies itself in the daily lives of men and women upon the plane of this present physical life.

Humanity everywhere, in a large and general sense, groups itself in accordance with this law.

For illustration, men whose lives are dominated by political ambitions, political motives or political interests, in general, are drawn together by this same Law of Spiritual Gravity and they form themselves into political clubs. They naturally gravitate to the common level of "politics."

Men and women who are attracted by the same ethical or religious creeds, principles and purposes gravitate together by virtue of the same law and form themselves into churches or societies. They meet upon the common level of the creed or ethical standard they adopt and the work in which they engage.

Men and women whose lives are dominated by the glitter and the license of wealth are drawn together by the common bonds of estheticism, vanity and licentiousness and form themselves into exclusive social sets. Under the operation of the same law they gravitate to the so-called fashionable sections of all the great cities of the world. Here they build themselves mansions and castles and surround themselves with all the beauty, luxury and license that wealth can buy.

Men and women who are ruled by the lusts of the flesh, but without the wealth to purchase social and legal amenities, gravitate together upon the common level of the brothel and the house of prostitution. By the same law they are found grouped together in the slums of all the great cities. In recognition of the moral and spiritual level to which they naturally gravitate the women of this class have come to be known with singular significance as the *"demi monde,"* or the under world of society.

And so it is with those who are moved to action by the nobler inspirations of life.

The Salvation Army, than which perhaps no single agency has accomplished greater good in its chosen field of labor, is drawn together by the same general law and does its work upon the common level of the public street.

It may be incidentally remarked in passing that the work of these earnest enthusiasts is effective because of their ability to carry their active sympathies with them down to the spiritual as well as the physical level of those whose emancipation constitutes the burden of their common labors. This is because they themselves have come up out of the same conditions and therefore fully understand them.

Thus the Law of Spiritual Gravity obtains upon all the planes and in all the conditions of life both here and hereafter, as far as it has been possible to follow its operations.

It exemplifies itself in all the departments of Nature and upon all the levels of individual life, so far as we know them.

With this primary and vital law of Nature, therefore, clearly in mind it is now possible for us to pass at once to an intelligent consideration of the post mortem effects of hypnotism and mediumship upon both the subject and the operator.

The law which binds a physically disembodied subject of hypnotism to its physically embodied hypnotist has been sufficiently considered in Part I of this volume. It now remains to note the results after the hypnotist also shall have passed through the gates of physical death and shall once more stand consciously face to face with his subjects upon the planes of spiritual life. Then it is that he obtains, perhaps, his first comprehensive understanding of the fundamental Law of Justice in its twofold aspect of Compensation and Retribution.

Under the Compensatory side of this law every unselfish act done in behalf of one's fellow man brings to the benefactor a definite soul reward. It lightens the Gravity of the Spirit and permits the Soul to rise in obedience to the law of its essential being to realms of greater light and fuller life.

Under the Retributive side of this same law every act of this life or the life to come, so far as we know, which purposely deprives a fellow man of that which of right is his brings to the wrongdoer a definite soul retribution. It increases and intensifies his Spiritual Gravity and in obedience to the law of his essential being he sinks toward the realm of darkness and spiritual death.

Under its Compensatory side every unselfish act which brings comfort, aid, joy, happiness or good to another carries with it the obligation upon the one so receiving to give in equal measure to those who need.

Under its Retributive side every act of this life or of the life to come, so far as known, which purposely deprives a fellow man of that which of right is his thereby fixes upon the wrongdoer the individual responsibility of righting the wrong himself if it be within his power, otherwise of rendering an equivalent service to those who need that which he can give.

Under the twofold aspect and operation of this great law the individual who knowingly and intentionally surrenders an inalienable right of the soul can never entirely recover it by his own individual effort alone. He must seek for and obtain the help of those who are able to give that which by such a surrender he has permitted to pass beyond the limits of his own individual powers.

When the hypnotist, therefore, emerges from the valley of the shadow of death freed from the encumbrance of a physical body he realizes that the demands of his subjects have long since matured. He finds those whose inalienable rights he has sequestered (and who have not yet been able by the help of others to regain them) awaiting his coming.

Their demands, being duly presented and verified in accordance with the "Statutes of Nature," are scheduled in the inventory of his fixed liabilities. Not only this, every such demand is a "preferred claim" under the law of its creation. It is therefore not subject to "discount." It cannot be compromised nor "prorated." It must be paid "in full."

The hypnotist, therefore, finds himself a spiritual mendicant, a pauper, a defaulting debtor. He is an insolvent, a bankrupt, without the benefit or advantage of an insolvency or bankrupt law or proceeding under which to relieve himself by scaling his liabilities. What, then, can he do?

There is but one alternative. He must either repudiate his liabilities and suffer the penalties which the law prescribes, or he must throw himself upon the mercy of the court and ask for time and opportunity to "work them out."

Fortunately, Nature is never impatient with those who honestly and humbly seek to discharge their just liabilities under her laws. She never demands more from her citizens than they are able to perform. To the hypnotist, therefore, she would seem to say: "These are your obligations. You alone are responsible for their creation. You, therefore, must liquidate them. While it may not be possible for you to meet them all at once, you can at least begin now. If you in good faith honor the law's demands you shall have whatever time the full limit of your abilities may require to make restitution. Go, therefore, and in the order of their maturity repay the debts you owe. By your individual service you may work them out, rendering to each and every creditor in rightful turn the full measure of his just demands."

Thus it is that under the Law of Retributive Justice the man who enslaves the souls of his fellow men, by the same act forges about his own neck the iron collar of servitude. In the realm of the soul the tyrant master becomes the slave of his own tyranny. Nor can he escape from this self-imposed bondage save by the narrow and steep pathway of servitude. He cannot claim emancipation for himself until the Law of Retributive Justice is fully satisfied.

A leading hypnotist of this country is reported to have recently fixed the number of his subjects at something like two thousand. He thus confesses judgment in advance in favor of each and every one of these individuals when he shall stand with them upon the common level of spiritual life. To whatever extent he has deprived each one of these two thousand subjects of the inalienable right and power of self-control to that extent he has irrevocably fixed upon himself the burden of retribution. In the same measure he has invoked upon himself the operation of the Law of Spiritual Gravity. Under its immutable provisions he must sink to the level of the law's demands.

Precisely the same law governs the relation of the spiritual control to its medium. The spiritual intelligence who deprives a medium of the power of self-control thereby, to the same extent, forges the chains of servitude upon himself. In obedience to the same law he must repair the injury thus wrought, if it be within his power, and if not, then he must render an equivalent service to those who need the help which he can give. There is absolutely no escape if he would rise to higher levels of life and achievement upon the spiritual planes.

The following, within the personal knowledge of the writer, will serve to more fully illustrate the meaning and the practical application and operation of the law:

Some years ago one of the leading physicians and surgeons of the middle west died. If his name were here mentioned there are still many of his old-time friends in the flesh who would be glad to acknowledge their indebtedness to his kindness and medical and surgical skill. A few months after his death a lady, who during his lifetime had been one of his patients, was visiting at the home of a friend who had become somewhat interested in the planchette. Out of curiosity and partly in reply to a banter from her friend she put her hand upon the instrument. To her great astonishment it immediately spelled out the name of the eminent physician.

Naturally this initial experience led to further experimentation, and in a short time messages of undoubted authenticity were received from the doctor to various friends and relatives whom he had left behind. This was followed by the organization of a "developing circle" at which the lady was soon developed as a trance speaking medium with the eminent doctor as her chief control.

Things moved along smoothly for some time until a great many of the doctor's former friends and associates became deeply interested in the developments. But in course of time, as it so often transpires, evil intelligences forced themselves into the environment.

The doctor then, for the first time, appeared to realize his mistake. He found, to his unspeakable horror and regret, that he had opened the door of control to the entire spiritual world, or to as many of that world as chose to exercise their power to that end. He then saw and understood the destructive nature of the process employed. He was forced to observe that it was not only sapping her physical vitality, but that she was being psychically destroyed as well.

Recognizing his own responsibility in the matter, and being a man of the keenest sense of justice, he undertook the task of protecting her from the domination of these vicious influences until such time as she could be educated in the power of self-control beyond the range of their malevolent influence. This task of education and reinvestment has thus far proved to be beyond the limits of the good doctor's powers. His subject is still a tractable instrument to whatever spiritual intelligences desire to control her. The eminent doctor, therefore, is now obliged to devote all his time and effort to her protection. Although he has learned the destructive character of the mediumistic process, it nevertheless often occurs that the only method by which he can prevent her from falling under the control of the most vicious and dangerous spiritual intelligences, is to control her himself. Although he has now learned that every time he controls her he violates the very fundamental law of her being, nevertheless he is placed in the unhappy position of being compelled to choose between two evils.

At the present time this innocent victim of mediumistic control would be pronounced by all regular physicians who do not understand the nature of her case to be a fit subject for the insane asylum. She would undoubtedly be sent to such an institution if it were not for the fact that the members of her own household understand, in some measure, the real cause of her condition.

While it is not at all likely, under all the circumstances, that she will live but a few years or possibly months more, yet however long her physical life may be prolonged, the doctor is bound to a most humiliating servitude from which there is no escape under the law of individual responsibility. But this is not all. When she also shall have crossed the troubled waters, he must still protect her and educate her and aid her until she is once more invested with the power of self-control.

Many pertinent questions are likely to present themselves to the mind of the student in this connection.

For instance: Did the learned doctor understand the law and its penalties at the time he first controlled this medium? Why did he control her at all? Do these evil spirits who are always ready to rush in wherever the door is opened understand the law? Do they know that by this same process they not only destroy the medium but at the same time bind themselves to further servitude? Do they know the effect this has upon their Spiritual Gravity? If so, why do they do it? etc., etc.

Briefly answering these questions:

1.   The doctor in this particular instance did not fully understand the nature or results of the mediumistic process at the beginning of his experiment. Had he known that it was destructive in its effects, there is every reason for believing from his known reputation for honesty and morality, that he never would have entered into the relation. His ignorance of the law, however, could not in the least mitigate its results in so far as the medium herself is concerned. Fire burns just the same whether one falls into it by accident or is thrust into it by design. The effects upon the doctor himself, however, present quite another question. The lack of evil intent would be in his favor and would somewhat modify the results.

2.   His desire to communicate with his friends in the flesh was doubtless very strong. It would seem that this is equally true of the very large majority of those who pass into that life. Nor should we be surprised that this is so when we remember how strong is our own desire to hear from those who have gone before us into that country. This simple desire to keep in touch with his former friends and relatives was doubtless the motive which prompted him to seek that method of communication. Nor can we find aught in such a motive to condemn. In this instance nothing but the process employed is subject to condemnation.

3.   Some of these evil spirits understand the law very fully while others do not.

4.   Those who have been in that life long enough to have learned the law, fully understand its effects upon themselves and the obligations they assume thereunder.

5.   They defy the law, however, and invoke its penalties for the same reasons that men in the flesh do the same thing. To an inhabitant of another planet where knowledge is never abused (if there be any such) it would doubtless appear strange that men will deliberately go on drinking liquor to excess when they know full well that it is only killing them. To one who has never experienced the effects of morphine, opium or cocaine it might also appear strange that any intelligent individual would ever become addicted to their use. But

these are phenomena with which we are all so familiar that we think but little or nothing of them. And yet, they fully explain why it is that spiritual intelligences will defy the laws of their being even though death be the result. It is because in the gratification of selfish ambitions and desires men often prefer to defy the law and suffer its penalties rather than obey it and earn its rewards. It is simply a matter of individual choice.

It must be remembered that the power of independent choice is an inalienable right of the soul. It is as absolute and indefeasible upon the spiritual planes as it is upon the physical. Men are therefore no more compelled to obey the law of life there than they are here. It is there, as it is here, a matter of individual choice. We all know that food is necessary to sustain physical life. Not one of us, however, is compelled to take it. We all likewise know that too much food is almost as dangerous to physical life and health as too little, but we are not compelled to stop eating when the law of health has been complied with. These are matters of individual choice. While we all know the law fully and understand the exact meaning of its penalties, we are nevertheless able to defy it if we so elect. But we cannot evade nor avoid its penalties.

There is, however, an important distinction between the position of the hypnotist and that of the spiritual control which might be overlooked if attention were not called to it in this connection.

The hypnotic process and the mediumistic process are in essence the same thing as far as they go. This has been fully developed in a previous chapter. But it must be remembered that the hypnotist is on the same plane with his subjects while the spiritual control is not. For this reason the hypnotist has an immense advantage in point of facility. He is therefore in position to accomplish vastly more harm upon the physical plane to both himself and others.

For instance: One professional hypnotist alone who is devoting his time and effort to his profession may, perhaps, within the period of a very few years acomplish the complete subjection and control of a thousand different subjects. One spiritual control, however, very rarely accomplishes the development of more than a dozen mediums within the period of an average physical lifetime. After a medium is once fully developed and the condition of psychic subjectivity completely established it is then possible for a thousand spiritual controls to operate successfully through the one instrument during a single year.

Thus, a single hypnotist, under the Law of Retributive Justice, may easily bind himself in the bonds of servitude to a thousand subjects, while a thousand spiritual controls may be able to divide among themselves the responsibility for the subjection of a single medium.

From this view of the subject it will be easily understood and appreciated that in proportion to numbers the hypnotist is by far the more dangerous factor in society.

It is also true that under the Law of Retributive Justice and Spiritual Gravity he is also the greater sufferer in exactly the same proportion upon the spiritual planes of life.

CHAPTER IX.

ADMONITIONS AND SUGGESTIONS.

I.

TO THE HYPNOTIST.

In accordance with the facts discovered and the principles demonstrated Natural Science is in position to declare with scientific certainty, and does so declare:

Hypnotism is a subjective, psychic process.

It is the process by and through which you obtain, hold and exercise control of the will, voluntary powers and sensory organism of your subjects.

By your own testimony, as well as that of every honest hypnotist who has ever testified upon the subject, you stand convicted of teaching and practicing a process which deprives your subjects of the inalienable right and power of individual self-control.

In exact proportion as you establish hypnotic control of your subject's will, voluntary powers and sensory organism you thereby and at the same time deprive him of the power of self-control.

In proportion as you deprive him of the power of self-control you thereby and at the same time deprive him of that upon which his individual responsibility and moral status depend.

In proportion as you deprive him of the free and independent control and exercise of those attributes and powers of the soul upon which his individual responsibility and moral status depend you thereby and at the same time rob him of those powers upon which he must depend for the achievement of Individual Immortality.

In proportion as you deprive him of the powers upon which he must depend for the achievement of Individual Immortality you thereby and at the same time condemn him to Spiritual Darkness, Disintegration and Death.

In the same proportion you, by the same act and at the

same time, invoke upon him the operation of the Destructive Principle of Nature in Individual Life.

In proportion as you deprive him of the free and independent control and exercise of any or all of the inalienable rights, faculties, capacities and powers of the soul you thereby and at the same time assume individual responsibility under the law of life for all that it otherwise holds him responsible.

In proportion as you divest him of the free and independent exercise of his own independent, self-conscious and rational volition you thereby and at the same time forge upon your own soul the chains of spiritual servitude to him, under the Law of Retributive Justice.

With all the power, authority and emphasis of universal language, Nature invests the individual human intelligence, ego, soul or entity, with the power of self-control and fixes upon him the primary duty of himself alone exercising that individual right and power, and discharging that duty.

The right and duty of each individual to at all times exercise the power of self-control involves in equal measure the concomitant obligation upon you and all mankind to respect that right and duty.

By your violation of this fundamental obligation and your infraction of Nature's law in relation thereto you deprive the soul of your fellow man of the one transcendent power upon which its Individual Immortality depends and stand convicted before the bar of Nature and the judgments of men, of THE GREAT PSYCHOLOGICAL CRIME.

You thereby and at the same time invoke upon yourself the irrevocable penalty which Nature prescribes therefor. You cannot evade it. You cannot avoid it. You can neither mitigate nor modify it. Alone you must walk the path of life and alone you must expiate this Crime against the fundamental Law of Justice and against the life and liberty of your fellow man.

II.

To the Hypnotic Subject.

As the crowning achievement of evolutionary development Nature has invested you, as a man, with certain distinctive and exclusive attributes and characteristics which distinguish you from the animal.

These are:

1. SELF-CONSCIOUSNESS, as distinguished from the simple consciousness of animal life and nature.

2. REASON, as distinguished from the simple intelligence of the animal.

3. INDEPENDENT CHOICE, as distinguished from the instinctive selections of animal nature.

4. Independent, self-conscious and rational VOLITION, as distinguished from the irrational, impulsive and instinctive volition of all forms of animal life.

Upon these distinctive and exclusive attributes and characteristics of your nature you must depend for all that enables you to rise above the level of animal life and animal nature.

Upon these alone you must also depend for all that makes you a responsible, individual intelligence.

Upon these and these alone you must depend for all that gives you a moral status among your fellow men.

Upon these and these alone you must depend for all your ability to achieve Individual Immortality.

The degree to which you are in undisputed possession and control of all these attributes of the soul at any given time determines with unerring accuracy the degree to which you are then a responsible, individual intelligence.

To the same degree and for the same reason you are then morally accountable to your fellow men.

The degree to which you are now in undisputed possession and independent control of your self-consciousness, reason, independent choice and volition, determines with unerring accuracy the distance to which you have risen above the plane of animal life and animal nature.

Whatever in any degree divests or deprives you of your own natural dominion and control over all or any of these distinctively human attributes of the soul, thereby at the same time and in exactly the same degree, robs you of your life, your liberty, your individual responsibility, your moral character and accountability, and the power upon which you **must** depend for the achievement of Individual Immortality.

Whatever in the least possible measure divests you of your independent control over these distinctively human attributes, capacities and powers of the soul, thereby at the same time and in precisely the same degree, reduces you toward the level of animal nature.

It is determined with absolute scientific certainty that hypnotism, in just so far as you become a subject of it, divests you of your power of independent choice and your power of will or volition.

To the exact degree, therefore, that you become a subject of the hypnotic process it divests you of your own independent control of each and every one of those distinctive and exclusive attributes and powers of the soul which lift you above the level of animal life and animal nature.

It takes from you your individual responsibility. It deprives you of your moral accountability. It dispossesses you of your power of self-control. It divests you of the powers upon which you must depend for the achievement of Individual Immortality. In just so far as it exists it robs you of the soul attributes which distinguish you as a human being, and reduces you to the level of your animal nature.

It makes of you a negative quantity, a nullity, a nonentity in the great world of activity, of thought, of accomplishment and achievement.

It destroys in you everything you possess that commands the admiration, the confidence and the respect of your fellow men.

It makes of you a mere plaything for the entertainment of those of your fellows who desire to amuse themselves at your expense.

Worst of all, it makes of you a dependent, a mere servant, a slave, a menial, a puppet, a serf.

It binds you to a base, an ignoble and a humiliating servitude both here and hereafter. With these facts thus plainly before you, to whatever extent you invite it, permit it, or knowingly and intentionally become a party to it, you thereby and at the same time become also an ACCESSORY TO THE GREAT PSYCHOLOGICAL CRIME.

As such, you invoke upon yourself the operation of The Destructive Principle of Nature in Individual Life. As such, you must, in addition, suffer the penalty which Nature prescribes therefor.

There is no vicarious atonement possible to those who deliberately participate in the commission of this vital offense against the law of individual life.

To the full measure of your own conscious and intentional part in it the crime is yours. To this extent you and you alone must expiate it.

III.

To the Genuine Medium.

All that has been said by way of admonition or suggestion to the hypnotic subject applies with equal relevancy, materiality, logic and force to you. But in order that you may not suffer injustice, by inference, in relation to matters therein considered, it is necessary that something be added.

The motives which inspire you are fully understood and appreciated. In just so far as you are moved by a sense of religious duty, or by a desire to relieve the sufferings and the ills of your fellow men and women, or by sympathy for the sorrowing, or by the importunities of friends and seekers after truth, or by your own honest desire for exact and definite knowledge of another life, or by the conviction that your mediumship is a "Gift" or a "Power" which you are in duty bound to dedicate to the world, your motives are fully respected and your intentions heartily commended.

Most unfortunately for you, however, it is not a question of motives nor intentions at all. It is the vastly more important question of results and results only.

No true religion ever has demanded nor in the very nature of things ever will demand of you the surrender of your individual responsibility, nor your moral accountability, nor your power of self-control, nor any of the faculties, capacities and powers upon which you must depend for the achievement of your Individual Immortality.

However desirable it may be under right conditions to obtain definite knowledge of a life beyond the grave, this cannot be justly nor rightfully nor lawfully done by any process or means which involves the sacrifice of individual life, or the surrender or suppression of any of the individual and inalienable rights and powers of the soul.

The law of Life is the law of Individual Development.

The law of Death is the law of Individual Subjection and Surrender.

You know full well that the men and women who to-day command the admiration, the confidence and the respect of their fellow men and women are not those who are under the domination and control of other intelligences.

Those who achieve individual success are those who employ their own intelligence and their own reason, those who exercise their own independent powers and rely upon their own independent judgments in all the affairs of life. This is the law of individual being both here and hereafter. In the realm of the soul itself science finds no exceptions.

If you have been flattered by the assurances of your controls, or have comforted yourself in the belief that your mediumship is a "gift" or a "power" conferred upon you by the gods as a badge of honor or a token of preferment, be not deceived longer, for such is not the case.

To whatever extent your mediumship has served to single you out from among the great general average of men and women, it stands for nothing so much as it does your own individual weakness and subjection.

To whatever extent it has given you a place in the seance, the circle, the cabinet or the pulpit is due to nothing over which you in your own right have dominion and control. Neither is it due to any knowledge or power which you in your own right possess. On the other hand, it is because of your lack of knowledge, your want of independence and your surrender of individual powers.

It is neither a "gift" nor a "power" of your own that paralyzes your will and makes of you a pliant and helpless tool to do the bidding of oftentimes selfish and irresponsible controls. It is neither a "gift" nor a "power" of your own that drags you bodily before a curious and oftentimes trifling, frivolous and deprecating audience and there compels you automatically to say and do that which your own intelligence would condemn and your own self-respect forbid if you but knew it.

The "power" that robs you of all you possess, which lifts you to a plane above the level of the animal, is not a "power" to be sought nor to be proud of. The "gift" that wrests from you the one transcendent power of the soul, the power of Self-Control, is not a "gift" to be prized nor one to command honest admiration.

You know full well that among the dearest possessions of the soul is the sovereign, independent power to command in your own right the confidence, the approval, the trust, the respect, the appreciation and the personal affection of your fellow men and women.

You also know, if you have studied the lives and experiences of other mediums, possibly you may know it from a personal experience, that in exact proportion as it becomes known that you are subject to the domination and control of spiritual intelligences your own reputation for stability of character, integrity, reliability, judgment and discretion inevitably suffers.

In your capacity as a mediumistic instrument you reflect to those upon the physical plane whatever degree of intelligence, honesty, wisdom or morality your controls desire to exhibit through you. Most of those who thus observe you are unable to differentiate between you and your controls.

When your controls are lofty in expression and exalted in thought you as their instrument lend yourself to the harmony of thought and expression. It is then that you appear to greatest advantage. When your controls are frivolous, coarse or vulgar, their spirit and intent reflect themselves through you, and it is then that you appear to great disadvantage.

And so it is that you are made the innocent victim of

those upon whom you thus rely for guidance, direction, protection and inspiration to life and action.

If you would be strong in your own right, either here or in the life to come, you must declare your independence from all subjection and from all subjective processes. You must assert your sovereign dominion over the faculties, capacities and powers of the soul upon which your individual responsibility depends. You must rise to the dignity and the majesty of self-reliance and Self-Control.

IV.
To the "Sensitive."

Perhaps there is no individual in society to-day who needs more to understand the laws of spiritual development than you. Certain it is that there is no member of society in greater danger of being misled by the subtle and seductive fallacies which are everywhere masquerading under the names of "Hypnotism," "Mediumship," "Occultism," "Mysticism" and "Spiritual Development."

If you have never carefully analyzed what it is to be a "sensitive," you may derive great value from a rational study of this subject. In that connection the following suggestions may be of service to you:

1. A "sensitive" is one who is more than ordinarily susceptible to the influences of his environment.

2. As the term is employed by spiritualists and occultists generally, however, it means one who is more than ordinarily susceptible to the influence of his spiritual environment.

3. In this latter meaning of the term it implies a negative or passive condition of the individual sufficient to make him or her receptive to the influences of the more positive intelligences on the spiritual planes of life.

4. It is found that by far the larger number of genuine "sensitives" are women. This is because of their generally finer and more highly attuned physical and nervous organisms. Hence it is that women, as a class, are more intuitive than men. For this reason they very often get things "out

of the air," while men are compelled to depend upon the more laborious and less expeditious process of reason.

5.   It often occurs that the genuine sensitive is dimly conscious of spiritual presences about him. He is also conscious that he receives thoughts and ideas that are projected upon him from the spiritual side of life. In the semi-conscious hours of sleep it not infrequently occurs that such an individual has visions. These often prove to be full of significance for the peculiar intelligence they convey concerning matters and things not at the time understood.

6.   This condition of sensitiveness may be the result of:

(a)   Heredity.

(b)   Prenatal conditions.

(c)   Conditions for which the individual himself is wholly responsible; such, for instance, as a negative diet, introspective habits of thought, insufficient nourishment, the use of opiates, narcotics, sedatives, etc.

(d)   The gradual refinement of the individual, physically, spiritually and psychically as a result of the evolutionary processes carried on by both the individual and Nature. It now and then occurs that under this process of evolution an individual is brought very close to the border line of conditions between physical Nature and the world of spiritual things.

(e)   Any two or more of these conditions combined may serve to produce the same result.

7.   Regardless of the exact method or process by and through which you have come to be a "sensitive," it is of vital importance for you to know that as such you have reached a state and condition fraught with the most momentous consequences, possibilities and responsibilities that can rest upon any individual, either here or hereafter.

For illustration: If you follow the negative or passive impulse of your nature under these conditions (which most of you do), or listen to the suggestions and advice of those who approve or practice the subjective methods or processes of mediumship, you will, without the least conscious effort on your part, fall into a subjective state or condition and ultimately become a medium.

Under this process you gradually lose the power of self-control. The process itself is so fascinating, so insidious and so gradually progressive that you do not discover this important fact until it is too late for you to retrace your steps alone. As a result, in the natural course of events, you begin to "see things" or "hear things," as the case may be. To your friends and relatives, as well as to every one else who does not understand such experiences, you are promptly pronounced "queer." In the largest number of instances this is but the beginning of the end. From this point the road is both broad and straight that leads to the insane asylum and thence to an ignominious death.

If, perchance, there should be any doubt as to the absolute truth of this statement, it may be fully verified by an examination into the lives and experiences of the insane in our asylums everywhere throughout the land. It will be found from a study of the individual history of these various cases that many of them were only simple "sensitives" in the beginning. The experience was both fascinating and pleasant. They yielded to the passive or negative impulses or tendencies of their natures, or perhaps to insidious suggestions from the spiritual planes, as is often the case. As a natural result, they soon began to "see things." It will be found, however, that in the larger number of instances they first began to "hear voices," or feel the touch of invisible hands or invisible presences.

With these experiences came also the irresistible desire to tell them to their relatives and friends. These, being ignorant of the true cause, became alarmed. The family physician was called in. An examination followed, with the usual result that the case was pronounced "delusional insanity." All such cases thus far have been sent to the insane asylums as the only institutions of the several states equipped with facilities for properly caring for those who are looked upon as mentally unbalanced or mentally irresponsible. It would astonish any intelligent individual who is not already familiar with the facts to know how many of these unfortunate individuals go on "seeing things" or "hearing things" or "feeling things," as the case may be, until death mercifully comes to their relief.

There is but one way for you who have not yet passed the point of mere "sensitiveness" to successfully guard yourselves from the unhappy results here suggested. If you would do this you must proceed at once to exercise your individual intelligence. You must assert your absolute independence of all subjective processes and conditions. You must maintain at all times the active, wakeful consciousness, and in the largest measure possible develop the power of individual self-control.

By following the lines here indicated you will gradually but surely rise above every tendency to subjection. When this has been once fully accomplished it is then possible for you, in course of time and conscientious work, under the personal instruction and direction of one who knows the law and the process, to become a natural and independent psychic without injury to yourself or harm to anyone.

But here again you are likely to encounter grave difficulties. You will find many self-advertised instructors who will not hesitate, for a valuable consideration, to undertake the hazardous task of guiding you over the dangerous road to the desired destination. With rare exceptions, however, they are entirely ignorant of the formula or process of independent spiritual self-development. As an inevitable result their instruction or guidance would serve only to lead you back again into the wilderness of "mysticism," where so many innocent, credulous and trusting souls are to-day wandering in darkness and despair.

But there are Masters who are able to guide you in perfect safety to the goal of independent, spiritual self-illumination. True, they are few in number. But even so, and notwithstanding they receive no fee for their services, alas, they are not overwhelmed with students who possess the Intelligence to take the instruction, the Courage to do the work, and the Perseverance to accomplish the tasks which such an instruction imposes.

It is, indeed, quite possible that if the course of study and the character, quality and scope of the work were laid out before you and you were then asked if you were ready to enter upon the task, you would hesitate to undertake it. And well you might, for a rational, spiritual self-development is the work of years, while mediumistic subjection and control, to one who is already a "sensitive" come almost immediately and without effort.

But even though you may not be prepared to undertake the process of independent development, it is nevertheless possible for you to avoid the pitfalls of subjection. In order that you may not fall a victim to the seductive charms of negation and self-surrender, it is of the most vital importance that you have clearly and distinctly in mind the difference between subjective and independent methods and processes. Then and then only will you be able to avoid the dangers which menace every "sensitive."

If, therefore, you would guard yourself from the blighting effects of mediumistic subjection, and preserve your independence and your powers as a sovereign, individual intelligence, you must assert your individuality. You must use your reason. You must maintain the highest possible measure of self-control over all the faculties, capacities and powers of your own individual being.

As a "sensitive" you stand at the parting of the ways. One of these leads onward and upward along the pathway of individual growth, development, acquisition, power, self-respect and the respect of your fellow-man. The other leads downward along the pathway of individual weakness, negation, inertia, self-surrender, degeneracy, self-condemnation and the condemnation of your fellow-man.

The one is THE WAY OF LIFE.

The other is THE WAY OF DEATH.

V.

TO THE SPIRITUALIST.

If you have followed the subject consistently and conscientiously to this point it will be perfectly clear to you that no attempt has been made to evade, avoid, ignore nor minimize any of the established facts upon which your acceptance of spiritualism is based. No effort has been made to disturb you in any manner whatsoever concerning the phenomena of mediumship nor the interpretations you have placed upon them. There is no desire to deprive you of the smallest grain of comfort to be derived from the great fact that there is a life after physical death, and that such a life is scientifically demonstrable. There is no wish to discredit the fact that mediumship embodies one of the methods and processes by and through which communication may be established and maintained between the two worlds of matter, life and intelligence.

While all this is true, it has nevertheless been conclusively demonstrated by the methods of exact science that the mediumistic process involves a violation of natural law. It is to this fundamental fact and this alone that you are asked in all sincerity and candor to apply your intelligence, your reason and your conscience. In this central and vital fact lurk the most insidious, subtle and fascinating dangers to "Life, Liberty and the Pursuit of Happiness."

It is a fact well known that the great body constituting the rank and file of Spiritualism are made up of those of you who are not mediums and who perhaps never will be. The largest majority of your number do not wish to become mediums. Many of you have been and are sufficiently close students and observers to have discovered for yourselves the destructive nature and effects of the mediumistic process. Many others of your number have intuitively sensed the danger in time to avoid it.

Even your leading journals, in recent years, have sounded the note of warning times almost without number. But in almost every such instance it is assumed, or is left by inference to so appear, that the dangers and the destructive results are all due entirely to the malicious work of evil spirits, who deliberately and intentionally destroy their mediums, and not to the mediumistic process itself.

Indeed, it does not appear to have thus far occurred to your leading thinkers and writers that the dangers and the destructive results are primarily due entirely to the medium-istic process itself and not to the spiritual intelligences who employ it or set it in motion. This, however, is the vital distinction. It is herein also that the remedy must be found.

The wisest physician on earth cannot paralyze the heart action of his patient without at the same time and by the same process destroying the patient's life. The doctor himself may be a seer or a saint, or he may be a villain and an outlaw. It matters not. If he employs a process which paralyzes the heart the inevitable consequence is death. Nor does his motive or intent have anything to do with it. It is the process employed which produces the destructive results, and not the character, motive or intent of the doctor who applies it.

Just so with mediumship. The destructive results are due primarily to the process itself and not to the personal character nor the motives nor the wisdom nor the folly nor the evil intent of those who apply it.

Whatever process paralyzes the will and voluntary powers of any individual is destructive in its nature and effects. It matters not who applies it. It matters not what name we give it. We may even name it "The Great Restorer" if you like, but this will in no wise change its action. We may call it hypnotism, or statuvolism, or mesmerism, or psychratism, or mediumship, or the Communion of Saints. This does not change its nature, its action nor its results. The mere adoption of a name cannot convert a destructive process into a constructive process, nor transmute death into life.

The dangers and the misfortunes and the desolations which follow in the pathway of mediumship are all due, primarily, to the great fundamental fact that mediumship is a subjective, psychic process. As such it paralyzes the will and voluntary powers of its subjects in just so far as it exists at any given time. Paralysis of the will, by whatever method or means accomplished, is a destructive process.

Nor does it in the least degree change the character of the process nor minimize its destructive results if, perchance, the subject of it should thereby become clairvoyant or clairaudient and as an incidental result thereof demonstrate thereby the existence of another life.

It is a fact well known to science that persons who slowly bleed to death, or those who starve, very often become both clairvoyant and clairaudient just before the transition we call death. This, however, does not sanctify the process of starvation nor glorify the practice of hemorrhage, nor in the least alter the destructive nature of either.

Quite aside from the rigid practices of the ancient ascetics or the diabolical and inhuman castigations of the barbaric religious devotees of primitive civilizations, it has been demonstrated that in this day and age of our race spiritual illumination does not necessarily involve ultra means or methods of any kind.

The time has come, in fact, when the same character of rational discrimination with which we examine other questions of science must be applied to the mediumistic process. However sorely we may be tempted to do so, we cannot afford to shut our eyes to the principle involved merely because we are interested in the phenomena of mediumship. We cannot afford to blindly indorse or approve this particular process or any other merely because it happens to afford us entertainment or amusement or even some degree of comfort and satisfaction. To do so would be to put ourselves upon a moral level with Nero, who is said to have accounted all things good which pleased him and all things evil which failed to do so.

If Spiritualism is to become a permanent, living factor in the moral and spiritual evolution of our race, you who represent its best brains, wisest thoughts and highest morals must come to the front and assert your independence. You must look beyond the mere phenomena of mediumship and recognize the demonstrated fact of science that the process back of them is destructive in its essential nature.

However radical the departure may be from the past and present position of your people upon this particular subject, you must insist upon the entire abandonment of every phase, form and degree of mediumship. You must turn your backs upon every process and practice which involves the subjection of one intelligence (or any of the faculties, capacities or powers thereof) to the domination and control of another. You must set the stamp of your uncompromising disapproval upon any and every process or practice which deprives the individual of the free and independent exercise of any one or more of the attributes of the soul upon which his individual responsibility depends.

Doubtless the question has already occurred to you: "How is it possible for Spiritualists to repudiate mediumship without thereby and at the same time renouncing Spiritualism itself?" This is indeed a searching question. Nor can it be answered in a single sentence. The following suggestions, however, may prove to be of possible value in that connection:

1. Spiritualism involves two distinct and separate phases of the same general subject.

2. One of these relates entirely to what is known as the phenomena of Spiritualism.

3. The other is confined exclusively to what is known as the ethics, or the philosophy, or the religion of Spiritualism.

4. The phenomena of Spiritualism are related wholly and exclusively to the various phases and forms of mediumship. They all, therefore, depend upon the mediumistic process for their production. This constitutes what may very properly be termed the purely mechanical side of Spiritualism.

5. But phenomena, of themselves, do not and cannot constitute a religion, nor a philosophy, nor a moral code, nor an ethical system by which to live a life. They simply constitute data from which a religious creed or a philosophical system or an ethical code may be formulated.

6. There is a process, however, wholly different from that of mediumship, by and through which all the data of mediumship and vastly more may be acquired by those who possess the Intelligence, Courage and Perseverance to properly fit themselves for its reception and school themselves to its proper use.

7. This process involves the acquisition of exact knowledge, the accomplishment of a specific work, and the living of a definite life. It is an independent, self-conscious and rational process. It is a wide-awake, a normal and an intelligent process. It is a process under which the individual at all times and under all conditions must maintain a normal and healthful control of all his intelligent faculties, capacities and powers. It is a process which enables the individual to see for himself, hear for himself and sense for himself the spiritual data and obtain for himself definite knowledge of another life. It is a process which demands Self-Control instead of self-surrender, and independence of volition instead of subjection to the will of others. In other words, it is in every respect a Constructive process. It develops a Master instead of a Medium.

As this volume is limited to the consideration of Nature's Destructive Principle, the process referred to must be reserved for another volume of this Series.

VI.

To the Minister.

To you, more than to almost any other individual in the community, society in general looks for its inspirations to higher ideals and more exalted achievements, as well as the development of a higher standard of morality and life.

To the extent that this is true your individual responsibility is increased and your obligation to society intensified. You stand in the position of not only a preacher of the word, an expounder of the law and an exemplifier of the life, but also in that of a voluntary, self-appointed, spiritual counselor and personal guide to those who are seeking knowledge of a life beyond the grave.

The very foundation upon which your profession and your life's work depend is the doctrine of another life. All your educational training has centered about this one fundamental tenet. The central purpose of all your schooling and all your study and all your preparation has been to fit you for the great life work of teaching this fundamental doctrine to your fellow-man.

All over our beautiful land schools, colleges, theological seminaries and universities have been erected and at an enormous outlay of time, energy and money are maintained for the sole purpose of equipping you for the proper discharge of your duties and responsibilities in the field of your chosen profession.

Notwithstanding all this, it would appear, from the unqualified statements of some of your most prominent and respected representatives, that there are those among you who do not yet know that there is a life after physical dissolution.

The following authentic incident of very recent occurrence cannot fail to command your intelligent interest and respectful consideration in this connection:

A meeting of select and intelligent gentlemen was recently held in the city of Chicago for the express purpose of listening to an address from one who has never, as yet, achieved the honorable distinction of ordination. On the other hand, it so happens that he is not even a communicant of any church nor a professor of any religious creed as the term "religious" is generally employed and understood.

Nevertheless, it so transpired that during the course of his address he spoke at some length concerning the existence of another life. More than this, he spoke "as one having authority." Those who heard him were impressed with the conviction that he was neither speculating nor guessing, but that he spoke from the standpoint of one who has had a definite personal experience.

Among his audience there seems to have been a most interesting exception in the person of one of the leading members of your profession. The gentleman here referred to is a prominent minister of the Methodist Episcopal Church. More than this, he is in good standing, and so far as known his orthodoxy has never been questioned by his superiors. He was at the time and is now the honored pastor of one of Chicago's conspicuous and prosperous churches.

After the conclusion of the regular address of the evening an opportunity was given to a number of the most prominent gentlemen present to express themselves upon various topics appropriate to the occasion. Among the number called upon was the reverend gentleman above referred to.

He arose, and to the astonishment of every other individual present delivered himself of a severe and almost bitter arraignment of the principal speaker of the evening for presuming to speak with assurance concerning the fact of a life after physical death and the possibility of its actual demonstration.

To the utter amazement of those who heard him, he declared without equivocation or mental reservation, so far as his words would imply, that the existence of a life beyond the grave is a subject entirely beyond the limitations of all human knowledge.

He declared, without exceptions or qualifications of any kind whatsoever, that no man ever has known and no man ever will know whether there is such a life until he has solved the great problem by the process of death itself.

In the same spirit of unqualified dogmatism he assured his audience that in the very nature of things it is absolutely impossible for one in the physical body to know aught of any life above or beyond the physical.

Perhaps the most impressive phase of this remarkable incident is the fact that the reverend gentleman did not appear to realize that his words were freighted with nothing but self-accusation and self-condemnation.

For perhaps a quarter of a century or more this same minister of the gospel has been preaching that there is a life beyond the grave. From many pulpits he has preached it to the multitudes. In the Sunday School he has unhesitatingly taught it to the children, the youth, the mature and the aged. At the hearthstones of his people, where he has gained admittance upon the basis of his personal integrity, he has repeatedly declared it. By reason of his assumed or supposed personal knowledge of it as a definite fact he has been able to comfort the living and allay the fears of the dying. With the unqualified assurance of a definite personal knowledge which none has dared to question, he has proclaimed it in triumph over the graves of the dead. Upon the solemn pledge of his own integrity and the good faith of his religion wherein it is embodied, he has drawn his salary as a duly ordained and active minister of the gospel and has thereby maintained both himself and his family during all these years.

But now, moved by a sudden impulse to rebuke the alleged assumption of one who dares in his presence to give expression to truths with which the reverend gentleman is not yet familiar, he unintentionally lets fall the mask of many years, and without knowing it publicly acknowledges his own duplicity and thereby pronounces his own condemnation.

This incident tells its own story. It needs no explanation. It embodies a most powerful sermon "To Ministers Only," and should commend itself to your earnest and thoughtful consideration.

In this day and age of scientific investigation and demonstration, when the limitations of human knowledge are being constantly extended, you cannot afford to dogmatize concerning the possibilities of human knowledge or human understanding. You cannot afford to thus put yourself on record among those who would prescribe arbitrary metes and bounds for the "knowable" and the "unknowable," or fix unalterable limitations about the "known" and the "unknown."

Do not mistake the purpose nor the meaning of these words. It is not intended to here impugn the value of Faith nor the necessity of Beliefs. Both are fully recognized and admitted.

But if you would command the continued confidence and respect of your fellow-men you must carefully differentiate between knowledge and faith, between the things you "know" and those you merely "believe." More than this, you must make the distinction so plain and so conspicuous at all times that your own people cannot possibly mistake the one for the other.

If you would maintain the commanding position you have so long held of healthful and beneficent influence among your own people and the community in general, you must not only believe and have faith, but you must do more than this. There are some things you must *know*.

And if perchance members of your own congregation should consult you concerning experiences which lie beyond the range of your own personal knowledge, you must possess the humility, the grace and the common honesty to confess your limitations rather than dogmatize with them concerning things you do not know.

It often occurs in these days of spiritual unfoldment that individual members of all the various churches come into definite and conscious touch and relation with their spiritual environment. Since this is a fact which has been verified times almost without number, it follows that any arbitrary denial of it on your part must, sooner or later, lead to your humiliation and discomfort as well as destroy your influence for good wherever your limitations subsequently become known.

Not long since one of your number who is widely known as an able pulpit orator and disputant, engaged in joint public discussion with a prominent Spiritualist upon the claims of Spiritualism.

Unfortunately for your representative, he permitted himself to be drawn into a discussion of mediumship as a fact. He took the broad position that all so-called mediumistic phenomena are nothing more than legerdemain, and that there is no such thing as genuine spiritual communication through mediumistic processes.

As every well-informed student of the subject would anticipate, the decision was overwhelmingly against your position. So strongly was this fact impressed upon those of your number who followed the controversy through to its conclusion that at a meeting of ministers soon thereafter it was wisely decided that joint discussions of this nature do not tend to advance the cause of religion and should therefore be discouraged.

The fatal error in this instance was that of denying the existence of a fact which has been conclusively demonstrated thousands of times over, namely, the fact that there is such a thing as genuine mediumship. The failure to successfully combat this one fact placed you at a disadvantage from which it was impossible to recover. The decision therefore went against you, and justly so. As a natural result of your failure in this instance, Spiritualism has gained an almost irresistible impulse at your expense, for all of which you are entirely responsible.

It is impossible for you or anyone else to successfully deny the fact of mediumship. It is equally impossible for you to successfully deny its phenomena. Neither can you successfully dispute the fact that by and through this process spiritual intelligences can and do often communicate with those yet in the flesh.

If you would successfully meet the Spiritualist you must meet him on his own ground. You must be prepared to admit all the material facts upon which he bases his claims and then stand upon the principle which lies back of these facts.

To admit that mediumship is a fact does not admit that it is right, any more than to admit the existence of murder is an admission that murder is right. To admit that there are genuine spiritual communications through mediums is by no means an admission that the process employed should be commended or approved, any more than to admit a forgery is equivalent to a declaration that forgery is right.

With a proper understanding of the destructive nature of the mediumistic process you are in position to fully and fairly meet every proposition which can be advanced in favor of any school or philosophy or religion which depends upon a subjective, psychic process as its substantial basis.

One additional suggestion may not be deemed out of place in this connection. If you have taken the time to familiarize yourself with the array of data already presented you cannot fail to be impressed with the position here taken upon the subject of ultra religious emotionalism. It has been established beyond all question that ultra emotionalism of any kind involves a subjective process. It is therefore destructive. It opens the door to complete psychic subjection and control. In the very largest number of instances where this occurs the result is so-called "delusional insanity."

Your attention is specially called to the demonstrated facts and to the principle which underlies them. These cannot fail to furnish you much material for serious reflection and earnest consideration. If they shall in any measure serve to furnish a motive and an inspiration which shall help you to lift your religious services and ceremonials from the plane of emotionalism to that of rationalism the purpose of this work will have been in part accomplished.

With the facts at your command there is no body of men in existence in position to accomplish greater good for present and future generations than you can do by an intelligent exposition of the Destructive Principle of Nature in Individual Life as it manifests itself in the subjective psychic processes of Mediumship and Hypnotism.

There is no field of educational work where the harvest is so abundant and ripe and the laborers are so few.

VII.
TO THE BENCH AND BAR.

There is, perhaps, no tribunal in existence to-day better prepared to pass intelligently upon the merits of any question involving legal or equitable considerations than the American Bench and Bar.

There is, without exception, no tribunal of the people to which the writer would more cheerfully or more readily submit a psychological problem involving fine legal discrimination and the application of a just and comprehensive ethical standard.

It has, indeed, been his long cherished hope that the occasion would naturally present itself whereupon he might have the honor of presenting to you, gentlemen, in a more direct and personal form, a number of the more important legal phases of the general subject covered by this volume.

Under the existing circumstances, however, nothing more will be attempted here than to respectfully call your attention in the briefest possible manner to a few of the important propositions upon which, in the nature of things, you will be called to pass legal judgment in the comparatively near future.

Perhaps no psychological proposition was ever more consistently or conclusively established as a principle of law than is that of "undue influence." Although a purely psychological problem, it is nevertheless a subject of which the courts have unhesitatingly taken judicial cognizance. More than this, so important has it appeared to you, and so persistently has it obtruded itself upon your attention, that to-day there is no question among you as to the absolute correctness of the central proposition involved.

In other words, it is now universally recognized as a fact that it is possible for the mentally strong to unduly influence the mentally weak under certain conditions and circumstances. Just what in law constitutes "undue influence" has been passed upon so often and from so many different standpoints, and has been defined with such exactness and perspicuity, that even the youngest and least experienced of your number has in mind a well defined and comprehensive understanding of the fundamental principle involved.

Notwithstanding this fact, however, it still remains for you to rationally and intelligently apply this exact and well defined principle of law to the specific subject of hypnotic control in all its varied forms and phases. In other words, hypnotism and mediumship exemplify a character and degree of subjection far beyond that known to you in law as "undue influence," even in its most definite, positive, unqualified and concrete form. And yet, with rare exceptions, the courts have not, as yet, taken judicial notice of either.

But the time is rapidly approaching and is, in fact, practically at hand, when your best intelligence must be applied to the just solution of numerous legal problems of importance growing out of the practice of these subjective, psychic processes.

In anticipation of this fact, it will not be deemed an impertinence to suggest that the following demonstrated facts may serve to somewhat facilitate your laudable undertaking.

1. By evidence which it is impossible to controvert it is established as a fact of science that to the exact extent hypnosis exists at any given time the hypnotist controls the will and voluntary powers of his subject.

2. Hypnotic control may be, and often is, established by and with the knowledge, consent and co-operation of the subject.

3. But where the hypnotist understands the process sufficiently well, and is strong enough, he may obtain such control without either the knowledge or consent of his subject.

4. Once the hypnotic relation is established, the individual thus subjected becomes the helpless instrument of his hypnotist. As such he executes the will of his hypnotist with absolute fidelity.

5. By the same unanswerable evidence it is established that a hypnotic subject under control may be compelled to commit any crime whatsoever that a criminal hypnotist may conceive and command, provided its execution be within the possibility of the subject's powers.

6. This is equally true whether hypnosis be induced forcibly or with the knowledge and consent of the subject.

7. Quite regardless of theories, both wise and otherwise, to the contrary, it is a fact to which your attention is specially called, that a considerable percentage of the crime of our own country in particular is, at the present time, inspired by hypnotic and mediumistic processes and practices.

8. Wherever this fact obtains justice universally miscarries to a very large extent. This is true for the reason that the subject alone is made to suffer the penalties of the law, while the real culprit, the hypnotist, goes entirely unpunished.

And yet there are serious legal difficulties to be considered in this connection. As soon as the courts have taken judicial cognizance of hypnotism and the hypnotic process as established facts, it must be expected that every criminal in the country will endeavor to profit by such a finding. It is not only possible but probable that criminals of every class will endeavor to excuse their crimes upon the ground that they were committed at the hypnotic "suggestion" of some one else.

This is, indeed, a phase of the subject that is sure to present itself. More than this, it is one that will call for the exercise of your best intelligence and finest discrimination. It is not impossible or even improbable that in the development of this subject as a legal proposition a few of the guilty may thus escape the just penalties of the law. But when necessity has made both Bench and Bar familiar with the principle and the process involved your intelligence can be safely relied upon to provide a complete remedy for such a contingency.

Furthermore, as an ethical proposition, it is far better that a few of the guilty should escape as a result of humane caution than that one innocent victim should suffer an unjust penalty as a result of carelessness.

9. Not only is a large percentage of the crime of to-day due to hypnotism and mediumship in their various forms and degrees, but by the hypnotic process civil wrongs are also accomplished with ease and facility, and the mentally passive or weak made the prey of the mentally strong. Your intelligence, unaided by further suggestions, will forecast the many possibilities which lie in this direction.

10. Your attention is especially called to the advertisements of the leading hypnotists and hypnotic schools, colleges and institutes in all the large cities of the central and eastern states. You will find them in many of the leading metropolitan dailies, weeklies and periodicals throughout the country. The nature and contents of these advertisements, as you will observe, fully sustain every statement here made, and vastly more.

11. Your perfect familiarity with the nature, meaning and scope of contracts, your experience in determining the motives of men from the nature and contents of their own deliberate, formulated utterances, and your perfect knowledge of ethical standards which fall within the line of "public policy," will enable you to quickly determine the status of the individuals and institutions here referred to.

12. If they do what they advertise and guarantee to do, then they stand before the community as self-confessed criminals of the most vicious and reprehensible character.   As such, they are a perpetual menace to society and morals.   In the event of such a finding, your appreciation of the responsibility resting upon you as guardians of public decency and the general welfare must impel you to the prompt application of every honorable means, method and power at your command looking to their immediate and permanent suppression.

13. On the other hand, if you shall find that they are unable to invest their prospective students with the knowledge or the powers they advertise and guarantee, then your trained intelligence will quickly grasp the salient fact that these advertisements are but a cunning means to an illegitimate end.   They constitute an important link in the chain of evidence, establishing the fact that these individuals and institutions are but so many individual and corporate criminals engaged in the unlawful business of obtaining money by false and fraudulent pretenses.

In this event every such advertisement sent through the United States Mails constitutes evidence of a criminal offense against the United States Government.   The law and the machinery for its enforcement are both entirely adequate to punish all such criminals and suppress their evil practices, as soon as the facts have been legally established.

Certainly no body of men in existence is so well equipped to deal fairly and intelligently with this subject and the problems it involves as the American Bench and Bar.   In the spirit of the most profound reverence and respect your attention is called to it in the hope that this brief and concrete presentation of the subject may, perhaps, suggest to you a line of duty and responsibility hitherto unobserved.

Another interesting line of thought which is in a way kindred to the subject under consideration is that which bears upon a class of crimes with which you are already familiar. It is a fact which the criminal statistics of the country will fully support, that drunkenness is the most prolific single cause of crime among our people.

But what is drunkenness as a psychological proposition? It is the subjection of the intelligence to the effects of a physical stimulant.

While this definition is one which you might be disposed to question at first view, its accuracy is well established by the position which you, in your legal capacity, assume toward the drunkard.

In those states and jurisdictions where drunkenness in itself is a crime, the drunkard is punished as a criminal for the act of getting drunk. This is upon the perfectly rational ground that even the drunkard (when sober) knows that it is a crime to get drunk. In the face of this knowledge, however, he goes and drinks himself into a state of drunkenness, well knowing the penalty therefor. Having knowingly and intentionally violated the law, he is punished accordingly.

But wherever a drunkard commits other crimes which are inspired by the influence of liquor over his intelligence and volition, you apply a wholly different rule. In this case you hold that to whatever extent the crime was inspired by the influence of liquor over him, to that extent he should be relieved from responsibility. This is upon the theory that he did not act of his own free and rational volition. And the rule is unquestionably correct.

The interesting phase of this proposition is in the fact that in the case of drunkenness you recognize the principle of domination and control, while in the case of hypnotism you do not. In the one case it is a subjection of the intelligence and volition of the individual to a physical stimulant. In the other it is the subjection of the same intelligence to the domination and control of another intelligence. The only difference, so far as the process is concerned, is that in the one case the dominating power proceeds from the physical plane, and in the other it proceeds from the psychical plane.

In the one case, where the admitted cause of the crime is an irresponsible, non-intelligent, physical substance called liquor, you excuse the subject (drunkard) upon the ground that the crime was inspired by the liquor and not by his own intent. In the other, where the inspiring cause of the crime is another intelligence, you refuse to excuse the subject upon the assumption that he alone was guilty.

But, reduced to its simplest expression, what is the principle involved? It is merely a matter of Self-Control, nothing more, nothing less.

When the drunkard absorbs enough alcohol it takes possession of his intelligence. In other words, it controls him. In proportion as he is controlled by the stimulant he loses his power of self-control. Just so with the hypnotic subject. In proportion as he falls under the control of an outside intelligence he also loses the power of self-control.

In proportion as the drunkard loses his power of self-control he also loses his sense of moral accountability and sinks to the level of the animal. He becomes the plaything of his own appetites, passions and desires, and is more a beast than a man. The same thing, in a slightly modified form, is true of the hypnotic subject.

This is why the principle of temperance (quite aside from the question of expediency) is, in essence, superior to that of prohibition. The man who is able to walk in the midst of temptations and has reached that degree of self-control where he is strong enough in his own right to live a clean life, is a greater soul in every way than he who must depend upon statutes to banish from his sight and reach the temptations of life.

There are many palliatives for drunkenness, but there is only one cure. That is the development of self-control sufficient to withstand by his own efforts the allurements and enticements of drink.

There is but one cure for hypnotic subjection. That is likewise in the cultivation of the power of self-control sufficient to withstand the assaults of all the hypnotists in the world.

Whatever view of this subject you may obtain, it is one which should command your immediate attention and enlist your most earnest and intelligent consideration.

While the hypnotic subject, in the largest number of instances, is a fit and proper object of commiseration and pity, it must be remembered that he is but the logical and natural result of professional hypnotism.

Although the criminal hypnotist who practices his insidious art in secret and under cover of darkness is a menace to society and a destructive agency more dangerous than pestilence or famine, it must not be forgotten that he also is a legitimate and sequential product of professional hypnotism.

Whilst the one is deserving of pity and the other of condemnation, neither must be held responsible for the initial evil. They are both but the results of an educational training received from the professional hypnotist or from the schools, colleges and institutes whose advertisements carry the noxious virus of moral leprosy into thousands of homes daily. And these destructive results will continue to abide with us so long as the cause which produces them—the professional hypnotist—remains unabated.

Whatever legal solution of this great psychological problem you may, in the plenitude of your wisdom, hereafter formulate, must of necessity be remedial and not merely palliative. To achieve permanent ethical results it must go to the primary cause, the fountain head of the evil stream, if it would check the ever swelling tide of infectious results.

And all this is entirely possible. Moreover, it may be done without in the least infringing upon the rights or natural prerogatives of individuals, or laying arbitrary and burdensome restrictions upon those who are devoted to the cause of science or to the conservation of the health or happiness of the people.

To you, gentlemen, naturally and rightfully belong the honor and the labor of formulating a legal remedy which shall successfully guard the present and future generations of our beloved people against the destructive power of the most seductive and insidious crime in the calendar of Nature, THE GREAT PSYCHOLOGICAL CRIME.

VIII.

TO THE PHYSICIAN.

For more than six hundred years the wisest and best men of the most progressive nations of earth have given their lives and their energies to the development of medical science. As a result they have evolved an empirical system which should command the respect as well as the admiration of all intelligent and unprejudiced students of science and patrons of progressive education.

The crystallized results of all this noble work are but imperfectly shown in the materia medica of to-day with which you are familiar and in accordance with which you have wrought many beneficent results.

No one but the fanatic, the deliberately vicious or the exceedingly ignorant will ever condemn you for entertaining a natural and modest pride in the merits of your profession and in the exact knowledge upon which it is founded.

But materia medica, as the average member of your school and profession knows and applies it, represents but one side of the great three-sided problem of Therapeutics in general. To such as these the existence of disease, as well as its cure, is a purely physical proposition. It is therefore perfectly natural and entirely consistent for them to limit their professional efforts to the purely physical aspect of the subject. In truth, they recognize no other.

To those who understand the great problem in its threefold aspect the comparatively meager results obtained by the strictly materialistic physician along purely conventional lines are entirely consistent with the limited view-point from which he proceeds.

But it is a matter of profound satisfaction to the School of Natural Science that the brightest, most intelligent, studious and progressive members of your profession are beginning to recognize both the spirituality and the psychology of medicine. Some of you (not many, it is true) have not only recognized the psychological aspect of disease and its cure, but you have gone further and inquired into the fundamental principle which underlies the entire subject of Therapeutics. Some of you have gone far enough along these lines to have demonstrated a number of interesting propositions not heretofore known or recognized by the acknowledged "Regular" schools of medicine.

thousands of times over, namely, the fact that there is such a thing as genuine mediumship. The failure to successfully combat this one fact placed you at a disadvantage from which it was impossible to recover. The decision therefore went against you, and justly so. As a natural result of your failure in this instance, Spiritualism has gained an almost irresistible impulse at your expense, for all of which you are entirely responsible.

It is impossible for you or anyone else to successfully deny the fact of mediumship. It is equally impossible for you to successfully deny its phenomena. Neither can you successfully dispute the fact that by and through this process spiritual intelligences can and do often communicate with those yet in the flesh.

If you would successfully meet the Spiritualist you must meet him on his own ground. You must be prepared to admit all the material facts upon which he bases his claims and then stand upon the principle which lies back of these facts.

To admit that mediumship is a fact does not admit that it is right, any more than to admit the existence of murder is an admission that murder is right. To admit that there are genuine spiritual communications through mediums is by no means an admission that the process employed should be commended or approved, any more than to admit a forgery is equivalent to a declaration that forgery is right.

With a proper understanding of the destructive nature of the mediumistic process you are in position to fully and fairly meet every proposition which can be advanced in favor of any school or philosophy or religion which depends upon a subjective, psychic process as its substantial basis.

One additional suggestion may not be deemed out of place in this connection. If you have taken the time to familiarize yourself with the array of data already presented you cannot fail to be impressed with the position here taken upon the subject of ultra religious emotionalism. It has been established beyond all question that ultra emotionalism of any kind involves a subjective process. It is therefore destructive. It opens the door to complete psychic subjection and control. In the very largest number of instances where this occurs the result is so-called "delusional insanity."

Your attention is specially called to the demonstrated facts and to the principle which underlies them. These cannot fail to furnish you much material for serious reflection and earnest consideration. If they shall in any measure serve to furnish a motive and an inspiration which shall help you to lift your religious services and ceremonials from the plane of emotionalism to that of rationalism the purpose of this work will have been in part accomplished.

With the facts at your command there is no body of men in existence in position to accomplish greater good for present and future generations than you can do by an intelligent exposition of the Destructive Principle of Nature in Individual Life as it manifests itself in the subjective psychic processes of Mediumship and Hypnotism.

There is no field of educational work where the harvest is so abundant and ripe and the laborers are so few.

VII.

To the Bench and Bar.

There is, perhaps, no tribunal in existence to-day better prepared to pass intelligently upon the merits of any question involving legal or equitable considerations than the American Bench and Bar.

There is, without exception, no tribunal of the people to which the writer would more cheerfully or more readily submit a psychological problem involving fine legal discrimination and the application of a just and comprehensive ethical standard.

It has, indeed, been his long cherished hope that the occasion would naturally present itself whereupon he might have the honor of presenting to you, gentlemen, in a more direct and personal form, a number of the more important legal phases of the general subject covered by this volume.

Under the existing circumstances, however, nothing more will be attempted here than to respectfully call your attention posed in him. By his subtle abuse of one of your most harmless, familiar and appropriate scientific terms, the term "suggestion," he has accomplished at least two false and fraudulent ends, both of which reflect discredit upon your intelligence as well as your integrity, and place you in a wholly false position before the world.

1. By his subtle misapplication of the word "suggestion" he would lead, and has actually led, the public to believe that the thousands of wonderful cures wrought by you through the natural and legitimate processes of normal, independent suggestion are, in fact, all due entirely to hypnotism and the processes of so-called hypnotic "suggestion."

This, as you well know, is as false as it is subtle. It is a fallacy you cannot afford to tolerate if you prize your future reputation for professional honor and personal integrity, for the time is at hand when the truth must and will be known.

2. By his artful abuse of this same innocent and respectable word he makes it appear that every member of your profession who employs normal, independent suggestion in his practice is a professional hypnotist engaged in the active practice of hypnotism.

He would convey to the innocent public (and has already done so with telling effect) the impression that every simple and normal suggestion employed by you to inspire in the minds of your patients a therapeutic faith, is but another phase of the black art by which he paralyzes the will and voluntary powers of his hypnotic subjects and makes them helpless instruments of his dominant will and questionable desires. He has even gone so far as to impress the thought upon the minds of the unsophisticated that the healthful, spiritual and physical magnetism which every advanced physician of to-day carries into the sick room as a healthful influence, is but another form of hypnotism or hypnotic "suggestion."

If you are not already familiar with these facts the interests of your profession as well as your individual interests demand that you become so at once. The time has come when they will meet you at every turn of your professional pathway. They will be thrust upon your attention whether you will it or not. In exact proportion as you come into possession of the facts and understand their meaning you will recognize the equivocal position in which you and your profession have been placed relative to the subjective, psychic process of hypnotism.

In view of the facts here presented, together with such as you may easily obtain independently, it may not be deemed presumptuous to suggest the natural and proper remedy. It is this: In all your public and private utterances, both published and unpublished, set yourself the task and charge yourself with the duty of hereafter clearly, explicitly and unmistakably differentiating at all times between normal, independent suggestion, which is at the basis of all therapeutic faith, and hypnotism, which is under all conditions and circumstances a subjective, psychic process of the most destructive character. Make it clear that so-called hypnotic "suggestion" is a misnomer and a libel and is at all times equivalent to an "irresistible impulse or command."

Set yourself and your profession squarely and unequivocally before the world as unalterably opposed to all subjective, psychic processes and practices, for the reason that they are destructive in their essential nature and as such deprive their subjects of the power of self-control as well as the ability to exercise those faculties, capacities and powers of the soul upon which their individual responsibility depends.

If you have followed the text of this volume from the beginning and have been impressed with its honesty and sincerity, it is fair to assume that the subject of insanity presents itself to you in a somewhat different aspect from that in which your profession, generally speaking, has heretofore viewed it.

Although it is conceded that the view here presented may not be, to you, professionally orthodox, nevertheless it is earnestly hoped that the facts recorded will be deemed sufficient to warrant at least a non-professional inquiry on your part along the lines indicated.

If such should be the case, then for your especial benefit in this connection it is here stated, for what it may be worth to you, that under and in accordance with the exact methods of Natural Science six hundred examinations have been made of an equal number of so-called insane inmates of one of the leading insane asylums of the country. Of the number thus examined 349 were found to be in a subjective, psychic condition, under the hypnotic domination and control of outside spiritual intelligences. These were treated according to the diagnoses in conformity with the methods of Natural Science. The results show 349 cures. In other words, out of the entire number treated not a single failure resulted.

This record speaks for itself. Indeed, it speaks more eloquently than all the theories, speculations, suppositions and assumptions combined, which constitute so large a part of the medical literature pertaining to the great general subject of insanity. This statement is made without prejudice, for the difficulties which surround and have accompanied the development of this particular branch of medical science are fully understood and appreciated. As far as your specialists have gone their wor has been most creditable in every particular.

In view of the record, however, it would appear to the writer that whatever views you may entertain concerning the causes of insanity in the 349 cases above referred to, the record in itself is worthy of your thoughtful consideration. The simple fact that all these cases were treated upon the theory of hypnotic control by outside spiritual intelligences, and the treatment prescribed was successful in every instance, should be sufficient to establish in your professional mind the reasonable presumption that the diagnoses were correct. Otherwise the logic of facts is without meaning or value.

IX.

To Master Masons.

What makes you a Mason?

The true Masonic answer to this crucial question indelibly impresses itself upon the mind, memory and moral consciousness of every just and upright Mason.

You who have pondered well its scope and its meaning and have heeded the timely admonition of the Master, know full well the responsibilities you assumed before God and man and your own conscience when you voluntarily took upon yourself the solemn and binding obligation of a Master Mason.

But why should the writer of this particular volume thus publicly approach you upon the level of your Masonic profession? By what right or benefit does he expect to gain admittance to your confidence or hope to enlist your active interest, sympathy and co-operation in the noblest cause that ever inspired the illumined soul of a Master Mason? Let the sequel answer

From the dawn of civilization to the present moment, two active and opposing forces have been engaged in deadly conflict over the destiny of human intelligence.

One of these has ever been the unfaltering, courageous and consistent champion of individual life, individual liberty, and individual happiness. The other has, with equal consistency and persistency, sought to dominate and control the life, intelligence and conscience of the individual and subject him to intellectual bondage and servitude.

The one has openly fostered the spirit of freedom and independence as a basic principle of individual and organic human life. The other has covertly sought to reduce the individual to the status of a mere instrument in the hands and under the domination and control of an aggregate organic will and design.

The one has dignified and emphasized the individual intelligence and appreciated its value to both itself and society. The other has persistently ignored the great fundamental fact of Nature, that the individual in his own right, as such, is invested with certain indefeasible attributes and certain inalienable rights, privileges and benefits which must be respected.

The one has recognized the fact that man's value to himself as an individual is the only sure and true measure of his value as an active, living factor in the social organism of which he is a part. The other has proceeded as if upon the assumption that man has but one value, namely, his value to the great aggregate body of which he is a part, and that his value, even in that capacity, is measured by the degree to which his individual will, intelligence and conscience are subject to the domination and control of that aggregate body.

The one develops individual Intelligence, Courage and Perseverance and a sense of Individual Responsibility through the power and process of a broad and liberal education. The other commands obedience and subjection through the power of Ignorance, Superstition and Fear.

At the very cradle of humanity these two forces arrayed themselves in an irrepressible conflict. At that point the struggle began. From that point forward throughout all the subsequent ages, even to the present time, it has continued unabated. At no time within the limits of authentic history has the conflict reached a more critical stage than in this, the dawning of the twentieth Christian century.

And who are the contending parties to this vital conflict?

Broadly and abstractly speaking, they are Light and Darkness, Truth and Falsehood, Construction and Destruction, Life and Death, the Widow's Son and the Ruffians. But more specifically and concretely, they are the two most powerful organic bodies of intelligence upon earth, together with the individual intelligences who have voluntarily arrayed themselves upon opposite sides of the two great principles involved in the struggle.

But to what great organic bodies is reference here made? It is sufficient at this time to state that one is the great organic body of Masonry, together with the parent organization from which it received its noble inspirations to Life, Liberty and Happiness.

What, then, is your place in this conflict? Where do you as an individual belong? Every just and upright Mason knows the answer. Every true and loyal Brother knows his place. Those whose privilege it is to walk within the sublime radiance of the Three Great Lights can never become the champions of Darkness, Falsehood, Death, Destruction or the Ruffians. Your place is in the serried columns of Light, Truth and Life, and beneath the radiant and glorious banner of the Son.

In common with all your Brother Masons, you revere the Order and the institution of Masonry, among other things, for its great antiquity. But do you know the real origin of this ancient Brotherhood? Perhaps not. Even the most learned historians of the Order to-day confess their inability to mark either the time or the place of its birth.

And yet the origin and the history of Masonry are known. More than this, they are matters of record. The record is authentic and unbroken. It is definite and certain. It runs like a thread of golden light backward to the very infancy of the human race.

Every Master Mason who has given the subject serious thought, although unable to fix the date or the location of its origin, has reached an unalterable conclusion. He has become impressed with the strange and almost startling consciousness that Masonry, in its present organic form, is but a continuation, transformation or metamorphosis from a more ancient organization whose records and history far antedate all that is known today as exoteric.

No more perfect illustration of what we term "intuitive knowledge" could be presented than this strange consciousness concerning the origin and history of Masonry. For it is indeed a fact that this mysterious intuition is but the conscious recognition of a sublime truth whose radiance has illumined the pathway of human liberty and human progress throughout the ages.

The Spirit of Masonry at every point in the journey of human life has spread its beneficent influence, like a protecting mantle, over the rights, duties, privileges, obligations and liberties of mankind.

No more striking illustration of this sublime truth is known to history than the spirit which everywhere manifests itself in the familiar records upon which our own beloved country depends for its organic national existence.

It was the Spirit of Freemasonry, as well as the Soul of a great Mason, that injected into our Declaration of Independence this sublime and living sentiment:

"We hold these truths to be self-evident: That all men

are created equal, that they are endowed by their Creator
with *certain unalienable Rights,* that among these are *Life,
Liberty and the pursuit of Happiness;* that to secure these
rights Governments are instituted among men, deriving their
just powers from the consent of the governed; that whenever
any Form of Government becomes destructive of these ends
it is the Right of the People to alter or abolish it, and to in-
stitute new Government, laying its foundation on such principles, and organizing its powers in such form, as to them
shall seem most likely to effect their Safety and Happiness."

It was the same Spirit, and a kindred intelligence, that
formulated these profoundly significant words constituting the
preamble of our National Constitution:

"We, the People of the United States, in Order to form a
more perfect Union, establish Justice, insure domestic Tran-
quillity, provide for the common Defense, promote the general Welfare and secure the *Blessings of Liberty to ourselves
and our Posterity,* do ordain and establish this Constitution
for the United States of America."

It was the spirit of Freemasonry that unanimously
selected a great Mason as the first President to inaugurate
our government upon the time-honored Masonic principles of
Equity, Justice and Right, for the preservation and perpetuation of individual human liberty.

At every point in the onward and upward progress of
our national evolution it has been the same broad, gracious
but uncompromising Spirit of Individual Liberty, together
with its unfaltering love of Human Freedom and its un-
quenchable thirst for Knowledge and Education, that has thus
far defeated the subtle and persistent efforts of opposing
forces to subvert and subordinate the power, the dignity and
the vitality of the State to ecclesiastical authority and control.

It has been and is the Spirit of Masonry, under the guiding intelligence of a great Mason, aided and supported by a
devoted Craft, that for more than a quarter of a century has
held aloft the sacred ensign of Human Liberty over the homes
and the people of our sister republic of Mexico.

To the same exalted Spirit from which the sublime Order

of Masonry has received its noble inspirations, and to the unselfish devotion of those who are able to rise to the level of this fundamental principle of Individual Liberty, present and future generations of our beloved people must look for the preservation and perpetuation of those inalienable rights upon which the government of a free and enlightened people must ever depend.

The body of this work has been devoted to an exposition of the Great Psychological Crime, as it is exemplified in individual life by the subjective, psychic processes of Hypnotism and Mediumship. The one specific purpose has been to present to the reader as graphically as possible a definite outline of the Destructive Principle of Nature in Individual Life. Of necessity, therefore, the subject has been limited almost entirely to its aspect as an individual problem of human life.

Let it be distinctly understood, however, that the same Destructive Principle of Nature by which one individual intelligence paralyzes the will and voluntary powers of another may, in a more general form, be invoked by organic bodies of individuals, if the purpose and intent be present and the aggregate will to execute them be sufficient.

This great fact has been profoundly demonstrated throughout the ages. It is written in letters of blood upon every page of human history. It constitutes one of the most fascinating problems of human life and human interest. It tempts the willing mind to further and more specific revelations.

But the limitations of this work have been reached. The task is finished. These prescribed limitations preclude further exposition of or reference to the two great Spiritual Schools, one of which has developed and the other dominated human intelligence and conscience throughout the ages; those two great, silent, powerful and vitally antagonistic currents which at their intersections have given to the world an Exodus, a Crucifixion, an Inquisition, a Protestation and a Reformation.

To ancient India and to Ancient Egypt clear, unbroken pathways run, backward to the organized centers of Intellectual Liberty on the one hand and Intellectual Bondage upon the other.

The selfish and ambitious misapplication of knowledge and the abuse of power are the unmistakable due guard and sign of Egyptian Black Magic.

The applied principles of Fraternity, Equality and Human Liberty have been and are the perpetual symbols of "The Wise Men of the East," and the purity of their perfect conception constitutes the spotless Badge of a Master Mason.

PAX VOBISCUM.

The Genesis of Dogma

If our modern scientific thinkers, investigators and writers could be prevailed upon carefully to tabulate under separate heads their "facts" and their "theories" and speculations concerning those facts, it would materially simplify the work of their students and readers and avoid the most prolific source of confusion which prevails in almost every department of scientific investigation and thought.

It is not in the spirit of hostility nor unfriendly criticism that this suggestion is offered, but rather as a friendly observation from one who has often encountered the perplexing difficulty referred to.

We all love to theorize and speculate upon the things that are out beyond the range of our definite personal knowledge. It is a part of our natures to do so. To many of us it takes the place of intellectual recreation and entertainment. This is more especially true among scientists and philosophers.

The scientist discovers what he recognizes as a "fact." His mind at once demands to know its meaning and value. If, perchance, it should lie outside the sequential line of those facts with which he is already familiar, he studies it, reasons upon it, speculates about it and theorizes over it until he reaches a conclusion. No matter how remote that conclusion may chance to be from the truth, if he is for the time being satisfied with it, he is strongly impelled to give it to the world along with the fact.

We all possess, to some extent, either consciously or otherwise, a feeling of admiration for the man who discovers a fact in Nature and gives it to the world. For this reason we are much inclined to entertain favorably whatever theories he may be impelled to present along with it.

Therefore, unless he is exceedingly explicit and thoughtful of the manner in which he distinguishes his fact from his theories and speculations concerning it, we who follow him fail to differentiate between them.

As a natural result of these conditions, the vast body of what we have been pleased to designate as "Science" is made up of a comparatively few demonstrated facts, mixed with an enormous quantity of theories, both wise and otherwise. This excessive adulteration has produced a compound which defies analysis and leaves the student in a state of almost hopeless confusion.

It is the purpose of this work, as far as may be possible, carefully to differentiate between the facts of science and the theories of men concerning those facts. For this reason special attention is called to the fact that in the preceding chapters will be found only such matter as has been absolutely demonstrated by Natural Science. The definite statements and declarations therein contained may, therefore, be accepted and classified under the head of "Facts Demonstrated," upon which the reader is entitled to draw his own conclusions and postulate as many theories as his intelligence may be able to formulate.

The specific intent of this supplementary chapter is to outline as accurately and as carefully as possible a few of the most important *theories* which the Wise Men of the ages on both planes of life have formulated relative to some of the facts stated in preceding chapters.

In order that there shall be no misapprehension nor uncertainty in the mind of the reader, these theories will be confined to a supplementary chapter by themselves, carefully labeled as such at the beginning.

The only reason or excuse for presenting them at all in connection with this work is that they will doubtless give to the intelligent student a valuable suggestion as to the specific lines of inquiry along which the most enlightened scientific intelligence throughout the ages has been and still is moving.

In Part II, Chapter IV, paragraphs 11 and 12, it is stated as an unqualified fact of science that animals, in the course of the years, disappear from the spiritual plane of the animal kingdom, and that they do not reappear (at least in identical or distinguishable form) upon any of the planes of spiritual life which are distinctively related to this particular planet.

The natural inquiry of every intelligent mind is, "What becomes of them?" The inquiry thus far remains unanswered so far as science is concerned. The Wise Men of both the physical and spiritual planes of life have brought to bear upon the problem all the knowledge and intelligence they possess. Thus far, however, the scientific demonstration lies beyond the limits of their understanding.

With a view to its possible solution, however, the following widely different hypotheses have been made the bases of their study and investigation:

First Hypothesis.

It is assumed that the disappearance is but a transition in the upward movement of the individual ego, or entity, in its evolutionary progress toward a higher state of individualized intelligence and being.

This theory involves the process of metempsychosis or transmigration, through the operation of which the animal ego is supposed to be transferred from the spiritual plane to the physical organism of a higher order of life and intelligence upon the physical plane. Here again it undergoes the progressive processes of physical growth, development, maturity, decline, old age and death, at which last named point it returns again to the spiritual plane one round higher in the evolutionary process.

Again, it is supposed to disappear from the spiritual plane and reappear in a higher order of physical life, only to go through the same process of physical growth, development, maturity, decline, old age, decay and death and reappearance upon the spiritual plane of animal life, each time representing a higher order of individualized intelligence and being.

This evolutionary process is supposed to continue until the highest form of individualized animal intelligence disappears from the spiritual plane of animal life, only to make its appearance upon the physical plane in the lowest form of human life and intelligence.

At this point in the evolutionary process involuntary metempsychosis, or transmigration, is supposed to cease and voluntary "reincarnation" begin.

To the foregoing general theory, or working hypothesis, the reader will be able to trace a number of the most conspicuous and interesting tenets of both theology and science as well as of ancient philosophies.

For illustration:

1. We have the doctrine of the transmigration of souls. This doctrine, as it has appeared from time to time upon the physical plane, is evidently referable to the foregoing theory, or working hypothesis of the Wise Men, concerning the disappearance of the animal from the spiritual plane of animal life. But it has also undoubtedly become confused with, or modified by, that other general theory of the Wise Men concerning the disappearance of man from the lowest plane of his spiritual life, to which theory reference will be made further on.

This is suggested as a most natural conclusion for the reason that the doctrine of transmigration, as it is generally expounded upon the earth plane, does not stop with the animal, but also includes man. That is to say, under this particular form of that doctrine it is generally held that the soul of man also may, at physical death, enter the physical organism of an animal, and that such an act is not necessarily a retrograde movement on the part of the intelligent entity.

A still further corruption of the original theory is found in the doctrine, or assumption, that transmigration always occurs at the instant of physical dissolution, and at no other time.

2. The doctrine of Transubstantiation is doubtless also referable to the same general source. Under this doctrine the Catholic Church has formulated the dogma that, in their celebration of the sacrament of the Lord's Supper, the literal substance of the body and the blood of Christ enters into the bread and wine used in the sacramental service.

3. The doctrine of "Reincarnation," as it is held and advocated by the exponents of Theosophy and some of the more ancient philosophies, is but another phase of the same general hypothesis applied to man in his evolutionary progress upon the spiritual planes of life.

The various exponents of this doctrine have developed a

most clever and forcible array of argument, which is both interesting and instructive, and is not easily avoided by those who hold to a different theory. It may not be improper to state in this connection that the analogies of science on both planes of life seem to support it, and some of the seeming mysteries of intellectual inequality among men appear to be accounted for by it.

Indeed, there are intelligences upon the spiritual planes of life who assert with unqualified assurance that reincarnation is a fact of Nature. There are also a few upon the physical plane who claim to have fully demonstrated its truth. But whatever the fact may be, it is—at least to the great majority of our western civilization—but a beautiful, ingenious and interesting theory. And thus it will remain, so far as this work is concerned.

4. On the purely physical plane the doctrine of the physical evolution of man from the plane of animal Nature would seem to be but another expression of the same general hypothesis. The search for the "Missing Link" in the upward movement of organic, physical evolution has been a search made upon the theory that man is but an ape evolved.

Upon the structural side of organic, physical life, more especially, this theory is strongly supported by an array of scientific data which no student of Nature can afford to ignore. But up to this time even the evolution of man's physical structure from that of the animal is held, by able exponents of physical science, to be nothing more than a "working hypothesis."

SECOND HYPOTHESIS.

The second general hypothesis of the Wise Men and of Natural Science holds that the disappearance of the animal from the spiritual plane is, indeed, all that it appears to be, namely, total disintegration, dissolution and a resolution of the animal entity back into Nature's elements, from which it came. This, of course, means total extinction of the animal as a separate, distinct and individualized entity.

At first view this hypothesis would appear to be in direct conflict with the very essence of the evolutionary principle. But a further study and analysis of the subject show that such is not the case, as the following suggestions will clearly indicate:

The facts of Nature on all the planes of life, so far as

the Wise Men have been able to observe them, everywhere suggest to the student of Natural Science the operation of what appears to be a Universal Intelligence. The forces, activities and processes of Nature, as far as we are able to follow their workings, appear to indicate a conformity to universal principles. Back of these seemingly universal principles the human intelligence searches in vain for the motive power or intelligence which formulates and operates them.

Notwithstanding our confessed inability to locate, circumscribe, define or identify the great Universal Intelligence which inspires and guides the forces, activities and processes of Nature, our individual intelligence intuitively recognizes its existence as a fundamental fact.

In so far as we have been able to trace the history of man there never has been a time when human intelligence has failed to sense that which to man has meant a Universal Intelligence. Even the professed disbeliever betrays his intuitive recognition of this Universal Intelligence in the very profanity he employs to emphasize his disbelief.

Although we are unable to locate, circumscribe, define or identify it, we all, nevertheless, have a name for it. Some call it "God." Others designate it as the "Father." Some name it "Law." Others term it "Nature." Some there are who give it other names. Others of us express our conception of it more fully in the term "Universal Intelligence."

Under this second general hypothesis, in all this upward movement of Nature we name "evolution," Universal Intelligence is engaged in the process of individualizing intelligence. The one object or purpose of this individualizing process, as it appears, is ultimately to evolve an order of intelligence which shall possess the knowledge and the power of indefinite self-perpetuation which is known to science as Individual Immortality.

In the animal organism Nature has not yet reached a point in the evolutionary process where the entity possesses that power. As a natural result the animal disappears from the spiritual plane of animal life in response to the law of its being, and, if the hypothesis be true, is resolved back into Nature's elements from which it came.

If this be true, the student is ready to ask, What, then, is the purpose of all the gradations of animal life, running from the amoeba to the anthropoid ape?

The answer in brief is, that in all this multiplicity of animal life, running through all its varied gradations, from the lowest to the highest, we see only the mechanics of a stupendous plan by and through which Universal Intelligence refines and raises the vibratory activity of matter on both planes of life, until it is capable of co-ordination with the Soul Element of Nature, which is individualized in man alone.

For a full consideration of the principle and process involved in the upward movement of evolution through all the kingdoms of Nature, the reader is referred to "Harmonics of Evolution," Vol. I of the Harmonic Series, Chapter VI.

In the chapter referred to, under the heading of "The Genesis of Physical Life," the facts of Natural Science which have a direct bearing upon this hypothesis are given with such clearness and detail that the reader cannot fail to grasp their significance and appreciate their scientific value.

THIRD HYPOTHESIS.

In Part II of this volume, Chapter IV, paragraphs 19 to 22, inclusive, under the head of "Facts Demonstrated," it is stated that man disappears from the lowest plane of his spiritual life by either one of two different processes, and in response to the operation of two different and opposite principles, viz.:

1.   Under the constructive principle and process of evolution, growth, development and progress, only to appear upon a higher plane, etc.

2.   Under the opposite principle and process of destruction or devolution he also disappears in a manner which corresponds, in every essential particular, with the disappearance of the animal.

It is also stated that in this second case he does not reappear (at least in identical or distinguishable form), upon any of the higher planes of spiritual life which are distinctively related to this particular planet.

The question of his destiny as an individual intelligence in this case is a matter of even more absorbing and vital interest to those who have undertaken its solution, than is the destiny of the animal.

But here again Nature seems to hold a secret which defies the detective powers of the wisest intelligences of both planes of life. No satisfactory solution of the great problem has yet been wrought out.

It is true, however, that many facts bearing upon various phases of the subject are known, and a vast amount of data has been accumulated. Indeed, it would doubtless be a matter of interest and profound wonderment to those who are not already familiar with the subject to follow the lines of investigation and examine the facts and the data that have been gathered and classified. The limitations of this work, however, forbid the opening of so vast a field of speculative interest.

Nevertheless, it is both relevant and proper to note briefly the fact that here also two working hypotheses or theories have been formulated, and that the facts and the data above referred to bear more or less directly upon the one or the other.

The first of these holds that man may, of his own volition, pursue a deliberate course of retrogression in conformity with the Destructive Principle of Nature in Individual Life, until he reaches that point in the downward path toward spiritual darkness, where he disappears as does the animal. But, according to the theory here under consideration, this fact does not necessarily involve his individual extinction or dissolution as an individual intelligence or entity. On the other hand, it is held that he simply falls below the point of co-ordination with the Soul Element of Nature, thereby loses his independent, self-conscious and rational volition, and reverts to the plane of animal life.

Here he begins again the evolutionary struggle under the guiding wisdom and power of Universal Intelligence, until once again he reaches the plane of human life. Here he again co-ordinates with the Soul Element of Nature, is reinvested with an independent, self-conscious and rational volition and given another opportunity to choose between the two alternatives of evolutionary progress on the one hand or devolutionary retrogression on the other. It is still within his power to choose the downward path. If so, and he persists in that choice, he must again descend to the plane of animal life and begin anew the evolutionary struggle under the guiding direction of Universal Intelligence.

This process is supposed to be repeated as often as may be necessary to develop in him the natural desire for the higher life, after which he proceeds of his own voluntary choice on the upward course of individual self-development to that celestial destiny of individual attainment and power which lies beyond the limits of our present understanding.

Fourth Hypothesis.

The opposite hypothesis holds that no matter from what heights man may descend, if he persist in his downward flight until he loses his independent, self-conscious and rational volition, under the law of his being he thereby forever forfeits the power of self-perpetuation and Individual Immortality.

In this case his disappearance from the spiritual plane means to him precisely what it means to the animal under the *Second Hypothesis,* namely, disintegration, dissolution, individual extinction and a resolution back into Nature's elements from which he came.

This fourth general hypothesis of Natural Science is deeply interesting in itself. But it becomes doubly so when considered in the light of theological dogmatism concerning the extreme penalty for sin.

It is well known that theologians widely differ in their views concerning the ultimate destiny of the persistent sinner. Their differences hinge, in a general way, upon their various understandings and conceptions of man's immortality.

Without taking into account the intermediate shadings, there are two general, theological dogmas concerning the immortality of the Soul, which, briefly stated, are as follows:

1. That man is inherently, intrinsically and essentially immortal. That he is so created. That immortality is a primary and essential property or characteristic of his individual being. That whether saved or lost, in a religious sense, he is in either event immortal and therefore can never die nor lose his individuality.

From this particular conception of the soul's immortality naturally follows the doctrine of eternal happiness for the saved, and never ending torture for the damned.

2. On the other hand, it is held that the soul is not inherently and essentially immortal, but that it may become so by conforming to the law of God—or Nature—upon which individual immortality depends.

In other words, under this theological conception man's immortality comes to him as the gift of God. It is the reward of his obedience to God's commands. Or, from the philosophic standpoint, it comes to him as the natural result of his own personal effort. It is the logical and necessary result of his obedience to the constructive principle of Nature which is the law of individual life.

From this conception of the soul's immortality it follows that the man who does not earn it, or who does not receive it as a gift from God, is necessarily a mere mortal and nothing more. In this case when death overtakes him he goes down to the grave, is eaten by the worms of the earth, his spirit as well as his body is resolved back into Nature's elements, and he perishes forever.

In this view of the subject, "The Wages of Sin is Death," and death in this case means total, individual extinction.

In closing this chapter the reader is once more reminded that it is a chapter of "theories" only. In it four general hypotheses have been briefly but carefully stated. They are presented without comment for what they may be worth. No attempt has been made to prejudice the mind in favor of or against any of them. On the contrary, it is suggested that even those who have at command all the facts and all the data thus far accumulated bearing upon the subject are still withholding judgment.

These four theories are here presented merely as a suggestion concerning the particular lines of thought and inquiry which have engaged the attention of those students of Natural Science who have endeavored to solve the great and absorbing problem of the ultimate destiny of animal and degenerate human life and intelligence.

About these four theories cluster an almost endless number of religious and philosophic speculations, opinions and beliefs which have occupied the minds of theologians and laymen, physical scientists and their students, philosophers and thinkers all down the ages, so far as we are able to follow the authentic history of civilization.

A few of the more conspicuous of these innumerable opinions and beliefs have also been stated, and their relation to the fundamental hypotheses of Natural Science suggested. These, it is hoped, will be of value, in that they may, in some measure, lead to a clearer understanding and appreciation of the manner in which a perfectly legitimate scientific hypothesis may be made the basis of innumerable religious dogmas and philosophic speculations which only serve to confuse the minds and warp the lives of the unscientific and the ignorant.

In Conclusion.

The author desires to say that the central purpose of this volume has been merely to erect guide-posts at the crossings and the partings of the ways which lead, upon the one hand, to Life, Light, Liberty and Immortality, and upon the other to Bondage, Darkness, Disintegration and Death.

It is intended only as an exposition of that which we escape by the power and the exercise of an intelligent Self-Control over the individual life.

Another volume will be given to the more inspiring theme of individual achievement under and in accordance with the same principle of Self-Control, the principle of MASTERSHIP in Individual Life.

END OF VOL. II.

Editor's Postscript

THE GREAT PSYCHOLOGICAL CRIME stands for a definite knowledge and a definite personal experiment, experience and demonstration, or it stands for nothing, and is of less value than its material make-up.

The subject matter of this volume and the ethics involved have a basis in Nature, in specific fact, in a definite school of learning and in an exact science, or the work as a whole is but the play of an unchained imagination and evidence of a deficient moral sense.

When an author passes from the familiar field of mere theory and speculation into the domain of unqualified statement, he places himself in a new relation to his audience, and is entitled to a different character of attention and investigation—assuming, of course, that he expresses himself in conformity with our common standards of sanity and good literature.

It is one of the mysteries of the human mind that the world, generally speaking, treats the theorist with far greater hospitality than it does the demonstrator. This is particularly true in that field we have come to designate as "Psychical Research." More popular credence has been given to a mere "working hypothesis" recently formulated by a voluminous theorist concerning the "Law of Psychic Phenomena" than to the accumulated and combined statements of thousands of honest psychics who for many years have proclaimed a personal demonstration of the continuity of individual life.

The theorist, however, has his place and his mission. Though he more frequently serves merely as a guide-post to the wrong direction, it sometimes occurs that the dreamer or speculator is the forerunner and prophet of the real scientist and the actual demonstrator.

The world is debtor to whomsoever passes on a really original idea or concept or plan that appears feasible, but when a man claims to have conducted a successful experiment, or to have made a personal demonstration, or to have gained an unusual knowledge—bearing upon questions vital to human destiny—he is entitled to a critical investigation by the best intelligence of his day, by the recognized schools of science and by the conservators of public morals.

Fifty years ago, when Bulwer's masterpieces, *"Zanoni"* and *"A Strange Story,"* appeared, they were accepted at their face value by his conventional world; that is to say, as weird fiction, having no higher purpose than to exploit their author's genius, and no deeper meanings than to furnish entertainment for mere lovers of romance.

It was neither perceived nor suspected that Bulwer had received a personal instruction, and had achieved a peculiar knowledge that inspired his powerful and picturesque pen to a character of literature that has not ceased to puzzle and delight his readers.

The real purposes and the real meanings which run through these works are clearly discernible to another of the same school. To another of that "August Fraternity" of whom that scholarly Englishman so reverently wrote, the common *Alma Mater* is vividly disclosed by a familiar code of sign, symbol and principle. Another of the same instruction knows to a certainty the work of the Entered Apprentice.

As a matter of fact, these two singular romances are carefully veiled expositions of the two oldest and most powerful centers of spiritual knowledge extant. They are, indeed, revelations of the loftiest pursuits and the most malign practices known to human intelligence.

Were there no other material evidence in existence than these two volumes themselves, the record of Bulwer's schooling is indisputably bound up in his works. To those who have the key these marvelous romances stand for true spiritual development and for hypnotic subjection, for Light and for Darkness—for India and for Egypt.

After fifty years another attempt is being made, less guarded, perhaps, but more definite, to throw additional light upon the same general subject.

While the world of liberal thought has enlarged its borders since Bulwer wrote, there still remain almost insurmount-

able obstacles in the path of those who have been privileged
to learn and are willing to share their gains with the world.
Fifty years ago a dogmatic theology and the limited data of
physical science barred the way to any rational public consideration of psychic phenomena, or of published personal
experiences and demonstrations in this particular field.   At
that time no properly instructed student of Natural Science
could have delivered his message to an Anglo-Saxon audience
except under skilful disguise.

Even to-day, with its broadened outlook, any adequate
published exposition of the knowledge, methods and purposes
of the great Spiritual School must encounter many perplexities.

While religious intolerance is less, individual skepticism
has increased, and it would almost appear as if the old dogmatic spirit of theology had transmigrated to the vigorous
and enlarged body of physical science.

Still other conditions shadow this specific educational
movement, conditions which furnish more problems than mere
indifference or skepticism or dogmatism.

When, by concerted effort, the silent, unseen forces set in
motion this New Thought wave, there was at the same time
made the condition and the opportunity for bringing to the
surface all the debris of the deeps.   Just as the troubled ocean
casts its driftwood and seaweed to the surface, so this profound psychical impulse has called to the social surface such
a company of "inspired revelators" and "seers" and "prophets" and "Messiahs," and such an array of metaphysical
"cults," "orders" and "movements," as to threaten obscura-
tion of the actual science and philosophy of the real powers
whose directing intelligence gave the initial impulse.

The one imminent and embarrassing possibility that suggests itself with every public utterance or publication of the
School of Natural Science is that its aims and purposes are
likely to be confused with the manifold claims of "inspired"
leaders, or with the unintelligible ecstasies of professional
"mystics," or with the commercial crusades of therapeutical
theologies.

The work in view, of which the Harmonic Series is a part,
is none of these.   The gradual development of the science
and philosophy of this series does not rest upon claims of "in-

spiration." This work is not in the material interests of any individual or organization. The School of Natural Science is not conducting an ambitious "movement," nor operating a commercial cult. It is not soliciting a material support on behalf of any "advanced" project. It is not selling instruction, nor seeking any character of personal leadership. It does not anticipate great popular interest nor an undue share of public attention and favor.

It has been just twenty years since the inception of this work in this country, and all this time has been consumed by the author of this volume in overcoming the perplexities and prejudices and materialities that have barred the way to a direct public or published presentation of his individual work.

The Harmonic Series, now in process of publication, is intended as a bridge between the definite, demonstrated and recorded data of the historical Spiritual School of Science and the definite, discovered and published data of the modern physical school.

When completed this Series will constitute *The Philosophy of Individual Life,* as taught to-day by the School of Natural Science in conformity with all of the demonstrated knowledge of all the schools.

While the Series, as a whole, will represent a joint literary task, it is not, however, a work of collaboration, as each volume of the Series will represent the individuality of its particular author and maintain its distinction of theme, scope and literary treatment.

In this particular instance the *editor* has no other part in THE GREAT PSYCHOLOGICAL CRIME than merely to relieve the author of all details of publication and preserve the continuity and relationship of the two published volumes of the Harmonic Series.

March, 1903. THE EDITOR.

THE HARMONICS OF EVOLUTION

By Florence Huntley

Volume 1. The Harmonic Series

This initial volume of Natural Science covers that universal principle of the individual Love relation in nature which operates through the mineral, vegetable, animal and human kingdoms.

The philosophy taught in this authorized volume means the dawning of a "New Day" in the intellectual and ethical evolution of the world.

Mrs. Huntley has sensed the very soul of mankind, understands its yearnings for what Drummond names "the greatest thing in the world, LOVE". She points out the pitfalls into which so many are continually falling, and erects guide-posts by the way which, if heeded, lead safely through the *here*, out into the *hereafter*.

To those who contemplate taking upon themselves the responsibilities of married life, as well as to all who have done so, this book will be a priceless pearl, to read, re-read, and read again; then heed, re-heed and heed again.

"HARMONICS of EVOLUTION" should be a part of every home where dwells one thought above the transitory, evanescent, sordid things of this life.

It opens the portals of the soul to a knowledge of the fact that *this* [life [has immeasurable possibilities and endless consequences which do *not* exist or obtain in the spiritual spheres.

A study of the philosophy set forth in this volume we are confident will repay you or anyone else for the time devoted thereto. It is a book to present to a friend, to take with you on a journey, to read in the family circle; in short, it is a "*traveling companion*" in Book form.

Bound in Interlaken, maroon-colored cloth.

Price $2.00 postpaid.

THE GREAT WORK

By TK

Volume III.   The Harmonic Series

This book is also from the pen of the author of *"the great psychological crime"*, and is a presentation, analysis and elucidation of the fundamental principle and working formulary of the Great School of Natural Science, which principle and formulary are known to the "Masters of the Law" and their students and friends as the *"constructive principle of nature in individual life."*

The author of "The Great Work" is the American Representative of the *great school of natural science*, a School which was hoary with age when the foundation of the great Pyramid was laid; a School which antedates all present authentic history and records; a School against which the waves of superstition and ignorance have dashed in vain, because its foundation is the rock of TRUTH.

To the intelligent *freemason* as well as the general reader this book is invaluable, for it puts before him facts in the history of that Ancient Order which heretofore have been *"buried in the rubbish of the temple."*

"The great work" is unique in that its statements are verified facts which every reader may prove for himself under right guidance if he but have the "Intelligence to know, the Courage to dare, and the Perseverance to do." The Philosophy taught in this book appeals to both Reason and Conscience, and is an inspiration to *"live the life and know the law."* Every student realizes that, if he so wills, he may be an heir to the Wisdom of the Ages.

The Great Work belongs in your Library.

Bound in maroon Interlaken cloth.

Price $2.00 Postpaid.

BRIDGING THE GREAT DIVIDE
between
THE PHYSICAL AND SPIRITUAL WORLDS

By A. Sophomore

A Clergyman, who is also a Psychical Researcher and Natural Scientist.

This is a very remarkable book to be written by a Clergyman, who, while "intuitively believing in immortality of the Soul, was not cognizant of any Scientific possibility that could raise this belief to a demonstrable certainty."

"Fortunately, however," as he says, he "was saved from making this humiliating statement, as an ultimatum of his researches, when his attention was directed to the volumes of the HARMONIC SERIES, wherein the bold assertion is made '*Life after Physical Death is a fact Scientifically Demonstrable.*'"

This book should be read by every seeking Soul.

It is beautifully gotten up. Bound in wine colored Interlaken Cloth. Gold stamped. Indexed, and contains 262 pages of closely written matter.

Price $1.00 Postpaid.

THE QUESTION BOX

A SERIES OF QUESTIONS IN NATURAL SCIENCE
ANSWERED BY TK

Author of
"THE GREAT PSYCHOLOGICAL CRIME"
"THE GREAT WORK," Etc.

This beautiful Volume is a compilation, in concrete form, of the many answers to questions propounded by readers and Students of the Text Books of the Harmonic Philosophy, and answered by the TK in *Life and Action*.

We believe it will be appreciated by the Readers, Friends and Students of the Work everywhere.

The book is beautifully bound in Interlaken cloth. Gold Stamped. Indexed, and contains 217 pages of solid reading matter.

Price $1.00 Postpaid.

Three-in-One

It gives us pleasure to announce the fact that we have completed an arrangement with one whom we believe to be the most artistic book-binder in Chicago, to be bound in *de luxe* form, 100 copies of the THREE-IN-ONE, Vols. I, II and III, of the Harmonic Series, under one cover.

These will be bound in genuine PERSIAN MOROCCO (Oxford Bible Style), the edges overlapping, to protect the "red-under-gold" edges of the book.

It will be printed on French Japan paper, and the HALF-TONES on French Japan plate. Black-water end sheets, ROUND corners, SILK head bands and SILK markers, English thread sewed, Genuine Gold Stamped "PHILOSOPHY OF NATURAL SCIENCE," and, if desired, the NAME of the purchaser stamped in GENUINE GOLD on the cover.

This complete THREE-IN-ONE beautiful *de luxe* book will be sent in strong box and sold for $12.00, post paid.

The Secret History
of
The Oxford Movement

By
Walter Walsh

This is an English publication and sets forth the various attempts of the Roman Catholic Church to Romanize the Protestant Episcopal Church and how far it has succeeded in accomplishing its purpose.

This book is, doubtless, the most exhaustless treatise on this now vital topic ever written.

It contains ten chapters and 293 pages. It gives the history of

The Society of the Holy Cross.

The Secrecy of the Ritualistic Confessional.

The Secret History of "The Priest in Absolution."

The Order of Corporate Reunion.

The Confraternity of the Blessed Sacrament.

Ritualistic Sisterhoods.

Some other Ritualistic Societies.

The ROMEWARD Movement, etc., etc., etc.,

The book is bound in cloth and sells for $1.00, post paid.

THE CRUCIFIXION

By an Eye-Witness

Volume II. Supplemental Harmonic Series

No book in recent years, regarding the Life and Work of the Master, Jesus, has provoked so much comment and discussion as this little book.

The story of the *"crucifixion"* is told by a friend of Jesus, an eye-witness to this historic event. The book is intensely interesting and holds the reader's attention to the end.

Besides giving a succinct account of the Crucifixion, it reviews the beliefs, duties and aspirations of the "Order of Essenes" of the childhood and youth of the Master, his initiation into the Order of which his Father and his Cousin John were also members.

It sets forth the parentage of Jesus, Joseph's flight into Egypt with his family; the child's visit to the temple; how he became lost; and finally, the incidents leading up to the Crucifixion a marvelous bit of Word-painting; the resustication of Jesus after being taken from the cross; his later travels and his final death some six months after the historic tragedy on Calvary.

This little book (to us) comes far more nearly giving a rational and intelligent report of the incidents in the life of Jesus than does the Bible.

Doubtless there are some discrepancies in the minor details, because Historians in any age are liable to err; but in a large general sense it appears to us undoubtedly true.

It cannot fail to interest you.

Bound in Interlaken cloth. Price $1.00 Postpaid.

PRICE LIST OF THE PUBLICATIONS OF
THE INDO-AMERICAN BOOK COMPANY
5707 West Lake St., Chicago, Ill.

*Note—These three morocco bound books $10.00